The hull of the *Bencoolen*, wrecked at Bude in 1862

HAWKER
OF
MORWENSTOW

Engraving of Hawker in 1864

PIERS BRENDON

HAWKER
OF
MORWENSTOW

(1803 - 1875)

Portrait of a Victorian Eccentric

With a Foreword by
JOHN FOWLES

JONATHAN CAPE
THIRTY BEDFORD SQUARE LONDON

FIRST PUBLISHED 1975
© 1975 BY PIERS BRENDON
FOREWORD © 1975 BY J. R. FOWLES LTD

JONATHAN CAPE LTD, 30 BEDFORD SQUARE, LONDON WCI

ISBN 0 224 01122 7

SET IN 12PT BEMBO 270 IPT LEADED

PRINTED AND BOUND IN GREAT BRITAIN
BY COX & WYMAN LTD
LONDON, FAKENHAM AND READING

To
ADELAIDE ROSS
and to the memory of
NICHOLAS

Contents

Illustrations

11

between pages 144 and 145

13 Pauline, née Kuczynski, Hawker's second wife, in about 1865
14, 15 Shipwrecks: the kind of spectacle with which Hawker
had been forced to become familiar
16, 17 Launching and beaching the Bude lifeboat in 1900
18 Hawker in 1870, dressed as usual in a claret-coloured coat,
a blue fisherman's jersey and sea-boots

The author and publishers wish to thank T. R. Sharpe for permission to reproduce Plates 3, 5, 6, 7, 11 and 12.

Acknowledgments

I owe gratitude to so many people who have given me help and advice over this book that there is not space enough to express my sincere thanks to each of them by name. I hope they will forgive this general acknowledgment. I must, however, specify my chief benefactors, none of whom, needless to say, is responsible for any faults the book may contain. I have received most kind assistance from Canon C. G. B. Davies, Mr Desmond Gregory, the Rev. Harold Lockyear, Mr Alan Munton, Mr Andy Noble, Mr Simon Nowell-Smith, Dr C. D. Peters, Mr Brian Stamp, Professor Nathan Starr, and Professor Charles Thomas of the Institute of Cornish Studies. I am particularly grateful to Mr Rennie Bere, Mrs Morwenna Hartnoll and Mr and Mrs Michael Kelly for allowing me to see and make use of manuscripts in their possession. I am indebted to many archivists and librarians, most notably to Mr D. S. Porter and his helpful and efficient staff at the Bodleian Library. Mr Porter's success in obtaining the co-operation of the Humanities Research Centre at Texas University (to which I am also under obligation) made this book very much easier to write. I have gained enormously from the criticisms of Mrs Judy Carver, Mr P. N. Furbank, Dr Vic Gatrell and Dr Michael Woodhouse, all of whom read the book in manuscript. As did Mr William Waddon-Martyn, who generously put at my disposal the Hawker MSS he owns as well as his vast store of erudition about Morwenstow past and present. My wife has helped me in literally countless invaluable ways. Finally, I must express profound gratitude to Mrs Adelaide Ross and her husband Nicholas, to whom I have dedicated this book. He collected the bulk of the manuscripts (now in the Bodleian) without which I could not have embarked on my task. She has given me unremitting aid and inspiration to complete it.

In addition my warmest thanks are due to John Fowles for his generous and perceptive Foreword.

Foreword

If before I read the text that follows someone had asked my opinion on the need for another book on Hawker, I should have made two very wrong guesses: first that, as with the tin in so many derelict Cornish mines, the Morwenstow lode had been exploited beyond further profitability; and secondly that (even if a trace or two of ore did remain to be streamed) Hawker's interest was essentially local. The great virtue of Piers Brendon's study is that it makes a nonsense of both these lazy assumptions. Those who like myself supposed that they had the man and his legend reasonably well pigeon-holed will know by the end of the first chapter that they had better think again; and those to whom Hawker's name means next to nothing, or perhaps nothing at all, have a fascinating meeting in store – one, moreover, that throws some very interesting general light on the Victorian mind . . . and beyond. Hawker may have largely turned, or appeared to turn, his back on his age. That does not make him any the less revealing of it.

He was rather more a unique character than a unique case, and may be classed as an early example of a cast of mind and temperament that became comparatively familiar, and very often notorious, in the later decades of the nineteenth century. Indeed, one might call Hawker's a rare but perennial species in English society, with Evelyn Waugh and Mr Malcolm Muggeridge as varieties of it from our own time. There were certainly in his own age a number of similars in career, life-style, religious belief, literary taste, even in secular foible and neurosis. I first came to him myself by way of another ecclesiastical odd man out, one of Mr Brendon's predecessors (and monstrously the least reliable, as he proves) in the list of Hawker biographers. Sabine Baring-Gould was rector – more accurately, squarson – of Lew Trenchard in Devon; a teeming melodramatic novelist (at least one lurid story, *In the Roar of the Sea*, owes a strong debt to Hawker) and miscellaneous writer, though he is more honourably remembered today for his invaluable folk-song collecting and for the hymn, 'Onward, Christian Soldiers'.

In Baring-Gould, too, there was the same fascination with the past, with ritual and decor, with the supernatural (another of the 159 books he published was entitled *The Book of Werewolves*) and folklore; the same love of esoteric practical jokes in his nonage; the same unfortunate gift for the kind of sarcasm that scars – and makes enemies – for life; the same curious juxtaposition of personal snobbery and public concern for the poor; even the same cry for help, during crisis, to Gladstone; and above all, the same susceptibility to the siren call of the early, and unreformed, church – accompanied by a total inability to tolerate those who had also departed from orthodoxy, but by the opposite door first opened by Wesley. Of the ecumenical spirit, and the proverb about people in glass houses, neither man ever showed a whit of awareness.

Then one thinks of 'Firm Father George' Drury, outraging his Suffolk parishes with his 'petticoats' and biretta, his incense and candles and bannered processions, his equally pugnacious loathing of Dissent; of Drury's *protégé*, Joseph Lyne, who became Father Ignatius. Both Drury and Lyne also felt obliged to flaunt their outsiderhood by the clothes they wore, and similarly could not resist translating their alternative spiritual worlds into stones and mortar. Mr Brendon cites other symptoms and examples of this highly eccentric syndrome and draws a striking parallel with perhaps the most famous of those who showed it: Frederick Rolfe, the self-styled Baron Corvo.

I am not quite sure what it is about such men that attracts even non-believers like myself, but I think it must be a blend of two things: their courage and their difference. Very few of them were fools and they knew perfectly well, whatever would-be innocent feelings of unjust persecution they exhibited, that they were not merely tilting at windmills, but running head first into the granite wall of received opinion and the established church. Fond to a man of the dangerous sport of bishop-baiting, all of them wished at least a substantial part of their isolations and 'martyrdoms' on themselves. But if they occasionally protested too much, they were also consistently men of conviction – even though this conviction may sometimes strike us today as being visibly more centred on self than on creed. From time to time this perverse probity was acknowledged by even their most truculent contemporary opponents: by Bradlaugh, for instance, in his famous public debate with Father Ignatius, where one has the impression that a mutual recognition of sincerity surprised both men out of their total antipathy on every other ground. Extremes have always their extremism in common.

The 'difference' I referred to is obviously of a very special – almost an aesthetic – sort. It cannot appeal to the thorough-going liberal or democrat, since these Anglo-Catholic and Romanizing storm-petrels were not only religious reactionaries, but social ones as well. That did not prevent them – at least in the case of Hawker and, more intermittently, of Baring-Gould – from being generous and caring parish priests. But their goodness in this is tarnished by their underlying political pessimism. They held a stubborn *de haut en bas* belief in a neo-feudal order, in a world where the duty of the lower classes is humbly to receive – and behave – according to their station. They were incipient patriarchs, in short, engaged in a kind of hopeless guerrilla war, anathema and jeremiad ever at the ready, against all onward time and social climate. To be fair, Hawker at his best was a benevolent and rather charmingly nostalgic patriarch – and in these days of urban civilization going to wrack and ruin, his backward Christian-rural Utopia may seem a shade less conservative than it was in the

17

context of his own age. Here is the final stanza of his very revealing poem on the theme, 'The Poor Man and his Parish Church',
written in 1840.

> O! for the poor man's church again,
>   With one roof over all;
> Where the true hearts of Cornish men
>   Might beat beside the wall:
> The altars where, in holier days,
>   Our fathers were forgiven,
> Who went, with meek and faithful ways,
>   Through the old aisles to heaven.

All such writing must of course be read from two viewpoints:
not only as general prescription, but also as gauge of self-know-
ledge. The poet's own ways may have been faithful, but he must
have been aware that the meekness he proposed (not always so
gently as here) for his parishioners was hardly a prominent trait in
his own character. However, since the central and unsolved political problem of our own century remains that of reconciling pity
for humanity with lust for authority, I think we should not be too
hard on the poet-vicar; at least he bore very clear practical witness
to the first concern, and did not try to shuffle out of the paradox
of the second.

This leads me to suspect that the deepest attraction of Hawker
and his kind lies in their having singled themselves out from the
great grey mass of those who have always adhered (if one can
adhere through inertia) to the most popular practical religion of
these islands, that of safe conformity. We may despise their
theology, their liturgical antics, their arrogance, their narcissism,
their malice, their combination of acute sensitivity to the romantic
past and seemingly wilful blindness to the realistic present, but
however long the bill of attainder we cannot deny them a colour
and style, a memorability. It is almost as if they sensed that their
age could not reach its full richness unless they went their very
individual ways; unless they cried their flamboyant no, where so

many muttered a tame yes. Nor were all the attacks and angers against their own epoch without substance, a mere cassocked premonition of Colonel Blimp's view of life. Our own age is still paying for some very grave Victorian fallacies concerning the destiny of man.

Inevitably there was a great deal of misery in the triple isolation, spiritual, psychological and physical, that such men condemned themselves to – or were condemned to by their natures; and I am not sure the most valuable part of Mr Brendon's book is not the analysis he makes of Hawker's very characteristic set of depressive and paranoiac neuroses, and of his opium problem. The kind of loneliness Hawker lived in is almost unimaginable today, and intense doctrinal feeling has shifted from the religious to the political domain. None the less, it seems to me that one can detect behind the historical circumstance a far more than merely Victorian human being. A number of Hawker's mental wens and warts are very nearly universal among writers; and also, I would hazard a guess, among working priests. The two vocations are both closely based on the word and on public performance, on a certain amount of play-acting – even on a strong degree of faith, though of rather different varieties; and after all, there was once a time when to be cleric or clerk was simply to change temporary function, not fundamental profession. I should be surprised if a modern member of either calling can read the secrets of Hawker's inner life without a sympathy founded on a feeling of identity. I most certainly felt it myself, and on more than one occasion . . . there, but for the grace of godlessness, go I.

All of us who know something of him have a favourite Hawker. To some it is the old impostor hamming it up with his jersey and sea-boots and the rest of his carefully cultivated eccentricities – the peg to hang good stories on, the excommunicator of his cat for catching mice on Sundays; to others, it is the crusty recluse, the hermit side of the tale; to others, the tormented and self-sacrificing pastor of a far from completely grateful flock; to many more, the memorialist of old Cornwall and the skilled minor poet . . . I say minor, but let me warmly echo Mr Brendon's admiration for *The Quest of the Sangraal*. It is strangely archaic and, to those whose ears and minds are more used to Clough and Arnold, atypical of its era, but it has a lasting power both in conception and in rhetoric. There are some truly magnificent images and lines, unsurpassed in Victorian blank verse – Mr Brendon discusses to what extent they were owed, like *Kubla Khan*, to the poppy; and I wish they were better known. Nor would any Cornish patriot (or the ghosts of Scott, Macaulay and Dickens, for that matter) let one of the shorter poems be called minor: if the Duchy ever needs a 'Marseillaise', the young Hawker provided it in 1825 with 'The Song of the Western Men' and its famous burden concerning the fate of Trelawny – or rather the fate of any 'foreigner' east of the Tamar who dared lay an axe to his neck.

But where we can all, Cornish or barbarian, join in treasuring Hawker is surely as one of that long national chain of literary characters whose summit and cynosure is Dr Johnson. None of them is clearly a great writer; but they were all great livers. What they have become in deed and anecdote, how they have been transmitted to us by their Boswells, matters at least as much as what they may still be in the formally composed pages of their books. However little those pages are read nowadays, however anomalous the lives may seem in the general run of their time, however flawed their creators as writers and human beings, such dramatically distinct and socially discrete personalities as Hawker's make not insubstantial contributions to the shape of the English imagination. Each forms a part not only of our knowledge of what it was to be alive in their day, but of what it still *is* to be English. We are a singularly humorous and bloody-minded race, as well as a sheepish and canting one; and we need our vicars of Morwenstow to remind us of that positive side of our character. They were seldom whole men, as this biography very plainly shows; but they live triumphantly whole in the racial memory.

The occupational hazard of eccentricity is the distortion by posterity, and the true portrait of Robert Hawker has, like a poorly restored canvas left to accumulate grime in an attic, been in urgent need of a good clean and the removal of some grotesque over-painting. I possess an old photograph of him. He stands in his familiar motley, half parson and half fisherman, a sad yet faintly comic amalgam of the Learlike and the bearlike, before the door of his church; with a wryly enigmatic face and his right hand extended towards the camera as if asking for something. It may perhaps have been no more than an invitation to his wife or his dog Ship to join him in the picture. But I should like to think the request was for what, on this hundredth anniversary of his death, he has at long last received from Piers Brendon: both the closely documented truth and a notably thorough and humane understanding.

1975   JOHN FOWLES

I

The Legend

Robert Stephen Hawker was born in 1803 and died a century ago, in 1875. Today he is known, if at all, as the highly eccentric minor poet who for more than forty years was vicar of Morwenstow, an isolated country parish on the north coast of Cornwall. His personality, career and achievements have provided intriguing footnotes for the historian and the literary critic. They have afforded lurid dashes of local colour for the travel-writer and the antiquarian. And they have constituted a subject of endless folk-tales, comic and curious, by which Cornishmen still earn themselves free drinks from gullible tourists. But amidst the mass of anecdotage, much of it fascinating and by no means spurious, the real interest and importance of Hawker – who was, in a paradoxical way, both violently at odds with his age and startlingly representative of it – has been obscured. The man has been lost behind the legend. From being flesh and blood in a breathing world he has been diminished to the quaint inhabitant of a Victorian strip-cartoon, the performer of bizarre antics, the victim of outlandish ideas. By such facile reductionism the present habitually exploits and patronizes the past. Yet it must be admitted that Hawker lends himself better than most to portrayal in a few crudely idiosyncratic lines. It is also true that character is sometimes most clearly revealed by caricature. So perhaps the best introduction to the historical reality is to be found in an examination of the salient features of the popular myth.

This depicts Hawker in the following terms. He was a youth of wild high spirits (what the Cornish still call 'a proper limb of Satan') who delighted in hoaxes and practical jokes. In 1824 he married his 41-year-old godmother in order to use her dowry to pay his way through university, and triumphantly rode up to Oxford with her behind him on the pillion. After a successful academic career, during which he won the Newdigate Poetry Prize, he was ordained and eventually made vicar of Morwenstow. Here he was a charitable, hard-working, Anglo-Catholic parish priest who restored the church, built a parsonage and a school. He also initiated the practice of holding Harvest Festivals, and diocesan and ruridecanal synods. But owing to the desolate remoteness of the 'iron bound' north Cornish coast and lack of sympathy from his parishioners, 'a mixed multitude of smugglers, wreckers, and dissenters of various hue', his true genius was stifled and he gradually became more and more peculiar. He wore highly unorthodox clothes decorated with odd ornaments, he studied weird antiquarian lore, practised strange forms of devotion, cultivated arcane superstitions, believed in the active agency of demons and angels, ghosts and brownies, talked to birds, invited his nine cats into church and excommunicated one of them when it caught a mouse on Sunday, and built a hut on the cliffs out of the timbers of wrecked ships, where he wrote romantic poetry and saw mystic visions. In later life he suffered from prolonged fits of melancholy, brought on by opium-eating and the nervous strain of burying in his churchyard the decayed and often horribly mutilated bodies of dozens of drowned sailors. When his first wife died, in 1863, he had an acute attack of depression, lived on nothing but clotted cream for a time and composed his masterpiece, *The Quest of the Sangraal*. He quickly remarried, this time choosing a girl forty years his junior, who soon presented him with three daughters. Twelve hours before his death, his mind wandering and under his wife's influence, he was accepted into the Roman Catholic Church.

Such is the Hawker legend. It contains some truth, some half-truth and some downright falsehood. But it is essentially misleading in its over-simplification. It takes no account of the context in which Hawker's life was lived. It distorts the perspective by concentrating on the dramatic lights and ignoring the subtle shades of his complex personality. It disregards the wisdom of Renan's apophthegm, 'La vérité existe dans les nuances.'

What gave rise to this myth? Partly, it was of Hawker's own making. He had a shrewd sense of the romantic nature of his situation and was enough of a mountebank to exploit it on occasions for dramatic effect and even for financial gain. But, ironically enough, it was another West Country parson, the Rev. Sabine Baring-Gould, who was chiefly responsible for creating and publicizing the Hawker legend. Baring-Gould had known Hawker slightly, having shared his interest in the ancient saints of Cornwall. They had corresponded, for example, over the knotty question of whether St Morwenna and St Modwenna were two persons or one, a discussion which Hawker abruptly terminated by declaring, 'I have twice received supernatural intimation of her identity, by dream and suggestion.' Such a conclusion, Baring-Gould considered, 'was clearly not that of a man of well-balanced mind'. Nevertheless, when Hawker died, Baring-Gould was quick to seize the opportunity of writing his biography. He had a large family to support and almost anything was grist to his mill for grinding out books. He was a staggeringly prolific writer. He manufactured 'literature' in a way that makes Scott and Trollope seem sluggards. However, he lacked any real education and certainly had had no formal training in history as an exact science. His sole resource was a memory which had been retentive in his youth but later became 'an unreliable lumber room'. His latest biographer gives an indication of his methods of composing history.

His unusual approach to the study of the Roman emperors was typical of his unashamedly prejudiced outlook on life in general. After long gazing at the portrait busts and statues he formed from the sculptured features his own impressions of the character of each. After that he wrote their histories in detail, but consciously or unconsciously these biographies had to be made to conform to that first impression.

Baring-Gould's life of Hawker was written in even more of a tearing hurry than was usual with him because he was anxious to be first in the field, and he had a competitor in the person of F. G. Lee – about whom more shortly. Baring-Gould had access to few original letters or documents, and he did not ask for the co-operation of Hawker's widow. Hawker's brother, Claud, provided him with a few snippets of authentic information but, for the most part, he had to rely on large-scale plagiarism – much of it irrelevant – from Hawker's published work, and on popular folk-tales. He was unabashed by this and frankly admitted that 'this is a gossiping book.' It is also a wildly inaccurate one. From the first sentence, which gets both the place and date of Hawker's birth wrong, via colourful inventions like the story of his wife's riding pillion up to Oxford, to the confident but erroneous remarks about Hawker's deathbed conversion, Baring-Gould's book is a work of fiction. Hawker's long-standing friend, William Maskell, reviewing it for the *Athenaeum*, exposed many of its sins of omission and commission, berated Baring-Gould for his 'reckless repetition of silly gossip', and correctly summed up the biography as 'partly a romance, partly a jest-book'. Others reacted in an even more hostile way and 'an action for libel was threatened against Mr Gould, who made the most humble apologies, retracted as much as he could and prepared a second edition.' Maskell also savaged the revision unmercifully. Apart from the fact that two pages and a few stories had been left out, 'there is hardly an alteration of the slightest intrinsic importance. The book seems to be a mere reprint; the mistakes and misstatements which we pointed out in our first notice remain, as if in contempt of truth and of all honesty of writing . . . [It is] a disgrace to English biographical literature.'

It is necessary to labour the point because Baring-Gould's book went into three editions (the last of which has frequently been reprinted), and is still widely read. Its popularity is understandable, for the book has the virtues of its vices. It is full of zest. It tells a large number of racy anecdotes and amusing jokes. It paints a garish, larger-than-life-size portrait of Hawker and sets it against the vivid background of his rustic sea-board parish. But while it is not surprising that the public should have preferred Baring-Gould's memoir to the long, somewhat stodgy, but splendidly full and accurate official *Life and Letters* compiled in 1905 by Hawker's son-in-law, C. E. Byles, there is no excuse for scholars and writers to do the same. Yet even they continue to read and quote Baring-Gould. To take a particularly flagrant example: a pamphlet recently issued, reprinted and praised in the press, *The Renowned 'Passon' Hawker of Morwenstow* (1963 edn) by H. R. Smallcombe, is based almost entirely on Baring-Gould and is correspondingly full of errors. Better-known authors, including Baring-Gould's biographer himself, and the distinguished literary critic John Heath-Stubbs, have been equally misguided. Thus the myth Baring-Gould created has not only been sustained, it has had new vitality breathed into it.

Hawker's second biographer, Frederick George Lee, did nothing to present his subject in a more realistic light. Indeed, he added a mythical accretion of his own. Lee was vicar of All Saints, Lambeth, and in some respects he rivalled even the vicar of Morwenstow in eccentricity. An advanced ritualist, he helped in 1877, shortly after writing Hawker's biography, to found the Order of Corporate Reunion which aimed to rejoin the Anglican and Roman Catholic Churches. In the same year he went to Italy where he was conditionally re-baptized, confirmed, made deacon, ordained priest and consecrated bishop by 'a mysterious triumvirate of prelates, the identity of whom has never been divulged, but who were popularly supposed to have been a Greek, a Copt and either a Roman or an Old Catholic'. He remained a clandestine bishop, denomination uncertain but apparently accepted as valid in Rome, while continuing to work as vicar of Lambeth, though six weeks before his death in 1902 he formally became a Roman Catholic. Thus in 1876 Lee was in a disturbed state, but he was obviously attracted to Hawker, whom he had met and corresponded with, because of the many views they held in common – hatred of Dissent and the Protestant Reformation, affection for Catholicity and ancient liturgy, belief in communication with spirits. Approaching a crisis in his own life, Lee drew strength from the Hawker whom he created in his own image. This was a drably propagandist figure, an 'exact theologian' who 'cordially fell in with the wise policy of those earliest Tractarian leaders'. He was also 'a Tory by birth and conviction ... absolutely untainted by "Liberalism," so-called'. In short, Lee's Hawker was a quirky, Anglo-Catholic conservative, like Lee himself. But Hawker, as will be seen, was entirely his own man. He always held aloof from parties both in Church and state, and affirmed the fact on numerous occasions. Nevertheless, Lee's addition to Baring-Gould's myth became established, and Hawker has been appropriated by some historians as 'one of the "characters" of the Church Revival'.

The reason why the myth was not scotched by C. E. Byles's *Life and Letters of R. S. Hawker* has already been suggested. That book is a quarry rather than a sculpt. Nearly seven hundred pages long, it contains a vast amount of original material arranged in a haphazard manner. It amounts to a form of biographical overkill, an excellent example of the Victorian 'Life and Letters' genre, by which the subject was entombed instead of being resurrected. Its advantages are comprehensiveness and heavy reliance on primary sources. Its disadvantages are unwieldiness and a tendency to pander to the proprieties. Actually, considering that Byles had a family interest in defending Hawker's reputation, he includes a surprising amount that is dangerously outspoken. But the approval of Prebendary F. C. Hingeston-Randolph, who evidently censored the book in proof, is a bad sign. He wrote to Byles, 'I think you are doing your work extremely well and with conspicuous judgement and discretion. You have certainly handled the more delicate subjects with all delicacy.' Hawker is not exactly muted by Byles's treatment, but he emerges somewhat fuzzy at the edges, more complicated than in Baring-Gould's memoir but less striking. At any rate, Byles's book has never been reprinted and is now extremely rare. Though it has provided the raw material for one brief academic treatment of Hawker and a few other sketches, it has singularly failed to drive Baring-Gould from the field. In spite of such massive over-painting, his is the portrait which lingers on in the public mind.

It is the aim of this book, a century after Hawker's death, Baring-Gould's travesty and Lee's misrepresentation, and seventy years after Byles's monument, to recover and present the true vicar of Morwenstow, by reference not only to the printed sources but also to a large number of unpublished manuscripts. The lapse of time makes the task easier in some respects and more difficult in others. The heat has gone out of many contemporary controversies and obsessions, and one can now examine such things as (to quote one pamphleteer), 'the abominable scandal of Hawker becoming a pervert to Rome', without becoming embroiled in partisan polemics. There is no longer any need for discretion about matters like Hawker's chronic financial troubles and the importunate begging-letters he sent to everyone from Gladstone downwards. One can freely print lines which would have shocked his contemporaries:

> Lo! When thy carcase of foul flesh shall writhe
> Fierce with its renal heat and wild with spasm . . .

The evidence in contentious questions, whether or not Hawker was a plagiarist or a poet, a mystic or a neurotic, a genius or a charlatan, can be weighed coolly and dispassionately.

However, what one gains in objective detachment one often loses in familiar insight. The Victorian period, though only a few generations removed from us in time, is in atmosphere a whole world away. Hawker's Morwenstow was backward even in nineteenth-century terms. He wrote to a friend in 1862, 'Did you ever hear that for every 100 miles you live from London, you must reckon yourself a century back from your own date? We therefore, who are 250 miles off, are now in the year 1610 in all that relates to agriculture and civilization.' As for Hawker himself, it is no exaggeration to say that he was nearer in spirit to the Middle Ages than to the present day. Educated in a Christian and classical tradition, he read few newspapers and fewer contemporary books (no scientific ones at all) and seldom moved out of the narrow circle of his segregated farming community. Intellectually and psychologically very different from his neighbours, he resembled them in that his life was dominated by local events and circumstances – the weather, the state of the harvest, superstition, 'the guesses, for they are no more, of a rural doctor'. Yet Hawker was only an extreme symptom of an endemic condition of nineteenth-century country society. Living, as they did, before the communications explosion, the cultural isolation of rural Victorians was palpable and overwhelming. It determined the whole tenor of their existence in a way which is almost impossible for us to understand without a great imaginative leap backward in time.

This book is based on the premiss that the historical imagination is better stimulated by particular, concrete, microcosmic analyses than by general, abstract, macrocosmic syntheses. But Hawker is not treated here just as a symptom or even as what one might call an anti-symptom of his age. He is celebrated for his own sake and in his own right, for the intrinsic interest of his life. Though, like his native cliffs of Morwenstow, Hawker's character was scarred with flaws and faults, there was also a raw grandeur about him. He was not a great man as a poet, a mystic, or even perhaps as a priest. But his courageous endeavours to overcome his own limitations and the restrictions imposed by his environment command respect and attention. His achievements were modest but his aspirations were as exalted as the beloved 'Hills of old Cornwall', 'so high that a man might hear the thoughts of God from their brow'. Hawker longed passionately for the vicarious immortality of a biography: 'Oh! that a voice unborn might blend my future name!' His heroic struggle in isolation and the strange warping of his rich personality earn him the right to be remembered. For Hawker was a true prophet in his yearning exclamation, 'What a life mine would be if it were all written and published in a book.'

Youth

Hawker is dead! that herald sent of God
To make to man his great salvation known.
Let Zion's offspring weeping kiss the rod
And gird their robes of deepest sackcloth on.

The subject of the rather dreadful elegy from which this verse is taken was not Robert Stephen Hawker. It was his grandfather, Robert Hawker D.D., who for nearly half a century before his death in 1827 had been vicar of Charles Church, the imposing edifice named after the Martyr King, in the northern part of Plymouth. He was a formidable Calvinistic divine and he exercised a considerable influence over his grandson, who was left in his charge for some of his most formative years. Thus it is with Dr Hawker of Charles that the life of the vicar of Morwenstow must begin.

Dr Hawker was born in 1753 at Exeter, where his grandfather and father had both been medical men prominent in city life, the former an alderman, the latter mayor. In youth he was 'frivolous, gay, and thoughtless', once going so far as to throw a lighted squib into a church full of people. However, he soon had to settle down, for when he was aged only nineteen he married a Miss Anne Rains, who was two or three years his junior. He went up to Magdalen Hall, Oxford, was ordained and, after a six-year curacy at Charles Church, was made vicar in 1784. Here he remained, refusing offers of further promotion, and labouring in the vineyard of the Lord with all the concentrated energy of one who believed himself a member of the elect by faith but, via the familiar paradox, felt he had to prove it by works.

He was a most eloquent extempore preacher who could, and did, quote much of the Bible by heart. He frequently visited London where George III used apparently to enjoy hearing him preach, often handing him a text just before he went up into the pulpit. Dr Hawker was also a prolific author and a powerful controversialist whose works were collected into ten heavy volumes after his death. He wrote on subjects of the day and on theological and devotional topics, and many of his pamphlets were specially composed for the minds, and priced for the pockets, of the poor. He started societies for the distribution of religious tracts, in one of which he was, as he wryly put it, 'the sole committee, chairman, treasurer, secretary, and editor'. Like many Evangelicals he was a conservative in politics, especially during the French Revolutionary period. He was a radical on the question of slavery. He proposed plans for its abolition and, in 1823, formed 'a society for the purchase of Plantations in Jamaica by way of ameliorating the wretched situation of the Negro'. Dr Hawker would have disapproved of his grandson who, in the tradition of the Tractarians, was to put slaves' salvation before their emancipation: 'So that you save the whole man, never heed his fettered limb.'

However, in two important ways, one ideological and the other practical, the grandfather did have a powerful influence over the grandson. The first was through his strong chiliastic intimations. Admittedly, many clergy (and laymen) interpreted the unprecedented changes brought about by the French Revolution and Industrial Revolution as heralding the end of the world. As one wrote in 1814, 'We are undoubtedly living in *the last days of blasphemous infidelity*, in that awful period which is *the peculiar reign of Antichrist.*' Such a millenarian reading of the signs of the times was indicative of bewilderment and incomprehension on the part of churchmen at the new world-order which was emerging. It was also a consequence of their unremitting awareness of living *sub specie aeternitatis.* No one attempted to convey his conscious-ness of living thus more earnestly than Dr Hawker. In a threepenny tract he implored those who studied the Scriptures to ask them-selves whether 'there can remain the shadow of a doubt to what age of the Church, more than the present, the blessed SPIRIT referred, when by *Paul* he said, that *in the last days perilous times should come!*' Robert Stephen Hawker spent his whole life in what he knew was a vain endeavour to prove his apprehension that the season of the apocalypse was nigh. A short time before he died, he saw a particularly brilliant crimson sunset over the sea and rushed to the window of his dining-room in great excitement, crying, 'It's the end of the world! I knew it was coming. I knew it.'

The practical way in which the Doctor influenced his grandson was in his charitable treatment of the poor and the suffering. Dr Hawker held the enlightened view that if 'the wants of the body are supplied, the mind will be left to more freedom, and be better disposed also ... to attend to *the one thing needful*', i.e. the saving of a sinner's soul. Thus he founded a number of societies for the relief of the poor. These he supported with generous donations, relying on the 'Almighty Banker' to supply his own financial needs. Funds from this source were not always forth-coming, and sometimes he and his family actually suffered hard-ship and want. But just as, later, nothing could discourage Robert Stephen's charitable impulse, so nothing could divert the Doctor from his prodigal course. After the disastrous harvest of 1817 he adopted the Sunday habit of selling a thousand sixpenny loaves to the poor at half-price, the difference being made up by the money he raised in his church. Dr Hawker was anything but an armchair philanthropist. He visited the most squalid quarters of his parish and personally saved many unfortunate girls from prostitution. These he often placed in the 'Female Penitentiary' which he had started (as an improvement on the workhouse) for the 'very numerous body of these wretched women' who 'for obvious reasons' abounded in Plymouth. And he took on the deputy chaplaincy of the garrison. This was no sinecure, for it involved the holding of regular services 'amidst the floating miasmata of the typhus, and the effluvia of other disorders'.

These were the works of Dr Hawker. The man himself is almost obscured in the remorseless piety of his hagiographer, whose tone can be gauged from the few words which he devoted to the Doctor's grandson and his juvenile poetry:

> the first shootings of the young vine, in its natural and unpruned luxuriancy ... might, under divine training, produce a vintage of richest clusters ... If his more mature muse still love to wander on the flowery banks of poesy, may he know what it is to drink largely of that fountain, whence Zion's minstrels drew their inspiration and their song – a song, which no man can learn but the redeemed of the Lord, Rev. xiv. 3.

No misgivings of this kind interfered with the panegyric lavished on Dr Hawker, who was safely dead. However, it is possible to read between the lines and discover a warm, amusing and sympathetic human being, one calculated to win the heart, though perhaps not the mind, of an impressionable, intelligent boy, whom he often rebuked, 'but always with a smile'. In spite of the uncompromising ferocity of his creed and the apocalyptic zeal with which he worked, Dr Hawker had a surprisingly tolerant and compassionate spirit, not unlike that of Cowper's friend, the Rev. John Newton of Olney. While the Doctor adhered to the strict predestinarianism of William Romaine, whom he invited into his pulpit, he was also friends with the Arminian John Wesley, whom he invited into his house.

Dr Hawker's devout nature and pastoral compassion can best be judged from this extract of a letter he wrote to a certain Mr Cox on the death of his son.

> While I was ruminating a morning or two since writing to you of Christ under your present bereaving Providence, our

morning portion (which my dear Caroline as our chaplain was reading) shook me forcibly. 'My beloved is gone down to his garden, to the beds of spices, to feed in the gardens and to gather lilies.' (Song of Songs vi, 2). So then, thought I, our dear Lord hath been gathering this sweet flower of my dear friends, your son, to transplant him into His garden in heaven. And are they weeping? Yea! It would be wrong not to weep, provided we sorrow not as others, which have no hope. Christ himself wept at the grave of Lazarus. Tears of nature mingled with grace are like the spiced wine of the pomegranate. But while nature weeps, GRACE triumphs. Your dear babe is gone. Where? Even where the Lord Jesus Christ hath taken him. Your son is where his spirit is. Apart from the body, present with Christ ... We call our body our home, and it is indeed, while sojourning through this wilderness. Yet it is but a sorry tabernacle for our spirits to dwell in, and until the Lord awakes them at the resurrection, glorified bodies, they are no more than sheaths and scabbards for so polished and bright a principle as our spirits ... Jesus the lovely, the all tender, the all sympathising Jesus be with you.

Such expressions are a trifle mawkish, no doubt, for modern taste, but of their sincerity and concern there can be no question.

Dr Hawker had eight children, three of whom became clergymen. The eldest son, John, was the best known. He was curate of Stoke Damerel, a village just outside Plymouth, where his nephew, Robert Stephen, was baptized on 29 December 1803. John was a popular preacher in his father's mould, though he spoke at such inordinate length, even by the standards of the day, that some at least were offended. The story is told of two sailors who missed their dinner as a result of staying to hear one of his mammoth sermons. Lest a similar fate should befall them, they subsequently beat a smart retreat from another church, convinced that the prominently displayed initials I.H.S. stood not for Jesus Hominum Salvator but for John Hawker of Stoke. In spite of heroic parochial labours, which included the founding of a 'House of Mercy for the Blind', where the inmates were 'snatched from the wretched employments which they are too frequently found in' and 'taught to earn their own livelihood by basket making', John was not preferred as vicar when the absentee incumbent died. So his friends raised subscriptions and 'a large and handsome Gothic Chapel was built for him, in the Parish of St. Andrew, Plymouth, which he named "Eldad;" that is, beloved, or favoured of God; and here he proclaimed "the truth" as it "is in Jesus", for upwards of sixteen years, preaching twice on each Sabbath-day.' John was so Low Church that he disappeared through the floor of the Anglican Establishment in 1828 when Roman Catholic emancipation was imminent. He opened 'Eldad', which was supposed to have been Church of England, independently of his diocesan bishop. He based his teaching solely on the Bible, which he considered unequivocal confirmation of his own Calvinistic creed. In the summer of 1846, one of his congregation reports, 'the Lord saw fit to visit his servant with gradual debility', from which he shortly died.

Of Dr Hawker's second son and fourth child, Jacob Stephen, the father of the subject of this book, less is known. Though he followed the family tradition of being an eloquent preacher and a committed pastor, he seems to have been overshadowed by the more forceful characters of his father and his elder brother. He embarked on a career as a surgeon in Plymouth and married Jane Elizabeth Drewitt whose father, Stephen, had come from Winchester and whose brother, Thomas, was a clergyman living in Cheddar, Somerset. Not much is known of her either, save that, in spite of poor health, she gave birth to nine children, the eldest of whom was the future vicar of Morwenstow. Robert Stephen Hawker was born at Charles Church vicarage, 6 Norley Street, Plymouth, on 3 December 1803. Sixty years later he wrote wistfully, 'I was at birth a harmless-looking, and, as poor mother used to say, a lovely little child.' Jacob Hawker soon changed professions, took Holy Orders and served as curate, first at Altarnun and then, when Robert was about ten, at Stratton in north Cornwall. Here he remained, being promoted to vicar in 1833, until his death in 1846. Jacob was never very well off, and when he moved was probably glad to leave his eldest son under the roof and in the care of Dr Hawker and his wife. Robert's grandmother had nursed him as an infant 'and was my first and latest friend as a boy'. Robert may also have stayed with his Aunt Mary, who was particularly fond of him and, having married a prosperous merchant, Thomas Hodson, helped to pay for his education. Thus Robert spent much of his early youth in the strict, though not unduly harsh, household at Plymouth.

From the few glimpses of Robert's juvenile self, to be found in his subsequent writings, it appears that he reacted early against this domestic environment, particularly the sternly restrictive creed of these 'Puritan church people', as he later denominated his forebears. Naturally he held

> For ever dear the life-bestowing breast,
> The arms that held us and the lips that prest.

But at the same time he yearned for an 'angel-guarded home' of his own, one where he might enjoy 'love for ever bright in woman's smile'. He escaped from grandparental restraint into the life of an unusually vivid imagination. As he was soon to write, 'Fair are the visions of the youthful breast'. In 'The magic of the *mind*', he found 'A charm to lure us and a spell to bind'. What stimulated him most was not the teeming life of the harbour but his own reading and, above all, the beauties of nature. As it did for many Victorians, especially Romantics and Tractarians, *The Arabian Nights* provided one of Hawker's earliest literary excitements.

The child is father of the man. I look back and I discern my ancestor, a shrinking apprehensive boy: clad in clouted clothes, hurrying through the streets away from the scorn of other boys, crouching among the pledges in a pawnbroker's warehouse in a reeky Plymouth street, to devour The Arabian Nights and with an imagery of mind even then creative, clothing that foul den with forms of fancy's mould until that Southside Street shop became the Palace of Aladdin's Lamp. And from that fountain evermore a world of beauty to inhabit, an orb of light divided from the darkness by the night of man's soul [sic].

By the age of ten he had read, among others, Shakespeare, Scott, Chatterton, Byron and Tom Moore. He soon began to write poetry himself, imitatively, yet with a genuine feeling for nature. At the age of thirteen, for example, he made lyrical mention of one of the dominant and recurring themes of his life.

> I love the ocean! from a very child
> It has been to me as a nursing breast,
> Cherishing wild fancies.

He was affected not only by the sea in which he swam naked as a boy, but also by the woodlands in which he roamed: 'I was reared among woods and always loved their leaves.' Subsequently he was often to muse in semi-poetic vein on the subject of trees, their voices in the wind, 'the groan oak, murmur beech, shriek ash', and their menacing shapes, 'knotted and gnarled like fierce Dwarfs in perpetual war'.

It was not long, however, before the young Hawker's inventive faculty found more exuberant outlets than poetry. The juvenile reaction against the pious orthodoxies of his parents, and more especially his grandparents, became an adolescent rebellion. He was sent to several preparatory schools, from which he ran away. He got into mischief at home by suggesting to Dr Hawker, with apparent innocence, revisions and improvements to a hymn which he knew perfectly well his worthy grandfather had himself composed. He acquired bad companions and embarked on a long series of practical jokes, some of them more cruel than humorous, by which he terrorized the neighbourhood and for which he is best remembered by modern Cornishmen. In some respects, too much has been made of these escapades.

Hawker was by no means unique. It has already been seen how his grandfather behaved in youth. A. L. Rowse, in his autobiography, describes the 'quite irrational pleasure' that late Victorian Cornish villagers took in simple jokes, 'playing a prank on people, some turn or other, giving them a fright, keeping up All Fools Day'. He even goes so far as to designate all this as 'genuine folk-creativeness in its own way'. Whether or not this is a correct view, one can surely see in these much-relished skylarks a crude response to the monotony and isolation of country society, a response which occurred in an especially acute form, and with a sharper edge of *Schadenfreude*, in far Cornwall. Perhaps I may be forgiven for illustrating the point with a family reminiscence of my own. In the late nineteenth century my great-grandfather was a yeoman farmer, with pretensions to being a country gentleman (he was M.F.H. of his own hunt), living at Stratton. He used regularly to visit Holsworthy market, drink far too much whisky and return home late, asleep in his trap. His clever pony knew the road home but could not open the gate of the drive, and many times my great-grandfather spent the night in an alcoholic stupor in front of that gate. At earliest dawn, after one such night, his two sons stole down from the house and, without awakening him, un-hitched the pony from the shafts of the trap, took him through the gate and hitched him up again. When my great-grandfather woke up to find the pony on one side of the gate and himself in the trap on the other he must have thought he was suffering from a sudden, violent attack of d.t.s. Horseplay indeed, but of a somewhat brutal kind. My great-grandfather never once mentioned the incident subsequently, but the rest of the family chortled over it repeatedly, told it and re-told it through the years with undiminished mirth. And it was merely one of many similar tales, some of which involved baiting people in a quite sadistic way, by which the long winter evenings were enlivened. But 'humour' was simpler and rougher at all intellectual and social levels among our ancestors. As a young man Goethe himself, doyen of European civilization in Hawker's youth, had participated in a number of uncouth practical jokes. Queen Victoria's son Edward, later designated by Hawker 'the baboon browed Prince' for his homage to Garibaldi and his neglect of charitable duties in the county of which he was duke, indulged in japes as well as scrapes. His idea of a good joke was to squirt waiters with soda siphons.

Hawker's youthful antics often had a certain savage quality about them. Indeed, all his life he remained capable of impetuous action though, as an adult, he usually sublimated it into barbed words. One of his earliest 'jokes' involved the persecution of three fashionable spinsters who had somehow antagonized him. Hawker gave a number of tradesmen bogus orders to deliver unwanted goods to them. When he finally arranged for a coffin to arrive at their door, the ladies actually left Plymouth and moved elsewhere. Another merry prank concerned an old crippled shop-keeper in Stratton named George Elias. When Elias was out one day Hawker entered his shop, locking the door behind him, hung a bundle of candles over the fire to melt and then began to make hideous noises from the back room on Elias's violoncello. The old man was appalled when he returned to the sight of roasted candles and the sound of tortured catgut, and rushed away for help, Hawker in the meantime making his escape. It was perhaps from this same shop that Hawker took the end of an enormous ball of twine and ran around Stratton tying the whole village up so that, as a local man put it, 'people passin' along was pitched on their noses without zackly knowin' why'. That Hawker intended no serious harm, to Elias at least, is evidenced by the fact that he subsequently helped him to avoid being evicted. His landlord had ordered him to quit and to advertise that the shop was to let. Elias, being illiterate, asked Hawker to compose the notice and as a consequence this discouraging rhyme was displayed in the window.

This house to let,
Both cold and wet:
In it you'll find no ease.
In winter you'll be froze to death,
In summer eat by fleas.

Hoaxes directed against the weak and ignorant always leave a sour taste in the mouth, but Hawker did not restrict himself to tormenting them. On one occasion he cut the mane of the local doctor's grey mare and painted the animal with broad black stripes to look like a zebra. He then called the doctor out with an urgent message, which obliged him to gallop through Stratton, an object of wonder and derision to the populace. Another time a local farmer was baffled by Hawker who persistently backed his horse through the hedge of his orchard and stole the apples. The man knew how the thief effected his exit from the orchard, but could not understand how he had entered in the first place. Hawker's most celebrated hoax was the best-humoured and the least harmful. This was his impersonation of a mermaid. For several moonlit nights, he sat at the end of the long Bude breakwater draped in seaweed, combing his locks and singing mournful dirges, to the consternation of the local inhabitants. Finally a farmer loudly announced his intention of peppering the apparition with buckshot, whereupon it dived into the ocean and was never seen again. Hawker's practical joking, then, was a predominant feature of his early life. It should be seen partly as a product of the natural effervescence of his personality, his bubbling, even manic, high spirits corresponding to the deep fits of depression by which his life was punctuated. Partly it was an adolescent revolt against the Evangelical discipline of home which manifested itself in a form by no means alien to the culture of his time and region.

Naturally Hawker did not settle down at school easily. He did eventually consent to board for a time at Liskeard Grammar School, but he resented pedagogic authoritarianism, worked sporadically and, though full of literary promise, never became an accomplished scholar. At the age of sixteen he left and worked briefly for a solicitor in Plymouth, He decided against the law as a profession and, his aunt paying, returned to his studies, this time at Cheltenham Grammar School. Founded in 1574, the school had, according to its historian, fallen during the first half of the nineteenth century 'in reputation and usefulness, so that only a few boys were ever on the foundation. The funds were mismanaged, the property neglected, and the school was of little advantage to the neighbourhood.' Or, indeed, to the pupils. Nevertheless, Hawker seems to have sobered down somewhat at this stage, probably because he had now determined to become a clergyman and recognized that it would be a struggle to achieve this ambition. Though there is no mention of any sudden or dramatic Evangelical conversion experience, there were undoubtedly strong religious motives behind his choice of career.

It can hardly be denied that there were also pressing social ones. Later in life Hawker wrote scathingly of his sister Caroline's aspirations for her son, Charles: 'His mother has brought him up with the vain silly idea that he is to be what nothing could make him – a gentleman.' But Hawker was almost certainly infected by a similar ambition in youth. For, of course, gentlemen could be made, as Hawker very well knew. English society had reached the transitional stage where university education could and did virtually convey gentility. Whewell, the Master of Trinity College, Cambridge, believed, for example, that a knowledge of conic sections made gentlemen. Like most Englishmen Hawker had sensitive, almost Pooterish, antennae for minute distinctions of class. He once wrote, 'I have always dreaded what the Irish call half-sirs and half-madams.' He must have realized as a very young man that he was in this invidiously intermediate position himself – a gentleman by virtue of his father's cloth, very much less than a gentleman because, to use the words of his frequent lamentation, 'how meagre in money were all my antecedents'. As a lawyer without a degree he would have been of dubious gentility: as a parson with one, nobody, least of all himself, could doubt his gentlemanly status.

It was only by diligent application that Hawker could take advantage of his aunt's generosity and realize his social and religious ambitions. But this did not prevent his continuing to write poetry. At the age of eighteen, while still at Cheltenham, he published a slim volume, entitled *Tendrils*, under the pseudonym of 'Reuben'. Though he had not yet found a voice of his own and his poems were imitative of Tom Moore and Byron, particularly as far as subject-matter and the use of anapaestic rhythms are concerned, his book showed promise. Moreover it adumbrated several themes which were to become central to Hawker's later thought and writing – the visionary faculty, vernacular superstitions and folk myths, love between the sexes, the poignancy of memory, nature. The last he hymned in a style which is pretty much Wordsworth-and-water, but with a passion which reveals it as a prime inspiration of his boyhood years.

> And I will hail thee, love thee as the flower
> Loves the young night-wind and the morning shower;
> For thou hast nurtured me, and thine the breast
> My infant minstrel lips in fear have prest,
> And thine the voice that cheered my trembling way,
> To song's high shrine with boyhood's tribute-lay.

In spite of these poetic endeavours, Hawker seems to have read widely, if not very systematically, at Cheltenham. As he later said, 'At sixteen I educated myself. No one helped me and I have been the better for it.' By 1823 he had earned himself a place at Pembroke College, Oxford, having completed his academic preparation in a characteristically romantic and unorthodox way. He recalled later how 'I lived for several months in a kind of hut upon the seashore, with a man who was a kind of half-fisherman half-wrecker; and his house was chiefly wooden, and I went there to study by myself, and what with the situation, the novelty, and the various incidents of the day and night, I do not think I was ever happier or more occupied with interest than there.'

3

Graduation

Pembroke was the cheapest Oxford college, and there is no evidence that Hawker's family could not afford to support him there until he took his degree. Baring-Gould's story that, when in 1824 his father announced that he would have to leave, Hawker immediately ran hatless all the way from Stratton to Bude and, arriving 'hot and blown', proposed on the spot to the rich godmother who had 'taught him his letters', is another piece of colourful invention. In fact, Hawker married in 1823, at nineteen, just the age his grandfather had been in the same circumstance. His bride, Charlotte I'ans, was forty-one, but she was not his godmother nor had she known him until his father had moved to Altarnun, when Hawker was about eight. She did, indeed, have an annuity of about £200 which no doubt eased Hawker's passage through Oxford, enabling him, for example, to pay his friend Jacobson to read with him for a term and a vacation. But, though no one was more conscious than Hawker of the disadvantages of poverty, he did not marry for money. Of course, he would not readily have admitted to such a thing even if it had been true, but all the evidence points to the fact that he doted on his wife passionately from the first, and remained a keenly uxorious man long after her fortune had been dissipated. In 1856 he described her as 'one of the best, most self-denying and noble-minded creatures that ever existed on the earth. She has been my inseparable companion with hardly an interval of two days.' In her old age he looked after her with care and devotion. In 1860 he wrote

touchingly, 'The continual stretch and vigilance, which are to me
a duty, almost master my mind and depress my bodily strength.
Still, thank God that I am able to nurse her and succour one who
has done as much as an army of modern women could do for
me.' At her death in 1863 he was desolated.

Charlotte was the daughter of Colonel Wrey I'ans of Whitstone.
He and his family spent part of the year living at Efford (or
Ebbingford) Manor, Bude, a beautiful old house which they rented
from Sir Thomas Acland. I'ans acted as a kind of local squire in
Bude. He was a just and benevolent man who, like Hawker after
him, exerted himself to rescue the crews and salvage the cargoes
of the many ships wrecked along the savage north Cornish coast.
'The Book of Wrecks at Bude', a manuscript cataloguing the 37
wrecks between 1756 and 1832, written by 88-year-old Jan Bray
in 1834 at Hawker's request, refers to the Colonel's 'great kindness'
and contains evidence to show that if saving goods from the sea
was a hazardous business, guarding them on the shore could be
even more of a problem. I'ans, though, was vigilant and determined. On one occasion, apparently, Bray and others were set to
make sure that a cargo of butter did not fall into the hands of local
wreckers. At about midnight, Bray records, 'eight stout men came
and they said they came for butter and butter they would have. A
battle ensued . . . The first man I engaged was one Cory, a blacksmith from Jacobstow. I gave him a blow in the peeping holes and
down he fell, his hat and wig fell on the ground and Mr Dennis
and I secured them . . . [etc., etc.]' I'ans was given a number of
tokens of thanks for his rescue-work, as was Hawker at a later
date.

The Colonel died in 1816, leaving four daughters, of whom
Charlotte was the third. In the words of one witness, she was 'tall,
fair, and comely, with suave and winning manners, and very
accomplished'. Another contemporary describes her as 'a person
of considerable attractions, well educated, fond of literature, a
good companion, and in every respect a lady'. 'Her face', according to Hawker himself, 'was indeed a perfect image of noble

Womanhood – oval – blue-eyed – with a nose slightly curved somewhat like my own – a firm mouth, and a forehead moderately high banded with soft light hair that never turned gray to the last.' 'Her form was as upright and her flesh as firm in later life as when I married her.' She had, moreover, a quiet but sharp sense of humour, very necessary in the wife of a man like Hawker. In this extract from one of the few of her letters which survive, her sly, Jane-Austenish amusement at the jockeying for social advantage in the Morwenstow neighbourhood is delightfully apparent. She complains of the

> most awful doings here. The committee of gentlemen consisting of William Sherm, Abrahams & Co., have decreed that no farmers or their wives or their sons or their daughters are to be admitted at the monthly soirées held at Stratton. Even the Sherms of Stowe are cut off ... This committee meeting took place last Tuesday and we have not seen any of the under-the-line ones since. I cannot tell you how they bear the disgrace! We had a card of admittance sent, but I cannot attend unless I can draw another line, and if I do there will be nobody left as I should certainly cut off all the rest. What high life below stairs we exhibit in this Stratton hundred.

Unlike her husband, who had no ear, Charlotte was fond of music and played the piano well. She had a distinct provincial brogue, which Hawker probably shared and which endeared her to him – he grew up before snobbery about accents, produced by the growth of the public schools, became rampant, and always loved what he called 'the Cornish twang or sing-song way wherein they do not converse but chant in their talk'. Charlotte knew German, and undertook a number of translations of literary works, damaging her eyes in the process. She was modest to a fault, never celebrating her birthday because she 'deems the day of life too deep for smiles', never allowing her likeness to be taken, so that there are no pictures of her in existence. Charlotte loved flowers and at Morwenstow 'enjoyed the *simplicities of life* – good bread, good milk and butter, good bacon (all our own pigs) and a good bed for nightly rest. She used to say that with her list we might very well do without the luxuries of a loftier life.' All in all, she was an admirable vicar's wife – busy, sympathetic, generous to others, yet 'abstinence itself' where her own needs were concerned. She was undoubtedly a good deal more universally loved in the parish than her tempestuous husband, who made enemies as well as friends. Her own devotion to him never seems to have wavered. After her death, one of Hawker's oldest friends wrote to him, 'her kindness and varied accomplishments, her wonderful memory, and cheerful conversation and her sympathy with your views all come back to me vividly.'

How did such a paragon of female high-mindedness and good sense come to attach herself to a wild creature like Hawker, young enough to be her son, and impoverished to boot? She did so in the face of opposition from her elder sisters, who harped on the disparity between their ages and the general imprudence of the match. Moreover, there seems to be a strong likelihood that Hawker made matrimonial overtures to one of these older sisters, who rejected him, before he proposed to Charlotte – uneasy shades of Mr Collins on his part perhaps, though happily none of Miss Lucas on hers. Probably Charlotte was first drawn to Hawker by their common love of literature, and he to her by the fact that as a youth he desired nothing more than to read omnivorously, and there was a well-stocked library and a well-informed guide to be found at Whitstone. There, according to one who knew them, 'Young, handsome, and brilliant, he was ever a welcome guest.' Even so, Charlotte must have had a vivid romantic streak to exchange her secure spinsterhood for a man who had nothing but a flamboyant reputation and prospects which in themselves were hardly very dazzling. The fact of the matter is that Hawker was then, as he remained throughout his life, highly attractive to women. He combined daredevil ebullience with poetic sensibility. He possessed a faculty for self-dramatization and a power of empathy. He was at once interesting and engaging. As far as Charlotte I'ans was concerned her marriage was a love-match from start to finish. The same could be said of Hawker.

The couple spent their honeymoon at Tintagel, where Hawker (like Hardy after him) first became interested in the Arthurian legends, about which his finest poem was written over forty years later, just after Charlotte's death. Then, at the beginning of 1824, they went up to Oxford, riding not on a single horse but in one of the numerous coaches which ran from Exeter. Being a married undergraduate, Hawker was forced to transfer from Pembroke to Magdalen Hall. Here he seems to have pursued a gay social life, entertaining his wife's two older sisters (so much so that he was nicknamed 'the man with three wives'), throwing champagne breakfasts for his friends and indulging his passion for sartorial extravagance, in every sense of that word. He later wrote, 'What money I have wasted in former days. I remember tailors' bills with annual averages of £20.' And he afterwards admonished a young friend,

> You are in what is called among snobs a fast College. I earnestly advise you to eschew its fast men. I am now suffering from the effects of silly and idle outlay at Oxford. I do hope that nothing will induce you to accept that base credit which those cormorants the Oxford tradesmen always try to force on freshmen in order to harass and rob them afterwards. No fast undergraduate in all my remembrance ever settled down into a respectable man. Ask God for *strong angels* and he will fulfil your prayer.

Apparently, in spite of his lavish outlay, Hawker did not consider that he had been a 'fast' man at Oxford.

Hawker's penchant for practical joking was not suppressed by marital responsibility or by academic commitments for, as he said, 'the University supplied but little excitement of mental kind'. He records one 'merrie jest' in *Footprints of Former Men in Far Cornwall*. It deserves to be quoted at length for two reasons.

First, it is a characteristic sample of Hawker's public prose (his
private letters, written impromptu, are much better). It is over-
elaborate and over-facetious, prone to archaism and allusiveness,
mostly affected but occasionally effective. The passage illustrates,
secondly, the unsophisticated, knockabout quality of Hawker's
(and many of his contemporaries') humour, with its willingness to
exploit the credulity of the simple and the uneducated.

There was an ancient woman, blear-eyed and dim-sighted,
'worn nature's mournful monument,' who had the far and
wide repute of witchcraft among the College servants and the
'baser sort' in the suburbs of the town; but in reality she was a
mere 'wreck of eld,' a harmless and helpless old creature,
who stood at more than one College-gate for alms. Her
well-known name was Nanny Heale. Her cottage, or rather
decayed old hut, leaned against a steep mound by the castle-
wall, and was so hugged in by the ground that, from a path
along the ramparts a passer-by might cast a bird's-eye look
down Nanny's chimney, and watch her hearth and home.
One winter evening certain frolicsome wights, out of College
in search of a channel for the exuberant spirits of their age,
were pacing, like Hardicanute, the wall east and west, when a
glance down the witch's chimney revealed a quaint and simple
scene of humble life. There she crouched, close by the
smoking embers, peering into the fire; and before her very
nose there hung, just over the fire, a round iron vessel, called
in the western counties a crock, filled to the brim with
potatoes, and without a cover or lid. This utensil was sus-
pended by its swing-handle to an iron bar, which went from
side to side of the chimney wall. To see and to assail the weak
point in a field of battle is evermore the signal of a great
captain. The onslaught was instantly planned. A rope, with a
hook of iron at the end, was slowly and noiselessly lowered
down the chimney, and, unnoted by poor Nanny's blinking
sight, the handle of the iron pot was softly grasped by the

crook, and the vessel with its mealy contents began to ascend in silent majesty towards the upper air. Thoroughly roused by this unnatural and ungrateful demeanour of her life-long companion of the hearth, old Nanny arose from her stool, peered anxiously upward to watch the ascent, and shouted at the top of her voice:

'Massy 'pon my sinful soul! art gwain off – taties and all?'

The vessel was quietly grasped, carried down in hot haste, and planted upright outside the cottage-door. A knock, given for the purpose, summoned the inmate, who hurried out and stumbled over, as she afterwards interpreted the event, her penitent crock.

'So then,' was her joyful greeting – 'so then! theer't come back to holt, then! Ay 'tis a cold out 'o doors.'

Extra-curricular activity of this sort was perhaps more the rule than the exception among undergraduates in pre-Tractarian Oxford. Witness the contemporary squib:

> Farewell stupid Oxford! away I must scud;
> As for *study*, I ne'er could get farther than *stud*.

It is easy to understand why lively undergraduates bade Oxford adieu in such terms. The university was situated in a small, sleepy provincial town with little to offer in the way of entertainment apart from walks and talk. Oxford was so remote from London that Black Will, the coachman, was able to keep a wife in both places, each remaining in ignorance of the other's existence for some long time. Even by the end of the nineteenth century, Hardy, in *Jude the Obscure*, could represent a villager who lived only twenty miles distant from 'Christminster' as never having visited the city and being vague about its exact location. The university itself was only beginning to emerge from the eighteenth-century torpor so eloquently, if jaundicedly, described in Gibbon's *Autobiography*. The dons, celibate, clerical, conservative, 'steeped in port and privilege', were decent easy men, who supinely enjoyed the gifts of the founder; their days were filled by a series of uniform employments; the chapel and the hall, the coffee-house and the common room, till they retired, weary and well satisfied to a long slumber. From the toil of reading, or thinking, or writing, they had absolved their conscience ... Their conversation stagnated in a round of college business, Tory politics, personal anecdotes, and private scandal: their dull and deep potations excused the brisk intemperance of youth.

It was a measure of Oxford's obscurantism that scientific studies were almost unknown in Hawker's day and never impinged on his mind at all. Although Professor Buckland had begun to give some stimulus to geology, his researches were thought by many to be dangerous. John Keble argued with him all the way from Oxford to Winchester on top of a coach about the eroding effects geology was having on Genesis, by making it difficult to accept Archbishop Ussher's authoritative dating of the Creation in the year 4004 B.C. Keble 'finally took his stand on the conceivability and indeed certainty of the Almighty having created all the fossils and other apparent outcomes of former existence in the six days of the Creation'. There may have been no overt antithesis between science and religion while Hawker was at Oxford, but Keble was not alone in discerning a growing tension. It is recorded that a certain Dr Kidd, 'after examining some delicate morphological preparation, while his young colleague explained its meaning, made answer first, that he did not believe in it, and, secondly, that if it were true he did not think God meant us to know it'. Thus, though mathematics was studied, scholarship was largely classical in the 1820s. And where it existed, it usually did so not for its own sake but for what it would bring its practitioners in terms of social prestige and ecclesiastical or academic preferment. Dean Gaisford of Christ Church gave undergraduates the following judicious advice at the end of a sermon: 'Nor can I do better, in conclusion, than impress upon you the study of Greek literature, which not only elevates above the vulgar herd, but leads not infrequently to positions of considerable emolument.'

Hawker would not have been unconscious of either of these advantages as he pursued his intermittent studies at the university. Like Mark Pattison and others, he gained neither help nor inspiration from his official tutors whose one talent, when indeed they possessed that, was a parrot-like ability to (in the slang phrase of the time) 'construe Thucydides "through a deal board"'. Hawker later wrote, 'I am self-educated from the Greek alphabet, which I learnt after entering Oxford, upwards.' In fact, he disliked the discipline of classical studies because it put a higher premium on memory than on originality as an intellectual quality. His mind, like that of the future Archbishop Whately (whom he resembled in various other ways), was 'an instrument rather than a receptacle'. Hawker was most stimulated by his diffuse and unsystematic reading of the early Church Fathers. For their whole ethos, especially their unscientific methods, their anxiety to surrender reason to faith, he felt a strong affinity. 'Were they', he asked, 'literal, exact, punctilious? I think not. They drew the sword and threw the scabbard underneath.' Occasionally his imagination was stirred and his concentration engaged by a particular writer. Plato he described as 'a vast Gentile mind imbued with every native and natural creed . . . manhood as far as it could go without Revelation, Moses at the foot of Sinai'. Generally, though, Hawker revelled in greedy eclecticism.

He was unwilling to fix his attention for long on any academic subject. Though he sometimes pretended to scholarship he had, as even his most ardent modern admirer could only conclude, 'a Notes and Queries mind'. Hawker's intellect was a capacious rag-bag stuffed with the shreds and tatters of learning, a magpie's nest full of glittering antiquarian trinkets. His 'Thought Books' tell the tale of wide but shallow reading. They contain tags in Latin, Greek, Italian, French, German and Hebrew, and quotations from or references to a broad range of authors – to name but a few, and to omit classical and religious writers: Dante, Racine,

Johnson, Gibbon, Goethe, Schiller, Scott, Southey, De Quincey, Talleyrand, Cobbett, Sydney Smith, Carlyle, Proudhon. Hawker's reading consisted more of dipping and skipping than of sustained study because, like many Romantics, he valued books for inspiration rather than information. His was the mind of a creator, a poet, a mystic. He read in order to generate the intense intuitional experiences which provided him with knowledge which he considered to be more profound, and more real and true, than that afforded by the senses. He later explained, 'There was a valuable usage in old times; I follow it now. When a theme of thought had been read in any book the reader used to shut it and to close his eyes and meditate on that particular theme and thus a great deal of knowledge came into the mind from without – from God's grace, from the Paraclete whose office is to fill the mind with good and holy thoughts.' In short, Hawker's mind was a lamp rather than a mirror.

Finding his own imagination much more interesting than the thoughts of others, Hawker derived no deep or lasting impressions from Oxford. His politics do not seem to have been coloured by the prevailing Toryism; he remained an anomalous combination of the reactionary and the radical. He never had any affiliation or commitment to a political party, writing in 1858 that he did not 'care one farthing whether Whig or Tory be in power'. Nor were his religious views much affected by Oxford. While he was at university the Tractarian movement was beginning to germinate, and most of its main proponents were his contemporaries, though he probably knew only Bloxam at all well. But though, like many who came from Evangelical backgrounds, Hawker did not find it difficult to assimilate the theological ideas of the Oxford Movement, he refused to adhere to a Church party. His closest friends at Oxford, both of whom subsequently became bishops, were the moderate High Churchman, William Jacobson, and the distinctly Low Church Francis Jeune. He later entertained at Morwenstow both the formidable High Church bishop, Henry Phillpotts of Exeter, and the Rev. George Gorham, who was

Phillpotts's Low Church adversary in a celebrated lawsuit over the vexed question of Baptismal Regeneration (i.e. whether Christians are 'born again' at baptism or have to be subsequently converted). Hawker 'always disclaimed the application of either of these words [High or Low Church] to myself'. He was adamantly independent. Throughout his life he was always too idiosyncratic to accept the role of orthodox discipleship. If Oxford influenced Hawker at all it did so by confirming him in his own individualism.

Though Hawker did not achieve high academic honours at university, he did manage to carry off the Newdigate Poetry Prize. His poem had no more and no less merit than those of other undergraduate winners in the nineteenth century, among whom are numbered some of the most distinguished names of the age – Ruskin, Matthew Arnold, Oscar Wilde. But it is interesting, and throws some rather ambiguous light on Hawker's character in one controversial respect. Hawker has been accused of having deliberately plagiarized the poem. George Murray, one of several Victorian critics who made the charge, wrote in 1853, 'As a notable instance of well-sustained and ingenious plagiarism, we may compare the Newdigate of 1827, on Pompeii, to Mr Macaulay's Cambridge prize poem of 1819 on the same subject.' More recently, a well-known scholar has agreed: 'The charge of plagiarism is not without foundation. A comparison of Hawker's *Pompeii* with Macaulay's earlier prize-poem on the same subject (1819) reveals structural obligations not otherwise to be explained.'

The case for the prosecution rests on the similarity of the overall scheme of both poems and the existence of a number of almost identical lines. For example, Macaulay wrote,

> With fillets bound the hoary priests advance,
> And rosy virgins braid the choral dance.

Hawker's rendering was

> Breathless they gaze, while white-robed priests advance
> And graceful virgins lead the sacred dance.

The case for the defence argues that there is no external evidence to prove plagiarism and that two near-contemporary undergraduates, tapping the same few classical sources, would inevitably throw up similar poetic ideas. Also, in 1826 Hawker had translated Schiller's poem on the same subject which his own (and Macaulay's) resembled in certain, admittedly slight ways. No sure verdict can be reached. It is possible that Hawker had read Macaulay's poem some time before he wrote his own and was half-remembering when he thought he was creating. Later he certainly recognized this propensity in himself and had *The Quest of the Sangraal* checked by a friend for unconscious plagiarism. On the other hand, Hawker's subsequent hysterical excitement, at times paranoia, on the subject of plagiarism – he seemed to consider that when he had treated a legend poetically the original became his copyright – may indicate guilt-feelings at a juvenile peccadillo of his own in this direction. It is also true that some of his literary methods were distinctly Chattertonian. And the fact that almost every other opium-eating poet of the period was guilty of plagiarism may be regarded as significant circumstantial evidence.

One thing, though, is clear. Hawker gave ample proof in his other work that his was no vicarious talent, that he was a poet in his own right. Even before he had composed *Pompeii*, he had published the ballad by which he is best remembered today – 'The Song of the Western Men'. It is based on a chorus (italicized below) supposedly written about the imprisonment of one of the Seven Bishops, Sir Jonathan Trelawny, by James II in 1688, but more probably referring to the incarceration in the Tower of the pro-Royalist Sir John Trelawny in 1628. The whole poem, when Hawker published it anonymously in 1825, was taken by four competent judges, Davies Gilbert, Scott, Macaulay and Dickens, to have been an original seventeenth-century popular song. The spirited rhythm and the stout provincial sentiments seemed to give it the stamp of authenticity.

56

A good sword and a trusty hand!
A merry heart and true!
King James's men shall understand
What Cornish lads can do!

And have they fixed the where and when?
And shall Trelawny die?
Here's twenty thousand Cornish men
Will know the reason why!

Out spake their Captain brave and bold:
A merry wight was he: –
'If London Tower were Michael's hold,
We'd set Trelawny free!

'We'll cross the Tamar, land to land:
The Severn is no stay:
With "one and all," and hand in hand;
And who shall bid us nay?

'And when we come to London Wall,
A pleasant sight to view,
Come forth! come forth! ye cowards all:
Here's men as good as you.

'Trelawny he's in keep and hold:
Trelawny he may die:
But here's twenty thousand Cornish bold
Will know the reason why!'

Nearly forty years after Hawker had written this ballad he reflected bitterly on its popular reception compared to the failure of his life at Morwenstow. 'All these years the Song has been bought and sold, set to music and applauded, while I have lived on among these far away rocks unprofited, unpraised and unknown. This is an epitome of my whole life.' It may have seemed so then. At the time he wrote the song, on vacation at a cottage in the lovely Coombe Valley on the southern boundary of Morwenstow parish, he was in the first flush of youthful optimism. Happily married to a wealthy woman, already successful as a poet and full of the promise of greater achievements ahead, about to embark on a career calculated to fulfil all his aspirations, Hawker could not but have looked with confidence towards the future. His rumbustious high spirits overflowed in more practical jokes, playing the ghost in Coombe Valley, releasing (in company with Francis Jeune) the pigs from their sties at Boscastle, so that they charged through the town and convinced the inhabitants that they were 'mazed' or bewitched – 'all the pegs up-town have a-rebelled, and they've a-be, and let one the wother out, and they be all a-gwain to sea huz-a-muz, bang!' Such light-heartedness did not deflect Hawker from the determined pursuit of his ecclesiastical ambitions. After taking his B.A. degree at Oxford in June 1828, he began to prepare for deacon's orders at his wife's house at Whitstone.

Once more, as he was to do yet again at Morwenstow, Hawker sought solitude in nature. Life, as he once defined it, was 'an omnipresent religious and personal interpretation of nature', and where better to fulfil this purpose than among the beautiful woods around Whitstone? There among the trees he could rhapsodize in tune with 'the soft eye music of slow waving boughs'. There he could absorb that scenery which 'enlarges a man's thoughts'. He later recorded, 'I built a kind of log hut in the wood, a mile from any house, and there read for Deacon's orders, only going home at night. It was one of my most peaceful periods of life. I learnt St. Paul's Epistles by heart there, and ever afterwards I used to revert to my Woodhouse with pleasure and regret.' Perhaps it is these remote, rustic huts, to which Hawker so often fled, which really epitomize his life. Only in isolation, divorced from the conveniences and complexities of 'civilization', distant from the pleasures and temptations of society, could he realize his true self and complete his unique destiny. When Bishop Phillpotts offered, in 1834, to prefer Hawker to Morwenstow, he expected him to refuse that cure and seek one 'in some district where access to congenial society would be easy to you'. Hawker accepted, obviously feeling that only in such seclusion could he travel in time as well as space far from Victorian England, which he damned (and not only in black moods) as 'a sea-girt charnel-house of crime', back to an era of faith for which he could feel full sympathy. He was clearly thinking of this kind of moral and spiritual fulfilment when he inscribed in one of his 'Thought Books', under the heading *Solitude*, the lines,

> Type of the Wise, who soar but never roam,
> True to the kindred points, Heaven and their home.

Many hermits, one suspects, are forced into their anchoretic role because the world, perhaps for sound reasons, dislikes and rejects them – T. H. White is a good modern example. The opposite was true of Hawker. He sought and embraced with a whole heart his solitary station on Morwenna's cliffs.

4

Morwenstow

Before being preferred to Morwenstow, Hawker was made deacon in 1829 and ordained priest in 1831. He served as curate in the small village of North Tamerton, about two miles away from Whitstone, until 1834 at a stipend of £90 per annum. Hardly anything is known about him during these years. He pursued his antiquarian interests. He continued to write poetry. There are indications that at this period of prosperity he lived more as country gentleman than country parson. Though he was later to abhor the killing of animals and to write 'I never take away life', he certainly shot birds as a young man and he may well have joined the considerable West Country fraternity of hunting parsons (which he was later to condemn). The bishop of Exeter had to enjoin him to move out of his wife's comfortable house at Whitstone, and into the parish, where he converted a cottage on the moor and, as it was surrounded by pagan burial-mounds (some of which he excavated), he called it 'Trebarrow' or 'a dwelling among the graves'. Hawker was apparently concerned to establish his respectability after his riotous youth. He wrote to Sir Thomas Acland in pique when he was omitted from the invitation-list to the laying of the foundation stone of St Michael's Chapel, Bude, in 1834. And he much resented having been, as he considered it, contaminated by association with two parishioners in North Tamerton whom he visited in all innocence as 'Colonel and Mrs Norris'. She was 'highly rouged and in my rural opinion improperly dressed. She talked largely about their place in

Norfolk.' Hawker was indignant when he eventually discovered the true identity of the couple – 'Lord Edward Thynne and Madame Vestris the opera Dancer'.

Still, no concern for his reputation at North Tamerton could curb Hawker's burgeoning eccentricity, and it is recorded that, like Robert Herrick before him, he kept a pet pig. The creature, named Gyp, was 'well-groomed and intelligent', and followed him like a dog in his parochial visitations. When Mrs Kingdon, his sister, objected to Gyp coming into her house at Whitstone, Robert would retort rudely, 'He's as well-behaved as any of your family.' Such peculiarities either did not reach the ears of the bishop of Exeter or were not enough to disqualify Hawker from the early preferment for which he had been marked down. Phillpotts's sole hesitation about promoting Hawker to Morwenstow was the one mentioned at the end of the last chapter. Hawker's gratitude to his worldly, pluralistic bishop was unfeigned. It expressed itself both in practical form, the seasonal gift of a pair of woodcock (much appreciated at the Palace), and in poetic – an unpublished stanza of verse:

> Let but one Name be cherished – his who gave
> Home to a Western heart on this dear shore,
> Where scenes long lov'd in youth still haunt the wave,
> The ancient Seawinds sigh – the native Waters roar.

To say that Morwenstow is situated in the north-east part of the Cornish coast gives, to those who do not know the area, a misleading impression. As Hawker himself once explained to a friend,

> When English people hear or speak about Cornwall I always find that they mean the region about Penzance which is in temperature and soil very like Madeira and the south and is unlike this bleak, bare shore of the Bristol Channel, called in old books the Severn Sea, as a country can well be. To give you a truly Cornish illustration – in that district they can produce potatoes three months earlier than we.

Morwenstow is indeed an awesomely bleak place, hemmed in by rough moorland to the east and so ravaged by storms from the Atlantic on its western border that the trees, when they grow at all (and Hawker's efforts to establish new ones always failed), bend inland to avoid the blast. The massive cliffs rise vertically to 450 feet in places and such is their height that on a clear day it is possible to see as far as the mountains of Wales to the north, Lundy to the north-west and Trevose Head to the south-west. To the west, as Hawker was fond of telling his visitors, there is not a speck of land between Morwenstow and the coast of Labrador.

The north Cornish cliffs have been riven over millions of years by streams and cataracts. There are seven sharp breaks in the rock-face in Morwenstow parish alone, and more up and down the shore, making coastal travel a nightmare of ascending and descending tracks. Hawker often described harrowing journeys amid ice and snow, gale and rain to Welcombe, a village in Devon just over his northern border, of which he was curate after 1850: 'Wellcombe [sic] Church is two miles and a half only from this house but the road is down one precipice (half a mile long) and up another, and this repeated twice without 100 yards of level on the brow between the hills. Nothing but Carrow my pony (Cornish for deer) could accomplish it.' It is hardly surprising that a man of Hawker's temperament should have been startled by a demon on one of his rides from Welcombe. 'As I entered the Gulph between the Vallies to-day, a Storm leaped from the Sea and rushed at me roaring – I recognised a Demon and put Carrow into a gallop and so escaped.' Even men with less imagination than Hawker might easily conjure up visions of the supernatural and succumb to panic in a place where the landscape and the elements conspire so fearfully together.

There is no real village of Morwenstow. The parish, which is very large in area, consisting of about 7,000 acres, comprises a few scattered hamlets, Woodford, Crosstown, Shop, Gooseham, Eastcott, Woolley, West Youlstone, several old manor houses,

Stanbury, Marsland and, most notably, Tonacombe, and a number of isolated farmsteads. These are joined by narrow, winding lanes, and separated by mixed pasture and arable fields, or by stretches of moorland on the high ground in the east, and woods in the western valleys. As in many villages which were originally Celtic, the parish church stands alone in the fields with only the vicarage and the glebe farm nearby. This delighted Hawker, who believed that people should not just drop into church but should make a special pilgrimage to the House of the Lord. The church's position is uniquely imposing and beautiful, for it dominates a wooded gorge with huge cliffs towering on either side and the sea before it. It seems likely that a church was first erected on the spot by one of the Irish missionaries who evangelized Cornwall between the fifth and seventh centuries. Certainly the Saxon font bears witness to the fact that the Normans built on a site which had already been for long occupied by a place of worship.

The name Morwenstow is an interesting combination of Celtic 'Morwen' (possibly meaning 'white or fair as the sea' or perhaps derived from St Morwenna) and the Saxon 'stow' (church), which suggests that the church was a going concern at the time when it marked the furthest limit of the Saxon advance into Cornwall, during the eighth century. Hawker's explanation of the origins of his church is a characteristic blend of legend and invention. He tells of Breachan, a Celtic king of Wales in the ninth century who had twenty-four children, one of whom was Morwenna, 'wise, learned, and holy above her generation'. Very often, in the words which Hawker put into Morwenna's mouth, 'from my abode in wild Wales, have I watched across the waves until the westering sun fell red upon that Cornish rock [of Henna-cliff], and I have said in my maiden vows, "Alas! and would to God a font might be hewn and an altar built among the stones of yonder barbarous hill."' According to Hawker, she fulfilled her wish. Unfortunately for this story there is simply no authentic information about the foundation of the church at Morwenstow.

Time has obliterated all but the physical remnants of Hawker's 'Saxon shrine'.

What is clear, however, is that from the Dark Ages until the coming of the motor-car Morwenstow remained a remote and inaccessible part of a distant and backward province. Bishop Grandisson's lament, on arrival at the diocese of Exeter in the fourteenth century, might have been echoed by any involuntary exile in the West Country until the twentieth: 'I am not only set down . . . in the ends of the earth, but in the very ends of the ends thereof.' Cornwall is geographically isolated, a peninsula surrounded by sea on three sides, with the Tamar river making a barrier on the fourth. It abandoned Celtic Christianity nearly three centuries after the rest of England. It was conquered later; the earliest stone crosses are 'primarily protests, silent and even unconscious, against the Saxon intruders, symbols of Celtic nationalism'. (Even today Cornish nationalism is not entirely defunct, and there is talk among some of erecting a *bona fide* Corn wall to keep foreigners out of 'Kernow'.) The Cornish language remained common speech in many parts of the county until Elizabethan times and was still used by a few as late as the eighteenth century. Even in the mid-nineteenth century visitors found that the Cornish 'peasantry speak a *patois* quite unintelligible to the people of any other part of England'. The French Revolution hardly had any influence in Cornwall, and Captain Swing and the Luddites raised 'scarcely an echo in the West'. Chartism made no progress there. The Industrial Revolution virtually passed the far north of Cornwall by. Indigenous customs and superstitions helped to cut the county off from the mainland. The few Roman roads which penetrated into Cornwall had quickly vanished, and even by 1760 it was said that there was hardly a stretch of highway in the county which was fit for wheeled traffic. Sir Christopher Hawkins's coach caused astonishment when it was first introduced during the 1760s, and there was little enough roadway for this amazing 'house on wheels' to run on, until the turnpike movement began to improve matters. Yet

1 Hawker in 1825, as an Oxford undergraduate

2 Hawker in about 1870 with his second wife, Pauline, and their
eldest daughter, Morwenna, in front of his vicarage

3 Hawker's vicarage as it is today, almost unchanged since his
own time

4 The shepherd's lantern, with candleholder, carried by Hawker to light his way from vicarage to church; the transparent panels are of horn

5 Morwenstow church today, as seen from the front garden of Hawker's vicarage

6 The footpath from Hawker's vicarage to the church

by 1794 one observer could still report, 'carts are not made use of in this county. Everything is carried on the pack-saddle.' Railways were slow to enter Cornwall – Hawker did not see one until 1845 and did not travel by rail until 1864 – and a line did not reach Bude until 1898, twenty-three years after his death. Even then it has been estimated that Hartland Point, what Defoe called 'a huge promontory, a mountainlike proboscis' to the north of Morwenstow, was the furthest land in the kingdom from a railhead. In short, one may extend a summary account of the landscape to cover Cornwall in almost all its aspects: 'Although of England it is quite un-English.'

Of course rural isolation was a commonplace among our forebears, and it has often been described, most evocatively in such classic literary studies of village life as Flora Thompson's *Lark Rise*, George Orwell's *Coming up for Air*, Laurie Lee's *Cider with Rosie* and Ronald Blythe's *Akenfield*. Railways relieved this isolation only patchily. Before trains arrived, travel was difficult and expensive. The poor seldom ventured far from home. When a new vicar took over the large parish of Wartling, Sussex, in 1866 he discovered that 'many' of his flock 'had never even seen the outside of the church, but only vaguely knew in what direction it was'. Hawker did not exaggerate when he said that, among his own parishioners, 'A visit to a distant market-town is an achievement to render a man an authority or an oracle among his brethren.' Even the wealthy avoided travel. In 1829 Dr Arnold of Rugby recorded, 'More than half my boys never saw the sea, and never were in London.' Distances seemed immense when laboriously traversed over bad roads on horseback or by carriage. The authoritative historian of Devon, W. G. Hoskins, writes,

The village of Bridford lay only nine miles south-west of Exeter by road, yet the rector tells us that when Napoleon's invasion of England was considered to be imminent the well-to-do families of Exeter made plans for flight to Bridford as though it were another continent. The same parson noted that in 1818 he buried three very old men who had been born in the parish, never lived out of it, and died in it. This is a more authentic picture of the nature of communications in Devon than any statistics about turnpike trusts and stage coach timing.

Yet Morwenstow was remarkably sequestered even by nineteenth-century standards. The flourishing state of the port of Bude Haven, which had what was arguably the most dangerous harbour in the country for the ingress and egress of sailing ships, is ample evidence of the difficulty of inland communication. More is provided by the remarkable construction of the Bude canal, with its convolutions, locks, aqueducts, inclined planes and tunnel. There can have been few country parsons who received *The Times*, as Hawker did in 1865, three days after it was published. As the Morwenstow population dwindled through emigration, so the meagre amenities and contacts with the outside world diminished. In 1864 Hawker wrote, 'Mine is without exception the most desolate parish for food in the country. We have no parish butcher – I remember when there were three – no carrier or coach, not even a shop.' It was not even worth the while of the Bude-to-Bideford carrier, who took a full day to cover the distance between the two towns, to pass through Morwenstow after 1858. Morwenstow had to rely on its own produce and on travelling pedlars and their packs. It was to be expected that Hawker, 'only fastened to the far world by the fibre of a Daily Post, granted by Lord Lonsdale as a special compassion to my loneliness', should often have bemoaned his desolate lot. Others were not less sensitive. A prospective curate refused to come to the neighbourhood because 'he could not live a week in "so isolated and dreary a place"'. On Lady Day 1862, Hawker recorded, 'A man in a farm near the churchyard leaves his place because of the noise made by the rooks and because "it is so lonesome".' Visitors could hardly comprehend how Hawker survived at all and they sometimes scarcely bothered to hide their contempt for his rustication. The distinguished theologian James Mozley, his wife and her two sisters, called at Morwenstow vicarage in 1863, as Hawker describes.

Mozley writes the literary articles in the Times and is what is called a great gun in the world of modern literature. He was quite full of the great world of Oxford and of London and he confessed that nothing would induce him to live in such a place as Morwenstow. The ladies also seemed quite to scorn so rural a place and when I said there was but little society they asked how any one could exist in such a remote corner. When I ventured to name books I was told that no one could always be reading. But they were very inclined to snub me in their mode of reply.

Hawker's parishioners did little to decrease his feelings of isolation. Though he resembled them in many ways and understood them in more, there was a great social, economic and cultural gulf fixed between the vicar and his people. Hawker described them as 'a mixed multitude of smugglers, wreckers, and dissenters of various hue', whom he had, respectively, to 'persuade' 'soothe' and 'handle'. This was a romantic oversimplification. There may still have been some smuggling but what had once been a flourishing industry was sharply on the decline by the 1840s and '50s. Wreckers, in the sense of men who lured ships on to the rocks, there were none in the nineteenth century (nor had there been for some long time before it). but there were plenty who combed the beaches for wreckage. Hawker often did have to restrain their instincts to plunder rich cargoes. These were a constant temptation because they seemed to have been sent so providentially – as this piece of doggerel indicates:

> The *Good Samaritan* came ashore
> To feed the hungry and clothe the poor,
> Barrels of beef and bales of linen
> No poor man shall want a shillin'.

Hawker was right in saying that there were numerous Dissenters in Morwenstow. He was told by a Methodist shortly after his arrival that his parish was 'the garden of our circuit'.

However, Morwenstow's population, as the parish registers prosaically reveal, consisted mainly of farmers, labourers and servants. Out of a population of 868 in 1861 there were approximately seventy yeomen farmers, sixty farm-labourers, numerous servants and a few workers in other categories – thatchers, cordwainers, carpenters, millers, blacksmiths, masons, etc. It was a poor and diminishing population (having numbered 1,074 in 1851), as Hawker explained: 'We have no mines, not a single manufactory and the introduction of machinery into agriculture has so diminished the need for farm labourers that there is nothing to allure men to settle in such a country.' It was also an overwhelmingly uneducated population though the literacy rate was surprisingly high. Seventy per cent of those marrying in the 1850s signed their own names in the parish register, which was well above the national average. If Hawker was not exactly, in Swift's ironical phrase, the one literate man in the parish, he must have felt himself to be a cultural exile, especially as there were no permanently resident gentry in Morwenstow. Admittedly the Waddon Martyns of Tonacombe Manor seem to have been present for some of the time, but because of their habit of favouring Dissenting tenantry Hawker's relations with them were not always cordial. His anguish at the departure of gentlefolk on one occasion is eloquent testimony of his need for some social and intellectual intercourse at his own level: 'It was indeed a gift from God to have a thorough lady and gentleman in the parish to appreciate the utterance of truth and the efforts of duty was indeed a happiness and is now gone [sic].'

Other factors besides their ignorance helped to separate Hawker from his parishioners. Though he sympathized with their poverty and did what he could to alleviate it, he could not but be alienated by the 'coarse brutality' which he so often witnessed in 'this barbarous neighbourhood'. Perhaps he was over-sensitive but callousness was an endemic feature of nineteenth-century life and it would not do to dismiss as entirely paranoid Hawker's cry, 'Human nature is bad, English nature is worse but Morwenstow nature is vilest of all.' He was horrified by his people's inhumanity to each other. It manifested itself in such incidents as the death from starvation of two children who had been driven out of the house by their mother to collect firewood, or in the occasional practice of a man's leading his wife to market by a halter and selling her to the highest bidder. Hawker loved animals and, like Charles Kingsley, believed that they had a future life, whereas his parishioners habitually treated them with cruelty. Bear-baiting, tail-piping, swallowing live mice, sparrow-mumbling (stripping the feathers off a live bird with the lips alone) and other horrors which had been commonplace in the Cornwall of Hawker's youth were no longer practised. But there was still a casual, perennial maltreatment of the brute creation which Hawker, who never sold his stock to a butcher, found repulsive.

A teetotaller himself in his later years, he hated the frequent drunkenness of his neighbours, deploring the behaviour of one Thomas Howard who went 'to the Blue Fox ... and undressed himself entirely before an assembled group', or of Lord John Thynne's agent, the lawyer, Shearm – 'The *wretch* is reeling drunk again. The boys pulling his coat and poking him with sticks as he staggers about ... His servants lock him in. He calls from the window and sends for a ladder. He descends in broad daylight and the magnate of east Cornwall [*sic*] takes refuge in a public house.' Hawker abhorred the long tradition of Cornish violence, and in his house (which he searched every night before going to bed) he kept a revolver 'as a defence, but except to intimidate I should not use it. If I were to kill a man I should be incapable by the canon of administering the Sacraments, besides the horrid gloom that would haunt all the rest of my life.'

Hawker was disgusted by the sin of extra-marital sexual intercourse which he described as 'the leprosy of England'. It was particularly prevalent in Morwenstow, he considered, because of the influence of 'that father of English fornication John Wesley'. According to Hawker, chapel girls justified their unchastity with the fine Antinomian argument, 'Sir I had a very clear witness of the spirit at such and such a time and come what will I know I shall go to heaven.' They had the opportunity for 'night assemblage under pretext of going to the meeting house'. As a result 'I swear that I never once in all my life married a Dissenting wife who was not about to become mother.' Such were the appalling consequences of having illegitimate children that those who failed to secure a husband often resorted to infanticide or to the services of a local man who performed abortions, unreliably, for a shilling. In the face of all these abominations, real and imagined, Hawker gave voice to loud and long jeremiads: 'This is the boasted century of civilization. It may be so in mechanical arts, but in decency, in morals, in religion how utterly degraded is this English nation.' He had moods in which he felt loathing and scorn for Morwenstow and all its works: 'My opinion of the people of this neighbourhood was always one of contempt.' He sometimes lamented, 'my desolation is more than I can bear.'

Fundamentally, however, Hawker recognized that the deplorable behaviour of his flock stemmed primarily from their abysmal poverty. Agricultural labourers in Morwenstow were paid in 1860 a pittance of eight shillings a week which, because there was no competition in labour from industry, was as low as any wage in the country. By 1845 they had been deprived of no less than 730 acres of common land and waste as a result of numerous recent enclosures, and apparently no compensation was provided by the landlords for the loss of grazing and gleaning rights. They received none of the usual perquisites like free cider or beer, except at harvest time. Hawker wrote, 'How they exist is a mystery, especially after the potato blight – 8/- per week, 1/- rent, 1/- fuel, 1/- groceries, the other 5/- for food and clothing, for often with four children they get no union relief.' It is interesting to note that although wages had only recently risen from seven shillings a week Hawker considered that the general standard of living had actually fallen. His remarks, which suggest that there was more of bleakness than improvement about the age, may make a small contribution to the debate which historians are conducting on the subject. Next to wheat, he said, the potato crop was

the principal staff of Cornish life. When I first came here, December 1834, 30 years agone, every labourer had his pig and his potato patch. But of late years both these comforts have disappeared together and the privations of the people have been in consequence extreme ... And amidst all they undergo, wages [of] 8/- a week they somehow live and so that they can get dry bread enough are content. And they increase. In the last three weeks I have had five baptisms!

Another shred of evidence is provided by an 82-year-old cooper whom Hawker visited in 1864. He attributed his recovery from cholera to the fact that he had been raised on cheese 'whereas children now and young people are fed so much on potatoes that there is no strength in them'. That the children managed to survive was indeed remarkable, considering the constant hazard to their parents' wages afforded by widespread use of the inequitable truck system (i.e. payment in kind – invariably corn in Morwenstow) and by long periods of under- or un-employment. These could be caused by a number of factors such as bad weather, gluts, slumps in the market, the bankruptcy of farmers (very frequent in Morwenstow) or the introduction of machinery. In 1861 Hawker reported, 'The policeman told me yesterday that in Kilkhampton many labourers have had only two days work in a week since the harvest and will soon steal or starve.' Crime was the last resort for desperate men who wanted to avoid the grinding discipline of the Stratton workhouse or the pauper's slow death on a dole of half-a-crown a week. The frequency with which the laws, particularly the game laws, were broken, in spite of the draconian penal code, is the best evidence for the degree of destitution which prevailed in north Cornwall during the nineteenth century. For Hawker it was also one of those un-mistakable 'signals of the end of all things'.

With such meagre incomes, it is not surprising that the lives of the working-class families of Morwenstow were coarsened and circumscribed in every possible way. Their diet was grotesquely restricted. They never ate meat, fish or cheese and scarcely ever vegetables apart from potatoes, garlic (that ancient north Cornish speciality described by Carew as 'the countryman's treacle') and the odd cabbage or onion. They seldom drank milk, beer or cider. In fact they lived almost exclusively on bread, potatoes and tea. This had to sustain the men for the long hours of hard labour which in many cases literally killed them. Hawker recorded that 'When they come to work they bring a little bag and it contains a hunk of bread two inches thick and four square. This is their dinner. If they can get a little milk and water or bacon broth to put in it they are as happy as kings. But if not they eat it dry.' They lived in conditions of such squalor that even the festering slums of the new industrial cities were salubrious by comparison. In 1880 a man from Holsworthy wrote a detailed account of housing in the area which is worth transcribing in full.

Probably the cottages in this district are as bad as, if not worse than, those in many other parts of England; that is to say, they are generally damp, deficient in room, ill-ventilated, without drainage, closet accommodation, or good water supply; and they are, for the most part, in a state of dilapida-tion. Many of them are literally hovels of mud, which, in the present day, most gentlemen would consider unfit for even the housing of cattle. In this neighbourhood we labour under the disadvantage of non-resident owners, and many of these cannot be aware of the actual condition of the cottages on their properties, or they would surely provide structures in which at least it may be possible to observe the decencies of family life. Overcrowding is necessarily frequent, and the promiscuous mingling of the sexes common. It is not unfrequent to find one sleeping apartment in which are huddled by night, husband, wife, and a family of three, four, five, or six children. What wonder that unchastity amongst the girls is so rife? Health and decency are defied by such arrangements, and comfort is not thought of. Degradation and want of self-respect are inevitable.

This is an accurate description of the state of affairs in Morwenstow in all but a single detail. At least one absentee landlord, the notoriously rapacious Lord John Thynne, knew exactly what was happening on his estates. Indeed according to Hawker, he pursued a deliberate policy which, together with the ambition of his nephew, the Rev. A. C. Thynne, rector of Kilkhampton, to win prizes in agricultural shows, had a disastrous effect on the population of the district. 'It is commonly said that from this and other causes the beasts on the farm have been housed and fed far far better than the labourers on the farm, and so they have been all around as Lord John Thynne has been pulling down cottages here for years till the workmen have hardly a decent abode.'

Obviously victims of malnutrition could put up little or no resistance to common scourges such as influenza, smallpox, diphtheria or the worst killer of all, Hawker's 'bete noir [*sic*]', scarlet fever. Rheumatism, caused by wet clothes which could not be dried for lack of fuel or changed for lack of alternative garments, was almost universal among the middle-aged and old. The appalling housing and sanitary conditions of Morwenstow, the propinquity of dungheaps and open cesspools to most cottages, helped to breed epidemic disease, most notably typhus and cholera. Hawker's letters are full of accounts of his visiting parishioners who succumbed to these diseases. In 1871, for example, he was horrified to find

typhus in Coombe, among the children of a labourer living near the sea in a solitary cottage which stands amid a vast volume of the pure breath of the Atlantic, the very last place where one would have looked for such an outbreak. Now father and mother and six children all sleep in one room and the results may be fearful.

Such calls must have been a traumatic experience, especially for a man given to nervous depression and hypochondria, as Hawker was. One can sympathize with his comic relief when another case of typhus occurred in the parish, 'fortunately in the house of a Wesleyan preacher so that I am released from the duty of visitation'. No one, of course, understood the causes of the prevalence of disease – Hawker's precaution of fumigating the church by scattering the floor with wormwood after the funeral of a victim was typically irrelevant. But then he believed that 'cholera spreads by atmospheric poison acting on the sick.' Even if medical knowledge had been more advanced there was no doctor nearer than Stratton and he, to Hawker's vociferously expressed disgust, evinced remarkable indifference to the illnesses of those would could not pay his fees. In 1848 the average age at death in Stratton was thirty-three years, nine months. The explanation to a visitor of what happened when an inhabitant of Bude was taken ill applied to Morwenstow all the year round: 'Well sir, you see, when the Quality's here in summer time, us sends across to Stratton, but in the winter us just dies a natural death.'

Actually, this is not quite true, for the people of Morwenstow all too often had recourse to magical remedies which accelerated their deaths unconscionably. Hawker narrated the following tale of the tragic consequences of superstition as late as 1860.

A farmer's wife afflicted with dropsical tendencies has been under the long care of Mr H. King. Some time ago I met him at the house on one of my visits. Said he in his reply to my questions about his patient, 'She is suffering from Medicine digitalis (foxglove) but that will wear off and I think she may linger for some years.' Three days agone her husband at her earnest entreaty resorted to an ancient man as they call him, an old labourer professing to be skilled in herbs (wild cucumber one). He brought her some decoction or other in a bottle and she took it. Not long after sickness ensued and in vomiting she ruptured a blood vessel somewhere in the stomach and on Friday he came for me. I carried her the Eucharist (she had been a communicant) and today a messenger arrives to tell me she has been dying and is not expected to live out this night. This is the second victim of this ancient of herbs within the last three months.

Given the kind of treatment to which orthodox medical men subjected their patients, the poor parishioners of Morwenstow might almost be forgiven for having resorted to ancient men. (My great-grandfather, incidentally, always called in the vet when he was ill.) Hawker's doctor, for example, once 'relieved' his 'ulcerated sore throat' by applying the hottest mustard plaster to his neck, followed by leeches, followed by cupping. In one sense this remedy can be said to have proved efficacious, for the external agony was so intense that the internal pain dwindled into insignificance. That is, until it was aggravated again by the doctor's lancing Hawker's tonsils and ordering him to gargle with a caustic solution. But the fact was that, on balance, medicine had advanced far enough to have done his parishioners more good than harm if it had been freely available to them. It was no longer true, as it had been as late as the seventeenth century, that the health of the poor benefited because they could not afford to pay for medical treatment. It may have been true that the rich, Hawker included, were more prone to valetudinarianism (that ubiquitous feature of the Victorian social scene) not just because it was a luxury which they could afford but because they were apprehensive about receiving cures which were worse than their diseases.

Yet though in general a sombre picture of life in Hawker's Morwenstow must be painted, it is not one of unrelieved gloom. Some compensations for poverty and isolation did exist, both for the vicar and for his parishioners. There was the universal 'exultation at the harvest home'. Indeed the harvest, with its opportunities for picking up a few vital perquisites, was usually a joyful season. Hawker wrote,

> A woman diligent will glean enough to make a bushel of wheat and each child, if active, half a bushel. This makes a comfortable addition to the year's earnings and the husband gains his regular wages. Meanwhile I do not know a more pleasant sight to see than the little ones staggering home with their sheaf of ears carefully bound up.

Hawker especially loved the obsolescent customs which accompanied the gathering-in of the corn, and his labourers seem rather to have played up to him, especially in 1863, after Charlotte had died.

> Some old usages are preserved here still. One when the sickle is first put in, 'God send out master a big load this year and health to eat it.' When they cut the last handful the man who reaps it runs off a little, crying, 'I have it', twice. The rest say, 'What have you?' Answer, 'A neck, a neck, a neck.' They all together shout 'They [the angels] save it, we have it.' Now a neck simply means a cut [i.e. nick] . . . And then the handful is wreathed with rustic taste and brought to me to keep till another year. They also, at saving the mow of wheat when nearly finished, they [sic] hoist a sheaf upon a pike and cry three times, 'If it's a cross I'll bear it. If it's a crown I'll wear it.' And this they call carrying the cross sheaf. They all know, and Cann in particular, that I like every ancient custom and so I think they practise it more here than perhaps in other farms. They cried the neck this year as though they thought to interest me, perhaps to cheer me.

Of course the harvest time was one of acute anxiety, and the safety of the crops was almost the sole preoccupation and topic of conversation in Morwenstow throughout the summer months, as Hawker's letters testify. One July Hawker wrote of the harvest, 'our worry is now unutterable.' The next, 'To me it is life or death in the harvest field and to how many more of my poor parishioners.' But the successful germination of the wheat, which Hawker was convinced was of 'supernatural origin', was the best possible cause for rejoicing. This had been done before 1843 in pagan fashion with beer and tumult. After that date Hawker held Harvest Festivals. He has a fair claim, though not an unchallenged one, to be considered the initiator of this service in the nineteenth century. He and his flock were thanking their Maker for freedom from famine for another year, for life itself.

Other seasonal celebrations illuminated the drabness of the yearly round in Morwenstow. There was the annual revel or feast on the date of the church's dedication. This too Hawker civilized. He wrote in 1864, 'it used to be a time of drunkenness and riot, but it is very far from that now'. More important, coming as they did in the misery of winter, were the festivities of Christmas. The church was gaily decorated and Hawker was generous in his distribution of beef and plum-pudding to the poor of the parish. He was also responsible for the improvement in the services and the carol-singing. He reported to a friend in 1861,

> When I retrace the twenty five years that are past I do discern a change for the better here. In 1835 the carols were almost disused. But when I urged them to revere the time 'when God the Lord was born' and wrote some new carols for them they imbibed a spirit of sympathy, and now, let me describe to you. On Christmas Eve the choir travels from house to house singing first outside then in and continues to do so a great part of the night. On Christmas day they sing, about six, in the Church. And the sexton decks the whole fabric with holly and ivy which the farmers give, that is to say the Church farmers allow to be cut in their woods. The ringers ring in the eve and the day ...

Such moments of recreation were scant recompense for the toil and hardship which were normally the lot of Hawker's flock.

But they did occur, and to omit them would be to present an unbalanced view of life in Victorian Morwenstow.

No one now imagines, except perhaps a few ivory-towered literary critics, that the organic society consisted of a happy, rosy-cheeked peasantry (their country's pride), bursting with the beer and roast beef of old England, fulfilled at their work in the wheelwright's shop, and expending their surplus energies by rushing out of honeysuckle-covered cottages to dance round the maypole. However, as even those most hardheadedly pessimistic historians, the Hammonds, admit, the antithesis of this idyllic representation is equally misleading. To suggest that rural life in the nineteenth century was uniformly miserable would be nearly as much of a romantic caricature as the optimistic account. The Hammonds were right to dwell on 'the assuaging influences of brook and glade and valley', and to remark that 'Men and women who work in the fields breathe something of the resignation and peace of Nature.' Hawker, who wrote near the end of his life, 'I never weary of the external aspects of nature', was surely not unique in finding compensation for the barren isolation of Morwenstow in the stark beauty of the land- and sea-scape. Nor, to strike a more prosaic note, could he have been alone in enjoying that most rewarding of seaside pursuits – scavenging among the rock-pools. In about 1850 Hawker wrote, 'We went yesterday to Marsland Mouth a beach two miles north of the vicarage where in half an hour I caught fifty enormous prawns, larger than any you sent from Widemouth. But the aged net gave way and I was obliged to withdraw. Still it was a great discovery.'

Society, too, in Morwenstow, though it was a hierarchy in which most of Hawker's parishioners were placed unequivocally at the bottom, possessed certain redeeming features as far as they were concerned. It fitted them as snugly as an old suit. There is little sign that they resented or even questioned the social order. They merely belonged to it, felt secure in its continuing stability. In so far as they thought about it at all they probably accepted the existing system of the rich man in his castle and the poor man at his gate as being one ordained by God. There is no record that charity humiliated those who received it. There seem to have been no independent spirits who withheld from Charlotte Hawker her habitual title of 'Ma'am', as Joseph Ashby's mother did from the vicar's wife at Tysoe because to address her so would have been an act of servility. The people at Morwenstow actually embraced sexual segregation in church instead of protesting, as Joseph Arch's mother did when the 'lady-despot' at Barford rectory decreed it. They were unconsciously and unresistingly dominated by what Dr G. Kitson Clark has called 'the continuing force of the logic of inequality underlying . . . the old system of social ethics'. Burke was a stronger influence in conservative Cornwall than Paine. Burke's classic formulation, doubtless popularized by the writings of Hannah More, and diluted in numerous sermons, was the ideological basis of Morwenstow society.

Good order is the foundation of all good things. To be enabled to acquire, the people, without being servile, must be tractable and obedient. The magistrate must have his reverence, the laws their authority. The body of the people must not find the principles of natural subordination by art rooted out of their minds. They must respect that property of which they cannot partake. They must labour to obtain what by labour can be obtained; and when they find, as they commonly do, the success disproportioned to the endeavour, they must be taught their consolation in the final proportions of eternal justice.

Thus Morwenstow was a society which looked towards the past rather than the future. It was a society in which rank, with its connotations of dependence, had not yet given way to class, with its connotations of antagonism. It was a society in which silver and gold had not destroyed what Dr Johnson eulogized, 'feudal subordination', and in which industry had not begotten what Carlyle execrated, 'cash nexus' relationships.

All this is not to suggest that the society of north Cornwall was notably harmonious or that the inhabitants were particularly tractable, let alone servile. They had no hesitation in breaking out into a good old-fashioned riot when the situation seemed to warrant it, as it did, for example, in Stratton in 1837 when the new workhouse was instituted. Troops had to be called in to quell the riot. Many of the more rebellious spirits emigrated – the population of Stratton Hundred declined by more than ten per cent in the 1840s. But those who remained were anything but cowed by the system or by their poverty, and Hawker bewailed the fact that 'none are so insolent as the lower orders.' The prevalence of religious Non-conformity indicated a common willingness to embrace social, and perhaps even political, dissent. What Mark Rutherford once said of the Dissenters, that they were 'the insurrectionary class', was certainly not true of those in north Cornwall. But E. P. Thompson's suggestion that the 'social energies' of Methodists, being 'denied outlet in public life . . . were released in sanctified emotional onanism' seems to be equally wide of the mark as far as the Nonconformists of Morwenstow were concerned. It was just that by preferring chapel to church (for what they considered to be good religious reasons – and what right have we to explain their clearly expressed motives in our murkily hypothetical terms?), they were incidentally asserting a degree of independence from the established order. This is exemplified by the periodic truculence of some of Hawker's Dissenting parishioners. He wrote in 1852,

We are in the midst of a fierce feud here, kindled by the Vennings and Arthur Trewin, about the choice of Wardens ... G[eorge] V[enning] gave it as sore as Satan blistered because I took him at his word about the farm. Well with all that long notice [for voting] and after canvassing the parish for votes, their whole party mustered but three ... I had plenty for myself. But they were insolent and I bullied them. I told J[ohn] V[enning] he had no business there, that he was a

Meetinger, as he was, he had never been in Church since 1849 when the window was put in. Said he never would till he was brought in as a corpse . . .

Such disputes and the periodic outbursts of violence which occurred in Morwenstow and its surrounding districts were expressions of temporary frustration and not of incipient revolution. In fact it is probably true to say that the prevalence of this kind of iconoclasm or letting off steam was an index of the flexibility, and thus security, of the old order. Certainly its foundations, firmly set in the social cement of deference, were unshaken while Hawker was at Morwenstow.

For, in the absence of a resident squire, he was the leading local gentleman. As such he was esteemed. Cobbett's description of the English gentleman as 'the most cruel, the most unfeeling, the most brutally insolent' of all God's creatures, would have found acceptance with few, if any, at Morwenstow. They admired, even revered, the 'great people' and were grateful for Hawker's influence with them. They took a lead from the gentry whose position and education they respected. The attitude of Tregarva, the saintly game-keeper in *Yeast*, would have found many echoes in Charles Kingsley's native West Country: 'I say, sir, that God makes you gentlemen, gentlemen, that you may see into these things.' In modern nostrils, no doubt, this kind of remark stinks of sycophancy. But it would hardly have had such a taint for people in early nineteenth-century Cornwall, as J. A. Froude's admirably generalized portrait of the 'average English incumbent' of the 1830s indicates. Froude, himself the son of a West Country clergyman, described the typical parson as

a man of private fortune . . . His professional duties were his services on Sunday, funerals and weddings on week-days, and visits when needed among the sick. In other respects he lived like his neighbours . . . He farmed his own glebe; he kept horses . . . he attended public meetings, and his education enabled him to take a leading part in country business. His wife and daughters looked after the poor, taught in the Sunday-school, and managed the penny clubs and clothing clubs. He himself was spoken of in the parish as 'the master' – the person who was responsible for keeping order there, and who knew how to keep it. The labourers and the farmers looked up to him. The 'family' in the great house could hardly look down upon him.

In many respects, though not all, Hawker conformed to this stereotype. He once explained, 'The Parson is my usual parish name,' – 'that is to say, the Person, the somebody of consequence among his own people.' In short, Hawker was the patriarch in a patriarchial society.

Thus, in spite of the appalling economic conditions which prevailed, there were a few mitigating circumstances about life in Hawker's Morwenstow. Perhaps the most potent were the least tangible – the agreeable sense of belonging to a familiar community, for example. Hawker himself felt this: 'I prefer the accustomed faces, all so well known, and I cling to the phrase "my own flock".' Moreover, in village life, founded on close personal relationships and fierce local patriotism, there was none of that disorientation which was so often the concomitant of the anonymous environment of the new cities. Of course the converse of this was a lack of privacy and even a feeling of claustrophobia, from which Hawker occasionally suffered. He once remarked that in country parishes such as his own 'every one's affairs are known to all the rest of the inhabitants and made common talk.' But even gossip is a binding activity, often a pleasurable one. Above all, there was among Hawker's parishioners a feeling that the social order was natural, given, unmovable, which bred in them a sense of, if not contentment, at least resignation. Such was the cosmic inevitability of the existing system, the '*vis inertiae*', that to envisage its amelioration seemed about as absurd as to look for bumper harvests every year. The isolation of

Morwenstow meant that change, even of the kind which was affecting society and living standards in other parts of the country, was almost unimaginable. The people of Morwenstow were inured to hardship. They had no alternative but to accept what they had and to make the best of it. Endurance had many pains but it also had some pleasures.

There was not much room for stoicism in Hawker's choleric temperament. He was almost invariably in a state of exasperation about some circumstance of life in Morwenstow, either his own or his parishioners'. Most notably, and most frequently, he dwelt on his own isolation: 'Mine is but a very bounded orb. My mere parish and my long loneliness has [sic] severed me from well-nigh all the "hum of men".' Yet though he sometimes cursed, sometimes lamented, his solitary state there is, paradoxically, no doubt that at heart he accepted it with his own brand of contentment. He was convinced that only in his remote eyrie could he find the necessary inspiration for his poetry: 'Every successful effort of the human mind was accomplished in the seclusion of the closet or the cell, never in the din of cities.' In Morwenstow Hawker had, as one romantically-minded witness put it, 'scenery around him well suited to his poetic moods. Wild moorland where the falcon floated and the chough chattered of King Arthur: a wide expanse of sea, over which you gazed from cliffs three hundred feet high: altogether a solitary legendary place, where a poet might live with much comfort.'

But Hawker did not cleave passionately to Morwenstow just because he found poetic fulfilment there. He was attracted to the physical beauties of the place as though by some overwhelming magnetic force. But he loved the people for their own sake and took his role as the pastor of his flock with uncompromising seriousness. His deep compassion for his long-suffering parishioners made him take on, single-handed, most of the work which is done today by the local social services. In spite of his poetic preoccupations, his eccentricities and his gusty capriciousness, he

83

was an excellent parish priest. Of course he operated very much within the social context of his era, as the father of his people, and his behaviour would often seem to the present age insufferably *de haut en bas*. But the fact remains, as the next chapter will illustrate, that Hawker gave to Morwenstow much more than he took from it.

5

The Vicar

Hawker began his ministry in 1834 with a series of grave disadvantages. The parish had had no resident incumbent for over a hundred years, and its business had been conducted by a succession of curates who seem to have made hardly any impression on the religious or social life of the community. This was one reason why Dissent, which was often hostile to the Established Church, was so strong in Morwenstow. There was not a single resident landlord in the district and there was no squire, not even a rich farmer, on whose secular arm Hawker could lean. This was a serious drawback from which his neighbour A. C. Thynne, who became rector of Kilkhampton in 1859, did not suffer. Hawker was quick to attribute Thynne's early success to the fact that 'the farmers are all his tenants and *must* be in their places in church . . . Tenants have no choice as to their Church duties but fully understand that they must fulfil them or depart from the land.' Hawker could exert no such leverage on his parishioners. He was not even (as so many of his brother clergy were) a magistrate, though as he wrote, 'in early life it was placed within my option to have attained to that distinction, but my tastes and habits are literary and retiring and the publicity of such an office would always be discordant to the thoughts and usages of my life.' Hawker had to rely on the power of persuasion to achieve his ends at Morwenstow.

Initially, at least, he was hampered by the hostility of his parishioners. It was to be expected that the people of Morwenstow, suspicious of strangers and wary of change, would resent the presence of a new and young spiritual ruler. They did so all the more because many of them remembered him from the days when he spent his holidays at Coombe Cottage. His reputation was enough to convince those who were not acquainted with him personally that this poetical practical joker was an undesirable addition to the parish. Hawker's reaction was one of wounded *amour propre*. 'The people of the neighbourhood looked coldly on me as a boy and youth. They never gave me sympathy or praise. And when ten years after leaving this very parish to begin life I returned as Vicar I acknowledge that I kept aloof from them.' Apart from having to overcome this antagonism, Hawker was obliged to contend with a number of other adverse circumstances – the fact that the church was seriously dilapidated, that the school met in a tumble-down cottage, that the most direct road to Bude and Stratton was often impassable at Coombe ford, and that the vicarage was an uninhabitable ruin. But he was entirely confident. Though he and Charlotte at first had 'to reside in a hired cottage of two rooms', he refused to be discouraged. 'Full of hope and burning with zeal I was about to accomplish great things ... My parish, I say, was to become a model on the Cornish Coast.'

It is significant that Hawker's first project in Morwenstow was the planning and financing of a public work to improve communications with the outside world. In 1836 he saw to the building of a bridge in Coombe Valley just downstream from the ford which flooded dangerously in wet weather. This had not stopped the people of Morwenstow from trying to use the ford and, according to Hawker's second wife, it had claimed the lives not only of cattle but of men. King William's Bridge was so named because the monarch, probably at the inducement of the vicar, who was skilled at wheedling cash from reluctant donors, subscribed twenty pounds towards its construction. Most of the rest of the money came from Hawker himself. No doubt the bridge was inspired by altruistic motives, but Hawker must have been glad to discover an early method of reconciling the community to his presence while at the same time diminishing the rustic isolation in which he found himself.

His next task was to construct a vicarage, which he did in 1837. Characteristically he selected a site which had both practical use and symbolic significance. This was a piece of ground where his flock of sheep sheltered from storms, a wise choice in 'a valley full of winds such as we inhabit'. The house was so placed that the only objects perceptible from its front were 'the Church and the Sea, the suggestions of both which are boundless [sic]'. Hawker employed no architect but himself adapted a model for 'a Clergyman's house, on a moderate scale' which he found in T. F. Hunt's *Designs for Parsonage Houses*. Though Hunt recommended the design as one by which 'frugality may be exercised without the appearance of poverty', Hawker finally raised an imposing Victorian-Gothic edifice. He added one or two embellishments of his own. The chimneys were all built to resemble the church towers of places where he had previously lived – probably Stratton, Whitstone, North Tamerton and Oxford – though the kitchen chimney, which must have been altered or put up later than the others, was shaped like his mother's tomb. Other ecclesiastical motifs were built into the structure, most notably the verse which was inscribed in the grey stone over the front door.

> A House, a Glebe, a Pound a Day,
> A Pleasant Place to Watch and Pray.
> Be true to Church – Be kind to poor,
> O Minister, for ever more.

It was perhaps not the most tactful stanza Hawker could have written, his stipend of £365 being rather more than twenty times the annual income of the average labourer in the parish. It laid him wide open to this anonymous satirical riposte which if it was, as seems likely, the product of a local pen, provides evidence that there were witty, articulate minds among his parishioners.

How different now the times we see
Since Jesus dwelt in Galilee,
And did poor fishermen prepare
His holy Gospel to declare.
No scrip or purse were they to take
But suffer for the Master's sake,
And not a single word did say
Of House, or glebe, or pound a day.

Hawker's charitable use of his money is its best justification. It may be more difficult to excuse the vanity of building a house which was grander than it need have been. At least one of his friends was critical, remarking to him, 'Ha! Fools build houses, and wise men inhabit them.' Hawker's reply was repartee not explanation: 'Just so, as wise men make proverbs and fools quote them.' But he did vindicate himself in a letter to another friend: 'I ought not to build a Shoppy Residence, I think, and as, like Absalom, I have no son, I will like him build me a pillar in the Bishop's Dale that I may be had in Remembrance among men. I would fain attract too a good Man here in every future generation.' Alas for this hope: though the vicarage still stands it is no longer the residence of the vicar, and if it were, its size and the cost of its upkeep would be enough to deter any prospective incumbent from taking up his post at Morwenstow.

Hawker next turned his attention to the school. For its continuing existence and success he, like many other rural clergy, held himself solely responsible. By 1843 he had designed (in the shape of a cross), built, furnished, financed and christened St Mark's School. It occupies a fine though exposed position on high ground near the hamlet of Shop in the centre of the parish. Nearby Hawker provided a dwelling for the schoolmaster. The school was a constant burden for Hawker and he claimed to support it partly by economizing on his own clothes – wearing a cassock instead of the normal black-suited clerical costume. Even so, as will be seen, he was always short of money after he had spent his wife's capital, as he had by the time St Mark's was completed. Until 1862 the school qualified for a small government grant towards its construction and equipment (these were first made available in 1843) and towards the teacher's salary. But after that date under the 'payment by results' system it was, like all poor schools, penalized. At least one of Hawker's schoolmasters, Patrick O'Carroll, blamed him for this state of affairs and resigned as a consequence, saying,

> I take this step very reluctantly and solely because you have in *no single instance*, (during my time in this school) complied with the requirement of the New Code of 1871. And although the greater part of my salary is the Government grant, you have not as yet put the school, (as you were in duty bound to do,) in the position to earn such a grant.

It is difficult to see what more Hawker, who dismissed O'Carroll as a drunken and 'malignant Fenian', could have done. He managed to extract £16 towards the master's salary from the local landlords, paid the remaining £4 himself and found the necessary money for extras such as books, slates and disinfectant, and school teas, at least one of which was given by his wife for as many as 54 children. As there were limits to the amount he could raise and the 'payment by results' system was hopelessly inequitable, the school had to forfeit its grant. What is more Hawker could only afford to employ such typical rural teachers as the poor, uneducated, one-armed John Littlejohns, who doubled as parish postmaster and could find no other work, or one Trood who had been a slave-driver in the West Indies and had startled Morwenstow by returning with a mulatto wife. Hawker himself supplemented the schoolmaster's instruction on Thursday mornings, and on Friday afternoons he catechized the pupils. If his sermons are anything to judge by, he was a good teacher. He was matter-of-fact and down-to-earth, but willing and able to stimulate the children's imaginations with tales of pixies and brownies.

In spite of the fact that St Mark's was run in this poverty-stricken, haphazard way it was a success. It outshone many other schools in the vicinity. At Barnstaple, for example, after twenty years of hard work by a dedicated vicar, his school received adverse reports from the Inspectors of education. By contrast E. P. Arnold, the brother of Matthew, and an HMI, wrote of St Mark's in 1874, 'I cannot help congratulating the vicar of whose uphill labours to support a school in this remote district I have been a witness for so many years.' Even better evidence for the efficacy of the instruction given at St Mark's is the high literacy-rate disclosed in the parish register. The efforts made by O'Carroll and his predecessors, who believed in improving their pupils' spelling by liberal applications of the rod, were crude but they seem to have worked.

Hawker himself acted as a benevolent despot who bullied and cajoled the people of Morwenstow into making their children attend school regularly. In one parochial decree, written magisterially in the third person (and given additional emphasis by a plethora of typographical variations, not here repeated), he announced that the vicar 'will not from henceforth show the same kindness to those who keep back their children from school as he will to those who send them'. In a sermon he pleaded persuasively, 'If you love your children do not keep them for your own indulgence away from Heaven, separate from church, absent from school. They will then breathe a thanksgiving over your grave.' But he gave pupils time off during the harvest and he showed his concern for them individually, often writing parents such notes as this: 'I am sorry to hear that Henry is unwell. If he is ever so much better tomorrow I hope he will not go out of doors.' That Hawker managed to kindle an enthusiasm for education is indicated by the fact that during the early 1870s there was a petition from parents of children at the school asking that geography should be added to the curriculum.

What was Hawker hoping to achieve by his educational endeavours? He seems to have valued education more for what it could bring in terms of social and economic advantage than for its own sake. In 1852 he offered his brother, Claud, practical help towards the instruction of his son, Willy: 'Education will be to him more than all the gold in Australia. In the present state of England by the time Willy is of age an uneducated man will be despised with thousands a year [*sic*].' Of course the higher education which Hawker envisaged for his nephew was different, both in content and in purpose, from the elementary schooling which he provided for his flock. But even for them he believed that certain practical gains could be achieved through careful drilling in 'the three R's'. He once admonished a subordinate who was seeking patronage to 'be careful to remember that there is a great disrespect in misspelling the names of people of Rank'.

However, Hawker recognized that, given the inertia of north Cornish society and the lack of economic opportunity, there was little hope that many of his parishioners would achieve much tangible benefit from their juvenile studies. This did not cause him to turn back on the instruction of the poor, as Voltaire and other enlightened men had earlier done. They had believed that since education could not be put to profitable use it would lead to frustration or subversion – as is sometimes the case among university graduates in under-developed countries today. Many Victorian churchmen also feared that education might endanger social and economic stability. As late as 1857 Bishop Wilberforce cautioned that 'they did not want everyone to be learned men, or to make everyone unfit to follow the plough, or else the rest of us would have nothing to eat.' However, the early nineteenth-century 'march of mind', exemplified by the Useful Knowledge Society, Thomas Arnold's 'Godless institution in Gower Street', London University, and the increasing number of Dissenting academies, could not be stopped. In the face of it the Church could not afford to take the aristocratic line of Lord Melbourne who remarked that he did not believe in education 'because the Pagets got on so damned well without it'. By the time Hawker came to Morwenstow the Church had decided that since it could not suppress education it must try to control it. For, as William

Howley, later Archbishop of Canterbury, said, 'the diffusion of knowledge, disjoined from religious instruction, stands in the same relation to ignorance as positive evil to the absence of good.' Or in the plainer language of the Duke of Wellington, 'education without religion would surround us with clever devils.' Provided that curricula were carefully controlled (reading, for Bible study, was often preferred, certainly by Hawker, to the dubious accomplishment of writing) and that everything was excluded which might give the poor, in Bishop Otter's words, 'a taste for the occupations or a relish for the pleasures of the higher ranks', the Church actually stood to gain. Moreover an access of religious citizens could not be bad for the state. Unfortunately for the Church, though, education turned out to be uncontrollable. The fact that some of the parishioners of Morwenstow wanted geography to be taught at St Mark's probably indicates that they had become well enough informed by their religious and vocational training to desire a more liberal and academic education for their children.

Hawker did not anticipate or encourage this. His dictum was, 'Happy they who only know enough to believe.' Like most other clergymen of his day, he believed that the purpose of education was not to convey independence but to explain to those in receipt of education the conditions of their dependence. It was designed to tutor the young in their duties towards their superiors. It 'should be dogmatic', he believed. 'Tell a child it is so, never why.' This the catechism pre-eminently did, which was why Hawker so favoured it and why, incidentally, Rousseau had regarded teaching it as 'the most heart-breaking stupidity'. Hawker's most scathing sarcasm was reserved for those among his flock who attempted to assert a right to modify or question the teaching that was handed down to them from podium or pulpit. This was to usurp his own function as shepherd. It was to threaten the stability of the total hierarchy. It was the germ of social dissent as well as religious. In a heavily ironical letter, apparently sent to a newspaper in 1844, Hawker wrote,

Will you suffer [me], Sir, to suggest one or two proposals which might tend to smooth existing difficulties [caused by current discussions and arguments about doctrine]. In the beginning of every week let the Parish officers and some of the principal farmers (I would not even exclude their wives) assemble in the vestry Room or elsewhere. Let them select the topics that shall form the subject of the clergyman's discourse on the ensuing Sunday. Let them point out the lines of interpretation in which they for the most part agree and which are most likely to suit the popular mind. On the Saturday let them assemble again. Let the clergyman submit his sermon to their perusal and if any statement excite contradictory opinion let its delivery or truth be put to the vote. Again in matters of practice during Divine Service the same plan might be proposed. Surely a doubtful rubric or a Church Canon might more safely be entrusted to the decision of a large majority than a single Bishop. Did not a majority decide in the case of the crucifixion of our Lord? Depend upon it Sir, a popular Church is a Church governed by the people.

This letter makes Hawker sound intensely conservative and, in his concern that education should strengthen the existing social fabric, he was, though not more so than many of his contemporaries in the Church. However, it is no contradiction to say that he believed in education as a progressive, civilizing force which it was his duty to disseminate as widely as possible through this 'primitive country'. He would undoubtedly have agreed with the aims of the Home and Colonial Infant School Society, which were 'to cultivate religious principles and moral sentiments; to awaken the tender mind to a sense of its evil dispositions and habitual failings, before it is become callous by its daily intercourse with vice'. Like Dr Johnson, Hawker favoured reactionary theories but in practice he was very often a radical. And his prolonged educational efforts did achieve practical results, not only in spreading literacy but in diminishing the violence, brutality and drunkenness which had been so prevalent when Hawker took charge of the parish. This reformation of manners can be seen as an attempt by Hawker to bring his people into conformity with the standards of the Victorian age, to rescue Morwenstow from the past.

The saga of Hawker's restoration of the church is a long one and reveals him in some characteristic postures. Early on in his ministry he used part of the material from the ruin of the previous vicarage to rebuild the vestry in which, among other things, Sunday School was held. Later he made various alterations to the inside of the church, restored the ancient rood-screen, demolished the gallery and banished the ancient box-pews. The last he probably disliked for many of the same reasons put forward by the High Church hymn-writer John Mason Neale – they were Protestant innovations, and they discriminated against the poor. At any rate, he seems to have followed Neale's example in attacking the pew system physically. According to Baring-Gould, when one recalcitrant farmer refused to sacrifice his enormous private pew Hawker called him to the church and in front of him smashed it to pieces with an axe. He completed his refurbishing of the inside of the church by taking the panelling out of the pulpit, on the bizarre principle that 'the people ought to see the priest's feet.' Equally strange was his reason for neglecting to improve access to the pulpit, which was through a tiny door and up narrow, winding steps. 'Don't you see that this typifies the camel going through the eye of a needle?' Perhaps Hawker relished the spectacle of visiting preachers being trapped in the pulpit when they failed to discover that the only way to make their exit was to go down the stairs backwards. Hawker would whisper to them, 'It is the strait and narrow way and few there be that find it.'

Almost as eccentric was Hawker's renovation of the outside of his church. Its roof was covered with shingles made out of seasoned oak, that is, as he explained, 'Tiles of Wood, – the material of the Ark, and of the Cross, that Deathbed of our Blessed Lord'. As early as 1820 the rural dean had recommended that slates should be substituted for the shingles which were, by 1855, in a serious state of decay. Then, in the teeth of local opposition, Hawker refused to replace them with the more durable materials which covered every other church in Cornwall. He announced to the public that

the Vicar is proud of this Shingle Roof and the hostile farmers have found it out. It has been their muttered threat and their shameless avowal that 'they would punish the Vicar by destroying his favourite Roof.' Since the late decision in the House of Lords, they have laid a crafty and malignant scheme to cover the church like a Cattle-Shed or a barn: and at the last Vestry, the paltry Penny in the Pound, for the usual yearly repair, was refused under the insidious cry of 'No Slate no Rate'.

Hawker appealed successfully for the money to replace the old shingles and brought in men to lay new ones. Because they were doing God's work in restoring church fabric, Hawker regarded these workmen, quite erroneously, as especially religious and insisted that they attend church, much to their indignation. Perhaps they repaid him by deliberately doing their job with tiles of unseasoned oak. At any rate the roof was not weather-proof for very long and Hawker's last years were plagued by the necessity of raising money to patch it up. It was slated in the end, but not until after his death. Hawker's reverent principle of build-ing the church out of materials which were both good and bad because this symbolized its Catholic inclusiveness was typical of his religious quixotry.

It must have been a weird experience for an outsider to attend service at Morwenstow church. The inside of the church, even the altar which was cluttered with used match-ends, was rarely cleaned. One clerical witness, having been taken on a guided tour by Hawker, described it with distaste in 1862. 'The Church floor was strewn with sweet-smelling herbs, – in fact carpeted with them, which however caused it to be always dirty. In fact *dirt* was over everything, vestry and pulpit very dirty. He said his cat always went with him to Church, and sometimes into the pulpit.' The congregation segregated itself by sex according to ancient custom, with which Hawker did not interfere. The women and children occupied the pews in the nave and the men sat in the side-aisles. The church was 'seldom half-filled' and at harvest-time almost empty because the farmers and labourers were 'worn out with toil'. There was no organ though a harmonium was introduced in 1866 to supplement, or perhaps supersede, the bass viol, two flutes and pitchpipe which had previously accompanied the singing. In the evenings there was no artificial light save that provided by a few candles stuck on the ends of the pews. The vicar, hidden from the congregation by the rood-screen, would range around the chancel, 'book in hand, and reading now in English, now in Latin. At certain points in the service he would prostrate himself on the ground before the altar, with outstretched arms in the form of a cross.' He was subject to attacks of nerves in church and recorded in 1862, 'Only a few years since it was not unusual for me to faint in Church and interrupt the service and terrify the people.'

Hawker was enough of a High Churchman to value the preaching of sermons less than the celebration of the sacraments. He illustrated the point by telling how he had once burnt a large number of his own manuscript sermons and used the ashes to fertilize his turnips. The crop was not improved at all. As he explained, the sermons were 'barren, all barren, like most modern discourses; not even posthumous energy'. More seriously, he told his congregation that there was much truth in the view that a minister had but two duties – to deliver the sacraments and to prepare his flock to receive them. 'For my own part now I would rather administer this Sacrament unto two or three sincere hearts than preach a popular discourse to a large multitude. And I am persuaded that this too is the mind of God.' After about 1847 Hawker followed the Tractarians' fashion of holding frequent communion services and, like them, he believed in the Real

Presence of Christ in the Eucharistic elements. He would not preach 'in my Master's presence'. By all accounts the services were conducted impressively. Hawker was perhaps the first nineteenth-century Anglican to wear vestments. At different times he dressed himself in a variety of garments, among them a magnificent purple velvet cope, white alb, stole richly embroidered in gold, a green-and-amber chasuble and scarlet gloves. He owed these and his various unorthodox additions to the service less to the Ritualist Movement (which, with his friend Bloxam, he preceded) than to his innate love of finery and his belief in the value of symbolism.

On the other hand Hawker retained, as vicar of Morwenstow, enough of the Evangelicalism of his youth to make him want to preach effectively. He avoided the fervid rhetoric so elaborately deployed by his father and grandfather, judging the 'language of persuasion' to be irreverent. It was 'like recommending Wares for Sale'. But he studied and practised the art of eloquence, which he defined as 'vehement simplicity'. He asserted that 'A ready and boundless grasp of the simplest and truest words is the real triumph.' He noticed that St Paul habitually used catchwords and he even regarded one of the functions of his poetry to be 'the arsenal of the orator'. It was the office of the priesthood, he considered, 'to unfold the mysterious mind of God – to utter his messages from on high in the human echo of the voice of the Lord'.

Sometimes this led him to address his congregations in high, mystical vein, on the subject of 'the colour of the soul', for example, or the ubiquitousness of spirits – 'the air is occupied with thousands of spiritual things that walk unseen both when we wake and when we sleep.' More often, though, his sermons were decidedly parochial and plain. He seldom indulged in intellectual exhibitionism nor did he, like so many clergymen of his day, preach above the heads of his rustic parishioners. But he gave the hungry minds of Morwenstow many 'themes for future thought'. Most frequently, he delivered straightforward, practical commentaries on the Bible. 'The chief end of [Christ's] appearance on earth, was to seek and to save the souls of men.' Salvation was only for 'the penitent and the believing'. The rest would perish in an awful material hell. A faithful life and, more important, a good life (Hawker's bias was distinctly Pelagian) would bring its heavenly reward. The Christian message was unambiguous. 'Plain, simple and easy is the instruction and so the poor have the Gospel preached unto them in a language which the poor may understand.'

The poor could not be expected to understand Hawker's mystical, or magical, view of the sacraments. But the vicar did attempt to communicate the importance which he attached to them. Baptism he believed to be '*another* birth', vital for salvation. It was 'A ceremony of Investiture with the order of Christ. An enfeoffment of the heir.' The efficaciousness of the sacrament depended, according to Hawker, on the correct performance of an elaborate ritual. The child had to be marked with the baptismal water three times, the sign of the cross being made on brow, breast and loins. There were other complicated hieratic manœuvres which were all full of symbolic significance, right down to Hawker's opening 'the Devil's door', as he nicknamed it, in the north wall of Welcombe church 'for the escape of the fiend'. This door was kept firmly shut at all other times. Hawker was particularly delighted when an infant cried at the appropriate moment 'to avouch the departure of the Fiend'. Hawker managed to convey the solemnity, if not perhaps the entire meaning, of baptism by his impressive manner of conducting the service. He once hammered home the lesson by demanding a fee of £1,000 for performing it. When his astonished parishioner protested that he could not pay such a sum, Hawker thundered, 'Don't you know that the sacraments of God are invaluable? that no amount of money can pay for them?' He calculated his effects with a showman's skill. As he complacently remarked, 'That will be repeated at every inn and hearth-side in Cornwall. It will teach them to appreciate the sacraments of the Church.'

Hawker set great store by confirmation. He worked hard at the 'harassing and laborious' business of securing and instructing as many candidates as possible for these triennial events. In 1868, for example, as was his custom, he visited every house in Morwenstow and Welcombe,

> to induce the children of dissenting parents and the lax and reckless of all ages to come to me for instruction and examination. Every evening for four weeks I had candidates here and of course some were very ignorant and others misinformed as to the nature of their duty and the service itself . . . I had to ascertain their knowledge of the Creed, the Lord's Prayer and the Ten Commandments as the law of the Church enjoins. I then taught them they were going to declare their belief in the Christian doctrine, to profess their intent to do as well as they knew in their station of life and to ask God for his grace to do so.

This is perhaps a rather prosaic account of Hawker's efforts. It does not convey the enthusiasm with which he roused each candidate to embrace his new role. 'You are about to take upon yourself the more immediate touch of the Holy Ghost. Soldier of the Lord, you have enlisted this day in a noble army.' Hawker was a more effective recruiting sergeant than any of his clerical neighbours. He managed to persuade a remarkable number of his parishioners to be confirmed – in 1868, forty-six from Morwenstow and twenty-five from Welcombe. In 1856 he recorded,

> I took in to Stratton (8 miles) in two wagons hired for the purpose 74 males and females, 60 from Morwenstow and 14 from Welcombe. At Stratton they all had cake and tea sent by Mrs Hawker as has been her usage for now six times (one in every three years). We had a drenching day of rain and yet all went and returned without injury.

Incidentally, Hawker's relief that such a simple local journey should be accomplished without accident says much about the state of the roads and the isolation of his parish.

Hawker hated taking burial services. As will be seen, the need to inter the decayed and reeking corpses of drowned sailors as quickly as possible became an obsession with him – an understandable one. He was hindered in his endeavours to bury the dead by the remissness of the distant Cornwall and Devon coroners. On one occasion it took the Cornwall coroner so long to provide a warrant to bury a sailor, who had already been in the water for eighteen days, that 'the atmosphere around for incredible distances is heavy with the poisonous taint'. It was only by 'drenching my men with gin for Bearers' that Hawker could bring the body to the grave at all. In 1861 the Devon coroner simply refused to hold an inquest on the body of a murdered child in spite of all Hawker's expostulations. 'It is beyond belief. His chief argument is "Because the corpse is *so small*, therefore its murder is too trivial for an inquest, and utterly beneath my notice."' Sometimes Hawker himself procrastinated unattractively over funerals. On at least two occasions he tried to use his powers to inter Dissenters where he pleased in the churchyard as a lever to extract money out of them for the church rate. When asked whether he objected to burying Dissenters he replied, characteristically, 'Not at all, I should be only too glad to bury you all.'

Churchmen received better treatment. Hawker was generous in dispensing spiritual solace and temporal comfort to the bereaved. Not least of his achievements in this field were his touching epitaphs. Some can still be made out on the mossy, slate tombstones in the churchyard. This one is on the grave of a child.

> Those whom God loves die young;
> They see no evil days;
> No falsehood taints their tongue
> No wickedness their ways.

> Baptized, and so made sure
> To win their safe abode
> What could we pray for more?
> They die, and are with God.

Infant mortality being so high, many such lines were needed to comfort stricken families in Morwenstow while Hawker was vicar. Like his grandfather, he was skilled at commiserating with the bereaved. On the death of his nephew's son he wrote, 'I can attempt no consolation, utter no word of comfort but such as will occur to yourself but I must assure you both of our most sincere sympathy ... I shall pray for his welfare tonight and I hope to greet him again one day in the measure of the stature of the fulness of Christ.' The consolations of faith were, for Hawker, as abundant as the manifestations of God.

> At the funeral of a child in this churchyard, the grave by a stunted tree, there broke in during the versicles an exquisite trill of song. It was last week. On looking up I saw a robin among the boughs not a yard from my head. We said the service together that Bird and I. At the close of every sentence came a still small sound like an infant's laugh, a cry of innocent gladness. From the Angel was it or the Bird? 'UBI AVES [IBI ANGELI].'

Apart from marrying them, Hawker performed two other services for the people of Morwenstow which he probably valued more highly than they did. He said Matins and Evensong in church every weekday. At 9.00 or 11.00 in the morning (the times seem to have varied according to season) and 4.00 in the afternoon the sexton would toll the church bell to announce the services, only stopping when Hawker shouted down the aisle, 'Now, John, three for the Trinity and one for the Blessed Virgin.' Often the only person in church with Hawker during these services was his wife, and he would then open with the words, 'Dearly Beloved Charlotte ...' Usually though, Hawker was alone; he was by no means George Herbert, and no ploughmen left their fields to join him at prayers. Hawker anyway regarded the daily service as being 'vicarious, intercessory and sacerdotal'. He said prayers '*for* the people, not with them even if they came but as the Prayer Book means, *for* those whose labours and duties suffer them not to join, that the voice of the Minister may plead twice every day for the absent and occupied sheep.'

There was a remote, medieval quality about Hawker's emphasis on intercession. Indeed, this quality pervaded his whole ministry. It was as though he was trying to create, by his building work, his educational efforts, his services with their attention to sacraments, ritual and prayer, a community of faith in the image of that which he believed to have existed in the Middle Ages. Of course, many in his own time, reacting against scientific materialism, industrialization and its effects, radicalism, utilitarianism and so on, shared Hawker's 'dream of order'. Few tried to realize it in quite such concrete terms.

6

❧❧❧❧❧❧❧❧❧❧❧❧❧❧❧❧❧❧❧❧❧❧❧

The Pastor

The division between Hawker's vicarial work, discussed in the last chapter, and his pastoral work, discussed in this, is an artificial one, made here simply for the sake of convenience: he regarded all his labours in the parish as being done for the greater glory of God. The word 'pastor' has an old-fashioned ring in modern ears. It conjures up visions of smug Victorian clerics distributing bundles of tracts and basketfuls of rotten apples to the deserving poor. Yet in an era when state aid was a heresy and self-help the orthodoxy, the pastoral care of a genuinely philanthropic clergyman, however patronizingly bestowed, could be of inestimable advantage to a poor parish. Hawker was such a clergyman.

He knew that it was as absurd to preach self-help to the helpless as it was to recommend (as had been done) fasting to the hungry. But it cannot be denied that he occasionally delivered pie-in-the-sky sermons to his congregations, in an attempt to reconcile them to the crusts that they were receiving on earth. He spoke of Heaven – 'What balm for all the trials and the poverty, and the pain of this brief condition. The days of the hireling may be bitter, but they will soon be over. The eternal morrow, the Resurrection of the just, in one hour will repay for all.' This kind of preaching might reasonably be regarded as the propaganda of the ruling class, what Charles Kingsley once called 'an opium-dose for keeping beasts of burden patient while they were being overloaded'. But Hawker did not offer spiritual prizes of the future as an excuse for ignoring temporal penalties of the present. He believed that charity was the 'essence of Christian principle'.

Like Carlyle, Dickens, Disraeli and so many others who belonged to the early Victorian phase of the Romantic Movement, Hawker was in rebellion against the harsh rationalistic creed of *laissez-faire* economics. Utilitarians, philosophical radicals, apologists for unbridled capitalism, believed that society was a machine in which each person, if left alone, would find his correct economic level. Lord Radnor epitomized the most ruthless version of this ideology in a statement to his labourers in which he explained why he would not increase their pay.

> If you cannot live upon the wages I and my tenants give you, it is a sign that you are not wanted here. Go to Lancashire, where wages are higher, and where, consequently, it appears you are wanted. You ask me to help you with land at an indulgent, that is, an artificial and untrue scale, of rent. I should only be giving you so much money. Thus I should be diminishing my own fair returns, and my own means of public usefulness; I should be checking the reproduction of capital; I should be enabling you to undersell less favoured labourers; I should be bribing you to stay where you really are not wanted, and cannot prosper, and at the same time seducing you from those who, being able to pay better wages, have consequently a better claim to your labour. I should be deranging the labour market to no effectual purpose.

The new Poor Law of 1834 gave legislative expression to the principle of *laissez-faire* by abolishing the 'interference' of outdoor relief in favour of that unavoidable, last-ditch refuge for the absolutely destitute, the workhouse. Hawker possessed no progressive theories about the organization of society but he knew suffering when he saw it being inflicted. Nothing became him more than his selfless pastoral endeavours to alleviate it.

Hawker was, to employ Louis Cazamian's expression, a reactionary interventionist. He had no radical solutions to economic problems. But he believed that *laissez-faire* did not work. The state had a moral and a political duty to relieve distress when and where it occurred. Only a national agency could do so effectively. About the famine conditions which existed in the winter of 1862, Hawker wrote, 'Nothing but a national revenue can suffice.' The government should not try to shuffle off its responsibility on to the landlords. 'The misfortune is national. The remedy should be national also.' Of course, this is not to suggest that Hawker was a socialist, or anything near it. As he himself said, 'I have no Radical or Liberal tendencies in my nature. As far as taste and judgement go my mind is cast in the old conservative mould.' But he did argue passionately against the provisions of the new Poor Law. He did vote against protection of corn, one of the few Anglican clergymen to desert the Tories on this issue. He did arouse antagonism among his natural allies in West Country society by championing the cause of the labourers.

Hawker was one of the first Victorian parsons to introduce the practice of holding a weekly offertory at the end of services in order to collect alms for charitable purposes, particularly the relief of the poor. A national row was building up on that subject in October 1844 when Hawker nailed his colours to the mast with a letter to the *English Churchman*. It must be quoted in full because it gives an insight into the scope of Hawker's endeavours and expresses his old-fashioned paternalistic view on the subject of charity. What is more it brought down upon his head the censure of no less a person than John Walter, the owner of *The Times*.

We, the Vicar and Wardens of the Church of St. Morwenna, commonly called Morwenstow, hereby make known our reception and disposal of 'THE OFFERTORY ALMS', devoted every Sunday as part of Divine Service, and of the monies found in the Poor Man's Chest, between the Festival of St. John the Baptizer 1843, and the Feast of St. Michael 1844: –

	£ s d		£ s d
Offered in Church	26 19 3½	Sent to the Church Building Society	1 0 0
Found in the Alms Chest	4 17 1½	Allotted to 11 men 1s. a week, 13 weeks	7 3 0
		Stolen by a Stranger	0 14 5
		Sent to the National Society	0 15 9
		Allotted to 19 men 1s. a week, 13 weeks	12 7 0
		Balance in hand	9 16 3
	£31 16 5		£31 16 5

In reliance on the collections of the current quarter, and on the above balance, we have allotted 1s. a week to 23 labourers from Michaelmastide to Christmas-day. We have chosen, as the objects of our charity, poor labourers, who had each a wife and four children to feed and clothe on seven shillings a-week, because such men are forbidden to be relieved from the parish rate. We have made in this donation of alms no difference between dissenters and churchpeople, but have ministered to the necessities of each, impartially, and alike. We anticipate a gloomy winter for the poor; the potato harvest, their chief article of food, has failed; the scantiness of the barley and oat-crops will throw many threshers out of employment, and we would fain therefore make every effort for their relief. We take leave, then, to transmit this our statement *to the absent landlords*, in order that if they should be inclined to give, by deputy, their alms in Church to the poor on their land, they may be enabled to do so, for Jesus Christ his sake.

Walter objected to the offertory less because it was irreligious or illegal than because the consequent alms-giving was retrogressive and harmful to the poor. As a result of his opposition to Hawker, the latter's biographers all implicitly dismissed Walter as a stony-hearted reactionary. He was not. His newspaper was sympathetic to the plight of the agricultural labourers and critical of the doctrinaire callousness of political economists like Lord Radnor. For example, it sharply denounced the 'wanton cruelty' of his explanation to his 'serfs'.

> Lord Radnor is well known to be a man ... that, if he chanced to take the theory of the non-existence of matter, would not hesitate to run his head against a stone wall in verification of the doctrine. Happily for the soundness of his occiput, he is not a Berckleian [sic]; unhappily for the labourers on his property, he is a political economist.

If *The Times* condemned the inhuman logic of the political economists, its owner might be expected to have supported Hawker's benevolent generosity. In fact, he found it anything but commendable because it was a resuscitation of the Speenhamland system, the distribution of a dole to agricultural workers which most believed had led to their demoralization and pauperization. Walter wrote,

> It is a revival of the old allowance system – of that system which was begun in Berkshire in the year 1795, and is now universally stigmatized. Here is an excuse for an employer to give deficient wages. We have the distinction again between the single and the married. If in this parish of Morwenstow seven shillings be the rate of wages for a man with a wife and four children, and the minister thinks eight shillings sufficient for six persons during a winter's week, how much will he allow to the single man? The absurdity and mischief of this scheme are obvious.

Thus it was not *The Times*, which advocated 'decent wages' instead of charity, but Hawker who was taking up an old-fashioned stance. In this instance Walter was on the side of the progressives – men like W. R. Greg who shortly let fly his tirade in the *Westminster Review* against paternalists of Hawker's type.

> *Charity*, – in various forms, in one or other of its multiplied disguises, – seems to be the only panacea which occurs to the Great ... One party advocates a more liberal poor law; another, shorter hours of labour to be enforced by law. In the view of some, *allotments* are the one thing needful; while Young England suggests alms-giving in the magnificent and haughty style of the feudal ages; and Lord Ashley commits his latest solecism, in getting up a society for the protection of Distressed Needlewomen. The same vulgar, shallow, aristocratic error runs through all. Everyone thinks of *relieving*, no one of *removing*, the mischief. The prevailing idea evidently is ... *to give benefits to an inferior*, not to *do justice to a fellow man.*

Though more circumspectly and with much less polemical vigour, much the same point was made by Walter in his attack on Hawker in *The Times*. 'One of our greatest statesman (I mean Mr. Fox) has said, that it was not fitting in a free country that the great body of the people should be dependent on the charity of the rich.'

Hawker had a real case to answer. He rebutted Walter's arguments with an impressive combination of gusto and forensic skill. He wrote haughtily, because he was confident that he completely understood the terms on which the agricultural labourers of Morwenstow lived, and was doing everything possible to ameliorate their condition. Walter was on the shaky moral ground of the theoretical philanthropist who advocates real present sacrifices by the poor for the sake of hypothetical future benefits. Hawker rebuked him for invading the tranquillity of his parish, bade him remember that he was 'an elderly man, fast approaching the end of all things, and, ere many years have passed, about to stand a separated soul among the awful mysteries of the spiritual world', and counselled him 'to beware lest the remembrance of these attempts to diminish the pence of the poor, and to impede the charitable duties of the rich, should assuage your happiness in that abode where the strifes and triumphs of controversy are unknown'. He set out his case. The local farmers were not being indirectly subsidized because the wages in Morwenstow *never* rose above seven shillings a week, whether alms were supplied or not. Hawker continued,

> Your argument, as applied to my parishioners, is this: Because they have scanty wages in that county, therefore they should have no alms; because these labourers of Morwenstow are restricted by the law from any relief from the rate, therefore they shall have no charity from the Church; because they have little, therefore they shall have no more. You insinuate that I, a Christian minister, think eight shillings a week sufficient for six persons during a winter's week, as though I were desirous to limit the resources of my poor parishioners to that sum. May God forgive you your miserable supposition! I have all my life sincerely, and not to serve any party purpose, been an advocate of the cause of the poor. I, for many long years, have honestly, and not to promote any political ends, denounced the unholy and cruel enactments of the New Poor Law.

Hawker may be accused of having connived at a monstrous compact by which the higher orders bought the humble obedience of the lower with a dole, but there is no doubt that he spoke in a spirit of compassion. Objectively, as Marx or Harriet Martineau would have argued, he was propping up an evil system of social subordination by palliating its worst rigours. But it is surely too much to expect Hawker to have let his people starve in the hope of thereby contributing to the advent of some Socialist Utopia such as William Morris was later to envisage. In fact, recent research has suggested that the dole system did not have such deleterious effects on labourers' economic and moral well-being as has traditionally been thought. It has been argued that the old Poor Law had affinities both in principle and practice with the modern welfare state, and that it was 'by no means an unenlightened policy'. But even were this not the case, the genuine humanitarianism of Hawker's charitable efforts, irrespective of their objective achievement is, in an era of Gradgrinds and Chadbands, its own justification.

Hawker did not just attempt to mitigate the symptoms of rural poverty. With what limited force he could muster, he attacked the disease itself. He used his vote against protectionist candidates, saying, 'I deem a tax on Bread Corn sinful and unjust, and I had rather my Rent charge should fall, than that it should ascend amid the cries of the hungry and poor for dearth of food.' This was quite a courageous step to take in the face of the almost universal hostility of his order, though, of course, many Nonconformist ministers took the same line, one even going so far as to pronounce that 'Jesus Christ is free trade and free trade is Jesus Christ.' Herbert Spencer claimed (no doubt with more bias than accuracy) that 'among the State-appointed teachers of rectitude' his own uncle was, with one exception, 'the only clergyman out of fifteen thousand who contended that the people of England, mostly poor, should not be compelled to buy corn at artificially enhanced prices to enrich English landlords'. Hawker believed that he was 'the only clergyman in this deanery whose silent influence has been felt and acknowledged by the friends of Mr. Gladstone'. Glebe-farming parsons traditionally followed the Tory landed gentry in protecting their own interests and Hawker, though never 'a political partisan – such a function is alien to my habits and tastes', probably came in for a certain amount of unpopularity among his clerical colleagues for his individual stand.

Hawker was outspoken in his endeavours to make the landlords improve conditions for their tenants so that they in turn could, if they heeded the vicar, pass benefits on to their labourers. He particularly supported Churchmen. But there was little that he could do even to protect the family of his sometime church-warden, Thomas Cann, from the exactions of their landlord. He reported to a friend, 'Martyn has treated the Canns like a brute

beast. Because John wished to receive the usual tenant's allowance, he has turned him out by main force, broken open doors and
windows. Every decent person cries shame. And it was done on
the vigil of Good Friday.'

Hawker did not conceal his anger, even though he also rented
land from Martyn. He told him 'that he had a God and that as he
dealt with John Cann and his crippled boy so he would be
requited'. In effect this was the language of impotence. The land-
owners of Morwenstow were as impervious to threats as they
were in general to appeals, public or private. Hawker managed
to wring from only a few of them small regular donations for
this school, and occasional ones for his church and other good
causes. He vented his spleen in letters to his friends. Lord John
Thynne, who would not 'relax his claims on any pretext of bad
times or losses', was 'notoriously not a giver, hard as the nether
millstone'. The Prince of Wales 'is the chief landowner here next
to the Thynnes and does not give a farthing to charity or school'.
After the hard winter of 1866–7 when all the charities were
exhausted he cried, 'The shame, the shame of the landlords,
carrying off 5000£ a year of the rents of our land and giving
back a paltry pittance of less than £20 in aid of club and coals.'
It was not just their hardness of heart which he lamented, it
was their lack of what Ruskin called *largesse* or chivalry, without
which the patriarchal system as Hawker understood it would
founder.

Because the farmers were under pressure and themselves poor
it is not surprising that they paid their workers so badly and were
not what Hawker called 'cheerful givers'. But though 'the result
was always so painfully small', he 'often appealed to their generosity by briefs or private missions around the parish'. Moreover he
was prepared to try to shame them publicly. He rebuked the
farmers in his sermons for their uncharitableness and 'for their
continued murmuring in the wilderness'. He printed an appeal in
which he set out the plight of the labourers, justified his efforts to
help them and berated his opponents.

Two farmers only had the audacity to allege that the effort was uncalled for; and a labourer of one of these must have gone barefooted to his work the whole winter had not the money for a pair of shoes been advanced to him by the victim of the parish.

For Hawker to refer to himself thus publicly – he often dramatized himself in private as 'The Victim of Morwenstow' – indicates how harassed he was feeling by 1861 as a result of local hostility to his crusade for the labourer. He was not deflected from his purposes or his prejudices. In 1863 he wrote, 'Give me evermore the labourer rather than the farmer in a parish like this.'

Nevertheless his physical and mental health was affected by the constant malevolence of the farmers. In 1852, for example, he told a neighbouring clergyman that 'a long and weary illness – produced by the way by the gross misconduct of my parishioners and chief among them your father's tenant at Marsland – has so cut me down that my duties are sadly in arrear.' There is a hysterical quality in many of the similar complaints to which Hawker gave vent. And his method of quelling the 'vile Rebellion' of five farmers in his vestry points to the overwrought state of his mind. 'I read the Exorcistic Service of the Western Church, in Latin of course. They knew not the meaning of the voice but those who inhabited them did. The five fled from the Room howling, as my Deacon will attest.'

As will be seen, Hawker increasingly suffered from a form of persecution mania. He often saw insolence where none was intended, and reacted violently to imagined insults. But he also received a good deal of genuine provocation from local farmers, particularly Dissenters, for what they considered to be his unwarrantable interference in their relations with their employees. When clergymen espoused the cause of the labourers, as a few did, they invited not only ostracism from their social superiors and equals but outspoken opposition from their immediate inferiors. The 'Radical Parson', William Tuckwell, who gave the labourer's

7 The interior of Morwenstow church today

8 The debris left on the shore beneath Hawker's hut by the wreck of the *Avonmore*, 1869

9 The coastline of Morwenstow; the upper bay is overlooked by Hawker's hut

10 Hawker's hut, built of timber from wrecks, on the cliff-top

11 The figure-head of the *Caledonia* in Morwenstow churchyard; in the background is the lychgate house where the corpses of drowned sailors were laid out for burial

12 Morwenstow church and churchyard

cause wide publicity, was made to suffer a number of slights in his parish. Professor J. S. Henslow, vicar of Hitcham in Suffolk, who 'stuck up for the rights of the poor', was faced in 1852 with a violent vestry-protest by farmers against his scheme for giving labourers allotments. Canon Girdlestone, who in the late 1860s organized the migration of labourers from Devon to better-paid areas, was told by a farmer at a vestry-meeting 'in language that cannot literally be repeated, that he was not fit to carry offal to a bear'.

Hawker lacked the evangelistic skill of a Tuckwell, the wealth of a Henslow and the resourcefulness of a Girdlestone. But he used what means he had to bring succour to his people. His pen was not the least effective of these. In one ballad especially, which John Keble told him 'quite haunts me', Hawker epitomized his feelings of compassion for the poor and his indignation at the conditions which they had to endure. With ironical insistence, he began by stating that they were, however treated by a brutal society, human beings.

> The poor have hands, and feet, and eyes,
> Flesh, and a feeling mind:
> They breathe the breath of mortal sighs,
> They are of human kind.
> They weep such tears as others shed,
> And now and then they smile.

The most obvious dehumanizing agent in Hawker's society was the new Poor Law which 'made poverty a guilt and interfered with Christian alms'. This he attacked, pointing to the indignity suffered by so many who now had to die inside the walls of the workhouse,

> Where the stern signal coldly calls
> The prisoned poor to pray.

The ideal was for the poor man to spend his last years surrounded by his familiar community, living in his own house

> Where roses round the porch would roam
> And gentle jasmines fall.

Hawker's condemnation of the social ills of the present was more sound than his prescription of a cure by means of a return to the organic society of the past. But in these respects he differed hardly at all from the greatest social critic of his age – Carlyle.

Hawker's propaganda was effective in stirring up the sincerest form of sympathy, that which expressed itself in gifts to his charities. Mainly, though, the burden fell on his shoulders. He accepted it, for 'the clergyman, limited as his powers of succour may be, is in reality in countries like our own the only poor man's friend.' Hawker's Evangelical upbringing had prepared him well for this role. He had no difficulty in reconciling his hierarchical view of society with his metaphysical opinion that 'The poor man ought to be called Master and Lord for so he is.' Hawker did not suffer from the tensions which afflicted the sometime vicar of Tysoe who

> had an aristocratic view of society and yet he was an evangelical Christian! He visibly alternated between stress on his own and his family's social claims and his wish to be a simple follower of Christ, between an ardent wish to bring about all possible unity in his complex parish and the sense that it ill became him as Vicar ever to accept any place but the first.

For Hawker there was no conflict between temporal and spiritual claims. For a man to fulfil his functions on earth he simply had to carry out the duties appropriate to his station. Charity was the function of the higher orders. Hawker was remarkable in that what he preached about that subject he also practised.

He was not alone, of course. Ecclesiastical historians (their inclination to look on the bright side confirmed by the tendency of churchmen to supply creditable evidence about themselves) instance many clergy who did as much, or more. But the prevailing impression remains, and it is particularly strong as far as the

West Country is concerned, that the Established Church concentrated what energies it possessed on its spiritual functions and attempted and achieved little in the way of temporal improvement. As F. G. Heath, a well-informed observer, concluded, 'one of the most striking circumstances in connexion with the movement of our peasantry for better wages, better houses, better treatment, has been the marked indifference exhibited towards the movement by the ministers of religion.' Not all church historians would disagree. The verdict of one is that the Church of England 'found practical action blocked by internal controversies' and dissipated its energies in the 'long battles with dissent'. Another admits, 'There was a grain of bitter truth in Charles Buller's witticism: "For Heaven's sake do not destroy the Established Church, it is the only thing that stands between us and Christianity."'

What was the range of Hawker's charitable efforts? In addition to the collections in church and the distribution of the money to supplement wages, he ran a clothing club and a coals club, organizations which were not uncommon and which proliferated steadily throughout the nineteenth century. He bemoaned the inadequacy of his clubs but clearly they were of considerable assistance to the poor. 'What can be worse', he wrote, 'than to know the wants you cannot alleviate? To be sure our clothing and coal clubs will assist a little ... The members pay a penny a week, 4/-4d. a year and I have usually collected subscriptions to make each ticket 10/- – when they are short the balance falls on me.' Hawker also supplied a great deal of food at Christmas time. In 1847 he noted, 'my beef this Christmas chiefly for gifts 303½ lbs. Groceries £3.0.0. Malt etc. £1.5.0. in all cir[ca] £12.' In 1872 he told a friend, 'On Christmas Day we had 40 people at dinner and gave away the cold meat and pudding next day to 30 more. We sold from our stock to accomplish these things and we shall be requited I am sure by a faraway friend on his Pay Night.'

Apart from feasts of this kind, Hawker apparently distributed

soup on a regular basis throughout the winter. He once complained that he had experimented with different varieties but his
parishioners would only drink bacon broth: 'As a rule the poor
dislike *unusual* food and soup is to country folks always a suspicious
fluid.' There were a variety of other periodic donations, such as
this one, rendered nugatory by the guardians of the Stratton workhouse (who were so hard-hearted that Hawker made strenuous
efforts to achieve 'the annexation of Morwenstow to Bideford
Union'): 'Mrs Hawker has been in the habit of giving the aged
who die calico for a shroud; they have now decided that if any
pauper receives a gift towards burial, the Union pay for the funeral
is withdrawn. Is it not fearful to live in such a fierce and savage
place?' It is difficult to assess the extent of Hawker's routine
charities. But his confidence that if the thief responsible for stealing
wood from Martyn's barn in March 1871 was a Morwenstow man
he was also guilty of ingratitude to the vicar, is impressive.
Hawker wrote, 'I have employed Papin the policeman to watch
by night and if he detects any one I shall exact punishment. If it be
done by a Morwenstow man that person must have received
money or other gift from me since Christmas Day. But the
ingratitude of this parish is fiendish.'

Not content with distributing regular aid, Hawker gave indiscriminately and often, it seems, capriciously. As his nephew said,
'he never knew how to keep [money]'. Hawker occasionally
committed that cardinal sin of giving assistance to the undeserv-
ing, thus, in Victorian eyes, undermining the gospel of thrift and
self-help, subsidizing imprudence and bringing the impending
Malthusian catastrophe a step nearer. Unlike many clergymen of
the Church of England he assisted Dissenters, passing it off with
the jesting remark, 'I like to give them a little comfort in this
world, for I know what discomfort awaits them in the next.' He
was never slow to unharness his horse from the plough and send to
Stratton for a doctor if a parishioner was ill, and when he could he
dipped into his own purse for the medical expenses. On freezing
winter nights he would 'stamp about the house, collecting warm

clothing and blankets, bottles of wine, and any food he could find
in the larder, and laden with them, attended by a servant, go forth
on his rambles and knock up the cottagers, that he might put extra
blankets on their beds, or cheer them with port wine and cold
pie'.

The sick and the dying, too, were given what comfort the
vicar could bestow. Visiting their bedsides was a duty to which all
Victorian clergymen paid lip-service and which most performed.
Even Julius Hare, who did not go in for 'constant, regular, vigilant
ministrations to the poor', made efforts to visit the sick though, as
they testified, communicating with them was more than he could
manage: 'The Archdeacon he do come to us, and he do sit by the
bed and hold our hands, and he do growl a little, but he do zay
nowt.' Hawker had no troubles on that score and was as conscien-
tious as any of his fellows. Every day, he reported, 'after prayers I
visit any sick or aged ones'. His letters are full of references to
being 'out in the parish on pony back now for I have many sick'.
Or to being 'obliged to ride to a village a mile off to baptise a
dying child'. Or to visiting the aged whose suffering was such
that all he could think of was the '*relief* of death'. He brought
material benefits as well as spiritual comfort – healing compounds
like calves-foot jelly, junket, soup or fresh produce from his glebe
farm.

From his own point of view, Hawker's expenditure on charity
was, like his grandfather's, irresponsible and improvident. It contributed to his financial worries, which began soon after he came
to Morwenstow and continued, with fluctuating degrees of
intensity, for the rest of his life. Of course, he was extravagant in
all sorts of ways, but he did make genuine sacrifices for the poor,
of which he was understandably proud. In 1855 he told a brother
clergyman, 'I thank God I have saved our Bookbox money'
(presumably for the school), 'this year by rigidly refusing every
atom of new clothes. It would be vainglorious if I were to tell you
the amount I have saved in twelve months by personal self-denial
– I mean on myself alone.' Towards the end of Hawker's life his

liabilities had so much accumulated and the expense of his young family was so great that he was unable to give as liberally to his parishioners as before. He said that the poor remembered his past alms and forgave his present disability 'but it cuts me to the very heart, even more than my debts to others, that I am so shorn of power for charity to them'.

In the circumstances, the poor people of Morwenstow could not but be thankful for the small mercies which the vicar did bestow. Evidence that they were is provided by their reception of Hawker's widow and daughters when they returned to the parish for a visit in 1879.

The *gentry* of Morwenstow were *civil* but not cordial, but almost universally we were kindly welcomed by the poor. Tom Lane who was *not* friendly when I went home immediately after my dear Husband's death, gave us this time a most hearty welcome, tears streaming down his cheeks. Dick Founde brought us potatoes from his little garden [etc.].

Of course, Hawker's efforts mitigated – they did not alter – the state of indigence to which most of his flock stood condemned. He could only have given a negative answer to Kingsley's pertinent question:

Can your lady patch hearts that are breaking
With handfulls of coal and rice,
Or by dealing out flannel and sheeting
A little below cost price?

However, Hawker's work had not been fruitless. Indeed, bearing in mind that he was a pessimist by nature, it would be reasonable to accept his own opinion that the over-all effect of his ministry had been to help his parishioners to take a few steps in the direction of moral progress. He wrote in 1862,

I do think that the Coast embraced by my own parish is improved within the 25 years of my own incumbency. They are certainly much more tender and respectful in their behaviour to the dead and there is also a change in their honesty of life. They did not steal a block or a rope from the two last wrecks in Morwenstow.

Certainly Hawker taught by example as well as by precept that charity was the essence of the Christian principle. Thus it would be fair, particularly as much will be said later about less admirable aspects of Hawker's nature, to let his second wife's pious if platitudinous lines stand as the verdict on his labours as vicar and pastor. She admonished her daughters

> That they should teach the future men to know
> Their Father's life was given for Morwenstow,
> That health and wealth were spent on Church and Poor
> And that his prayers are for her evermore.

7

Shipwrecks

Enough has been said about Hawker's work in Morwenstow
to indicate that for him isolation did not mean tranquillity. By
the time his major building-work in the parish was completed, in
1843, he had settled down to a regular daily round which, provided it was not interrupted, brought him some sense of security.
With a few seasonal variations and some changes as he grew older,
Hawker's programme went thus. He rose quite early and had
breakfast at 8.00. He then said morning prayers and visited his
parishioners, especially the old and the ill. For the benefit of a
friend Hawker took up the story of 'one day that you may understand the year'.

Dinner at one, Tea with it, We neither of us touch at any
time beer or wine. After dinner I read (while Mrs Hawker
works or knits) aloud ever since her eyes grew weak. At four
Church, for evening service. Tea at five. Then arrives the
[letter-] bag, newspapers etc. Letters to be answered. MSS
written by me in bits as they come. More reading. About
eleven bed. And thus with the variety of people of the parish
coming to see me or with something to ask for and with calls
too from strangers who arrive from different quarters, thus
glides away year after year – except when some inquietude
breaks in ... and then I am so broken down and shattered
that the old routine is gone and I cannot command myself to
read or write or think or pray as I ought.

All sorts of interruptions frayed what Hawker described as 'my naturally thrilling nerves and fibres' – battles with local gentry and farmers, problems on his own glebe, family troubles, Dissenting hostility, crime, debt. But nothing reduced him to such a state of prostration as the shipwrecks so frequently hurled up on his angry rocks.

In the days of sail, the coastline of north Cornwall was a magnet for wrecks. There were no fewer than eighty-one vessels cast ashore at or around Bude between 1824 and 1874. Westerly gales swept across the Atlantic with stupendous fury in the winter. Wind and wave together were capable of wreaking havoc, of destroying the breakwater and tearing down the lock gates of Bude, for example, or of tossing fifteen-ton boulders around Morwenstow beach like pebbles. It has been estimated that a single roller of Atlantic ground-swell can fall with a pressure of over three tons per square foot. Spray from ocean storms carried ten miles inland, as far as Holsworthy. Tennyson came to north Cornwall to 'be alone with God' because he had heard that he would see 'larger waves there than on any other part of the British coast'. Another traveller claimed that the sea at Morwenstow roared more loudly than in any other part of Cornwall; it often made 'a series of sharp explosions, like field guns at a review, followed by deeper detonations, as of heavier guns'. Frail sailing ships in the funnel of 'the Severn Sea' stood little chance against what Hawker called 'the storm – the blast – the tempest shock'. There was no hospitable harbour on the north Cornish coast and little enough shelter under the lee of Lundy, itself a dangerous obstacle to be given a wide berth, especially in the dark. There was much truth in the old Cornish saying:

> From Padstow Point to Lundy Light,
> Is a watery grave, by day or night.

Two circumstances about the Morwenstow coastline contributed to Hawker's anguish over the wrecks. The first was that the prevailing current tended to throw up detritus from the sea on to his shore. Hawker believed that the current set directly across from Labrador, and it is true that 'once, in 1843, a huge pine trunk of a tree floated ashore in Morwenstow, with the branches rudely lopped off, coated with Barnacles and sea-weed, just as it had floated in a raft down some American river.' This current still makes Morwenstow a good place to go beachcombing; one man who does so today remarks that 'my own experiences of this coast entirely endorse Hawker's accounts'. These were grim. After storms, the waters of the Bristol Channel were often, as Hawker graphically put it, 'peopled with corpses', and his 'nervous terrors' about what each tide would bring in were accordingly 'great'. Sometimes it was a bloated body which had only become light enough to rise to the surface and float, after ten days or more of decomposing in the water. More often though, and this was the second circumstance which tormented Hawker, the sailors had been mutilated, literally cut to pieces on the rocks. Frequently, dismembered limbs were found – an arm, a leg, a hand. When the *Caledonia* was wrecked, 'a mangled seaman's heart' was discovered. After a wreck in 1859 five out of seven corpses buried by Hawker 'had no Heads – cut off by jagged rocks!!' Unrecognizable lumps of human flesh, known locally as 'gobbets', were collected in baskets. All were buried with decency. As the years went on Hawker found it increasingly difficult to undertake this physically repulsive and psychologically agonizing task with equanimity. But he struggled to overcome his nervous debilitation and always fulfilled what he considered to be his duty towards the mortal remains of dead sailors. Which was more than can be said of some neighbouring clergy. In 1862 Hawker lamented, 'I very much fear the old wrecker's spirit is by no means departed from Bude.' A human trunk had come ashore on the sands there, and had been washed out by the next tide, 'when its silent appeal for burial was found to be in vain'.

Hawker had to exert himself to prevent his people from stripping the wrecks that came ashore at Morwenstow. As has been said, Cornishmen regarded these, not unreasonably, as a bounty of

God to compensate for poverty, a harvest of the deep to be gathered in with thanks. Even the seamen were not immune from mishandling. There was a long-standing superstition, based perhaps on the diabolical behaviour of Cruel Coppinger, that

> Save a stranger from the sea,
> And he'll turn your enemy.

This did not, in fact, prevent Cornishmen in the nineteenth century from making heroic efforts, often fatal to themselves, to save lives. But their disrespectful attitude towards the dead horrified Hawker. It was summed up in the laconic reply given to an ingenuous young curate when he excitedly asked a native what he should do about a body, apparently drowned, which he had found on the shore: 'Sarch 'is pockets.' The Cornish child's prayer was supposed to be, 'God bless Father 'n Mother an' zend a ship ta shore vore mornin'.' A few clergymen probably added their own orisons to those of the children, just as in the past they had often connived at, and in some cases assisted with, the smuggling. Parson Troutbeck is said to have offered up this supplication, 'Dear God, we pray not that wrecks should happen, but that if it be Thy will that they do, we pray Thee let them be to the benefit of Thy poor people of Scilly.' In the face of the poverty and unity of the people of Morwenstow, Hawker's stand for legality and righteousness was a bold one.

It was first put seriously to the test when the *Caledonia* was wrecked in 1842. Hawker managed to prevent his parishioners from plundering more than a few fragments of the ship for fuel. The *Caledonia* was a fine vessel of 200 tons, homeward bound from Odessa. One September night she was caught in a hurricane and hurled on to the rocks at Sharp's Nose, a headland just south of Hawker's vicarage. The longboat had been carried away by the waves and only one member of the ten-man crew managed to scramble ashore. The rest perished. Hawker described the scene at daybreak. The ship had been shattered into broken pieces by the fury of the sea. The rocks and the water bristled with fragments of mast and spar and rent timbers; the cordage lay about in tangled masses. The rollers tumbled in volumes of corn, the wheaten cargo; and amidst it all the bodies of the helpless dead – that a few brief hours before had walked the deck the stalwart masters of their ship – turned their poor disfigured faces toward the sky, pleading for sepulture. We made a temporary bier of broken planks, and laid thereon the corpses, decently arranged. As the vicar, I led the way, and my people followed with ready zeal as bearers, and in sad procession we carried our dead up the steep cliff, by a difficult path, to await, in a room at my vicarage which I allotted them, the inquest.

Hawker helped to look after the lonely survivor, Edward Le Dain of Jersey, who in gratitude ransacked his island, whenever the vicar afterwards wanted a cow, for 'the sleekiest, loveliest, best of that beautiful breed'. It took some time to find the remaining corpses, or pieces of corpses, but eventually all were interred after a number of moving ceremonies. The figurehead of the *Caledonia*, 'the relique of the storm', was placed over the captain's grave. The white wooden statue with sword and shield, in a remarkably fine state of preservation, still stands in Morwenstow churchyard.

The year after the *Caledonia* came the *Phoenix* of St Ives, which foundered on a reef after hours of unavailing effort to tack away from Morwenstow's fatal shore. All hands were lost. Hawker told the story, no doubt with his usual artistic embellishments, of how one member of the crew had a brother who came up from St Ives to search for his corpse. Eventually it was found, almost at the low-water mark. It was recognized by its shoe, for only this was visible. The rest of the body was inextricably jammed under a fifteen-ton boulder. All the endeavours of Hawker and his parishioners to move this mass of rock, in the brief moments allowed by the ebb-tide, failed. The brother's anguish was 'thrilling to behold and terrible to hear. "O! my brother! my

brother!" was his sob again and again, "what a burial place for our
own dear merry boy!"'

Eventually Hawker asked the engineer from the Bude canal to
come to his aid. He did so, bringing with him two windlasses. In
the late evening, iron chains were attached to the rock and it was
hoisted up far enough to enable Hawker to pull out the body.

To our startled view and to the sudden lights, came forth
the altered, ghastly, flattened semblance of a man! 'My
brother! My brother!' shrieked a well known voice at my
side, and tears of gratitude and suffering gushed in mingled
torrent over his rugged cheek. A coffin had been made ready,
under the hope of final success, and therein we reverently
laid the poor disfigured carcase of one who a little while
before, had been the young and joyous inmate of a fond and
happy home. We had to clamber up a steep and difficult
pathway along the cliff with the body, which was carried by
the bearers in a kind of funeral train. The vicar of course led
the way. When we were about half way up a singular and
striking event occurred, which moved us all exceedingly.
Unobserved, for all were intent on their solemn task, a vessel
had neared the shore, she lay to, and as it seemed had watched
us with night-glasses from the deck or had discerned us from
the torches and lanterns in our hands. For all at once there
sounded along the air, three deep and thrilling cheers! And
we could see that the crew on board had manned their yards.
It was manifest that their loyal and hearty voices and gestures
were intended to greet and gratulate our fulfilment of duty to
a brother mariner's remains. The burial place of the dead in
this churchyard is a fair and fitting scene for their quiet rest.
Full in view and audible in sound for ever rolls the sea. Is it
not to them a soothing requiem that

> 'Old Ocean, with its everlasting voice,
> As in perpetual Jubilee, proclaims
> The praises of the Almighty!'?

Trees stand, like warders, beside their graves, and the Saxon
and shingled church, 'the mother of us all,' dwells in silence
by, to watch and wail over her safe and slumbering dead.

In this and other accounts of his experiences of wrecks which he
printed, Hawker tended to dramatize himself as the resourceful
spiritual suzerain who performed his grisly duties with compassion and calmness. There is no reason to doubt his compassion
but he did not always take quite such a prominent or judicious
part in the rescue-work as he claimed, and he became increasingly
tortured by the task of finding and burying the corpses.

Only a month after the *Phoenix* came the *Alonzo*. All her crew
were drowned. Hawker was particularly struck by the 'strong
expression of *reluctant agony*' on the faces of the corpses when they
had drifted ashore. The 'struggle of the conscious victim in the
strong and cruel grasp of the remorseless sea was depicted in harsh
and vivid lines on the brow of the dead'. When he had placed their
bodies in his churchyard, Hawker found that he had buried
fifteen sailors in just over a year. Perhaps it was his desire to escape
from this accumulation of misery which caused him to build his
third and final hut. He constructed it from the timbers of the
wrecked ships and placed it on the cliff-top where it still stands,
commanding a magnificent panorama of sea, sky and coastline.
Here he often came on fine evenings and read to his wife. Here he
conducted much of his correspondence with the outside world.
Here he won solace in composing his poetry, retreating from the
assaults of reality into the fastness of his imagination. Unclouded
by so many of the fleeting preoccupations of his era, Hawker's
mind drew pure inspiration from the timeless vista at his feet.

In 'the ever-striking scene of the Sea' he found 'a storehouse of
incident and imagery'. He took his temper from the ocean and
saw in its changing face reflections of his own moods. The deep
could seem a type of glistening Paradise, a 'Mirror of Heaven':

Fair visions haunt those waves – sweet dreams arise –
And billows bathed in glory, bound to meet the skies.

while Hawker's own cliffs, scene of lonely miseries, sometimes aroused

> Gloom, gloom! for me – the mountain clothed in cloud,
> The shore of tempests when the storm is loud,
> Where wild winds rush, and broken waters roll,
> And all is dark and stern, like my own wintry soul.

In different vein, though, 'Morwenna's Strand' could become a rocky fortress of faith, valiantly resisting 'the baffled army of the waves'. Hawker was not a dupe of pathetic fallacies but a seer of sacramental visions. He did not credit nature with human feelings but with divine vitality. God's 'spirit thrills the conscious stone'. Directly echoing Newman, Hawker speculated: 'What if all material things are but sacraments of God? This created universe, with its stars may be a mere galaxy of Symbols fraught with Spiritual and interior life.' Of all the 'lifted emblems' in God's 'vast Revelation', the most awe-inspiring was the sea. Living beside it, Hawker was constantly reminded of the omnipotence and immanence of the everlasting Deity. The obvious corollary of this was the feebleness and irrelevance of the ephemeral creeds of nineteenth-century man – industrialism, utilitarianism, positivism and the like. To the believer's ear the sea spoke of the past, of an age of faith. From his eremitic cell on the cliff-top Hawker heard 'the pulses of the ocean bound Whole centuries away'.

However, the sea often wrenched Hawker's mind painfully back to the present, as it continued to deposit its wrecks, with their cargoes of corpses, on his shore. His epistolary descriptions of them, penned at white-hot speed in moments snatched from his rescue-operations, make fascinating reading. They also show, particularly the unpublished ones, how the sea, which afforded Hawker his chief imaginative stimulus, also helped to shake his mental equilibrium. In 1862, for example, the *Bencoolen* was wrecked at Bude and it provided Hawker with the twenty-eighth sailor he had to bury under the trees by the southern wall of his churchyard. His excited accounts of the wreck and its aftermath give a good indication of the psychological toll exacted on him by such events.

Hawker reported that in the afternoon of 21 October

a hull was seen off Bude wallowing in the billows. All rushed to the Shore. At Three she struck on the Sand close to the Breakwater – not 300 yards from the Rocks. Manby's apparatus was brought down – a Rocket fired and a Rope was carried over the Ship. The Mate sprang to clutch it – missed – and fell into the Sea to be seen no more alive. 'Another Rope!' was the cry. But from the mismanagement of those in charge there was no other there. They then saw the poor fellows – 34 – (two lost before) constructing a Raft and launching it. A Call from the Life Boat, one of large cost provided with all good gear kept close by. She was run down to the Water. A Shout for Men – none – A few of the Hovillers, pilot men, got on board, but refused to put off – Conceive the Scene – the Baronet [Sir Thomas Acland] shrieking in vain – all Bude lining the Cliffs and Shore – Well well – to abbreviate a horror, The Raft was tossed over. About six were washed ashore with life in them, Four corpses, and the rest were carried off to Sea dead – 26 corpses are somewhere in our Waters, and my men are watching for their coming on shore. The County gives 5/- for finding each corpse, and I give 5/- more. Therefore they are generally found and brought here to the Vicarage where the inquest and the attendant events nearly kill me.

Hawker was furious at the refusal of the lifeboat-men to go to the rescue of the *Bencoolen's* crew and characteristically attributed it to their Wesleyan 'Sneakism'. Even Sir Thomas Acland was 'roused almost to frenzy' by the lifeboat's failure. But there were no experienced sailors available to man it, the surf would have made launching suicidally dangerous and at a subsequent inquiry the lifeboat-men were vindicated. Hawker was not convinced and wrote his bitter little ballad, 'A Croon on Hennacliff'. It purported

to express a raven's gratitude for the cowardly generosity of the
Bude men in providing him and his 'hungry mate' with such a
'savoury supper'.

> 'Cawk! cawk!' then said the raven,
> 'I am fourscore years and ten:
> Yet never in Bude Haven
> Did I croak for rescued men. –
> They will save the Captain's girdle,
> And shirt, if shirt there be:
> But leave their blood to curdle,
> For my old dame and me.'

Hawker's venom was no doubt partly inspired by the terrors
that he experienced over the burial of sailors. He reported to Sir
Thomas Acland that, eighteen days after the wreck,

the too accustomed message arrived at my door: 'A corpse
ashore Sir, at Stanbury Mouth', – a little creek a mile south of
the Church. My staff went about their work. Six bearers with
a rude bier were called to bring the dead. A letter written and
sent by a policeman to the Coroner, and my lych-gate-house
on the Vicarage premises got ready. At six o'clock notice
came that they were nigh and I went out into the moonlight
to meet them. I receive the dead sailor at my gate and with
the sentence, 'I am the Resurrection and the Life.' And it
always moves me to soothing thoughts, that no sooner is the
bruised and broken and nameless stranger cast up by the seas
than the Church greets him as a son and proclaims his right to
inherit a glorified body and a life everlasting. I saw when they
had laid him on the ground that he was a fine, tall, and
shapely man, very little disfigured. Above the common in
aspect and with a pair of thin elastic boots on. My people at
once thought it was the Captain so I sent off a messenger to
Bude describing him. Then the doors were shut that the
sexton and his wife might wash and shroud the corpse. A

carpenter came to measure for the coffin and at midnight all the last duties were done.

If we could have had a visit from the coroner next day, the work of mercy would be done. But we are always obliged to wait for the tardy proceedings of that official person, Mr. Good, who forgets that a body already a fortnight dead and, as our people graphically say, 'looking for the earth long ago', must try our nerves and nostrils very cruelly. Indeed, in a very few hours the air is tainted a long way off. Next day, Wednesday, Captain Jones arrived from Bude to identify, if he could, the man. But he was an utter stranger to him. At last, on Thursday at noon, arrived a policeman with the letter from Mr. Good and a warrant to bury. So we laid him in his rest not far from that oak tree, making my group of silent seamen twenty-eight!

> They came in paths of storm,
> They found this quiet home
> In Christian ground.

Again startled! 'A woman Sir, has brought a man's right foot, picked up at Combe.' So we have put watchers on the spot on the look-out for the rest of the body or another. No other bodies have been gathered from the tide but there is a strong suspicion that the broken hull with full ten feet of sand washed into it contains in a kind of temporary burial some of the thirteen still unaccounted for, and this is thought from the fearful effluvium around the wreck at low water. They have not yet dug into this sand because they have loftier duties to perform . . . but when this is done, no doubt they may yet discover the dead.

As a result of this letter Acland ordered an excavation to be made into the sand, and at least one corpse was found.

In these accounts there are indications of the strain exerted on Hawker by this wreck and others. He explained to his most intimate correspondent, Mrs Watson, that what afflicted his nerves most of all was not physical but metaphysical terror.

I keep up my nervous tissue at the full tension of resolve but the reaction will come and how can I help breaking down. You know not the rushing thoughts, the thick-coming fancies of the sleepless and vigilant night. All that I have read comes back upon the mind – the Rabbinical tenet that until the body is interred the separate soul can win no rest.

There is no doubt that Hawker, superstitious by nature, dwelling in that lonely house where his ears were so often assailed by 'beating rain, howling wind, moaning chimneys', believed himself to be haunted by the spirits of the unburied dead. It was to be expected that Hawker's shaken mind should dwell on ghosts. His 'Thought Books' are full of references to them. For example, '*Ghosts*. I have seen men in dreams who never knew that they appeared to me.' Or again, '*Ghosts*. Pale and eyes without life. Spake. No sound but the words are felt all through. They thrill like an echo.' Hawker was 'fully persuaded that the dead are cognizant ... of all that occurs among men'. He asked, 'who can doubt that things spiritual commune with the *unslumbering* soul in dreams?'. With such acute apprehensions of the ethereal world, Hawker had good reason to tremble at the prospect of wrecks.

He spent anxious hours in his hut watching the skies for gales. He told a friend that 'a principal theme of my thought is the weather.' After an especially violent storm, during which his normally reliable barometer (known to the farmers as 'Parson's Glass') had remained at 'Set Fair', Hawker wrote, 'I have been compelled to solve that and other wonders of the weather by my real opinion that God is angry with this land. And so I think and fear. In all that is called material success England prospers – in wealth in arts and arms – but that is of the Earth and Earthly. Demons may be the authors of that ...' Thus Hawker interpreted bad weather as yet another intervention of the divine providence which was constantly superintending terrestrial affairs. Not only was he forced to participate in the national doom, brought on he believed by the accumulation of English sins, but he had to suffer a personal fate in the shape of wrecks. He saw himself as the particular target of providence, whose activities were, of course, impenetrably mysterious. Sometimes it afforded him angelic protection, while at others it permitted demons to afflict him. In 1859, for example, the schooner *Milo* of Sunderland was sunk on the glebe rocks 'a little south-west of MY HUT'. The last of its sailors to be buried was a

> nameless Officer who was found upon my beach with face upturned as it were for a quiet grave 'beneath Morwenna's Shade'. Among the epithets one is THE CRUEL SEA ... is it not deserved? ... In the night of the storm a Prince-Demon twisted off in one clutch slates, rafters and all a fourth part of the roof of my barn ... Yet, strange! No! Natural, – only a few shingle were shaken off the Church, although a circle of storms onslew the roof.

Hawker felt himself peculiarly to be the victim of unaccountable cosmic caprice. The unenviable terms of the tenure of his existence were never more forcefully brought home to him than when wrecks were cast up on his shore.

Thick and fast they came during Hawker's last years at Morwenstow. The winter of 1863 was a particularly stormy one and December saw two shipwrecks. One of them occurred with brutal suddenness; the other was a protracted ordeal. Hawker witnessed the first when he was called to the cliff-top to see a ship in distress during 'a hurricane'.

> The vessel was a schooner, her sails nearly gone. We watched as she tacked twice within a mile of the shore and after about an hour all at once, while we stood with our eyes fastened on her, she keeled over and went down. The waves closed over her and her crew are floating in the water out of sight until they are washed ashore.

The weather did not abate, and a few days later Hawker recorded,

At night rockets sent up at sea terrified our country people
out of their wits. They thought it something supernatural. On
Friday morning just at daybreak I was called up. A vessel
coming ashore on Vicarage Rocks. I went out, Cann with me.
She was not coming ashore but anchored a mile off, her masts
all gone and they were on the glebe beach. The English flag was
hoisted upside down at half height of a spar. We saw many
people on board running to and fro. I came in and sent off a
messenger to Bude with a letter to the Master of the Lifeboat
telling him of the event and begging him to put off with his
men to save the lives of the sailors. He did make one effort and
only one. The surf at Bude was too strong. But although provided with a truck and wheels they did not take her to another
place and try her there. A coastguard came to tell me this.

We went out on the cliff again. Mr Valentine [a clergyman
who lived in Morwenstow for a time] had arrived. When we
reached the cliff we saw a bustle on board and presently a
boat was lowered and five men got into her. She did not try
to come ashore on my own cliffs but made upward north
towards, or rather along, Wellcombe and Hartland. Mr V.
and myself then got our ponies and rode on the cliff, the boat
rowing onward ... We rode thus many miles, the boat all
the time keeping off shore and afraid to land. At last the boat
drew near the shore where a peer and creek ran out towards
the sea and we were able to see them land. It turned out to be
the mate and four men sent off from the ship to try for help to
get the others off. We sent them on to Clovelly to telegraph
for aid and we ourselves came back. They told us she was the
Margaret Quayle, 1,000 tons laden with salt from Liverpool
to Calcutta. She was driven into this Channel on Thursday
night and after beating about a long while they had sent out
two anchors and cut their masts away. The crew were 24 so
that there were still 19 on board.

The mate achieved no success at Clovelly and Hawker was driven nearly desperate by the situation. 'Before my very window at the bottom of my valley this ship at anchor with 19 Souls hovering between life and death and the poor Mate and Seamen imploring me continually with tears to rescue their companions . . . My very heart is broken when I am so racked and strained.' He went to Clovelly himself on the Saturday afternoon in an attempt to persuade the fishermen to go to the rescue but both bribes and expostulations failed to move them. In this they were undoubtedly sensible and Hawker, in his agitation, was unreasonable. Two Bude men had almost been drowned in their attempt to launch the lifeboat. More lives would have been put at risk if the Clovelly men had embarked. Eventually, on Sunday, the captain and crew of the *Margaret Quayle* managed to patch up a damaged ship's-boat sufficiently to reach Clovelly by themselves. They left two dogs on board whose mournful howling 'quite overcame' Hawker. At his insistence these were finally brought to land.

As successive winters advanced, Hawker heard the winds and watched the waves with mounting distress. His churchwarden remarked on the fact in 1864: 'Why Sir when we used to find the dead Sailors on the Shore, and carry them in, you didn't use to give way, but now I see you weeping when you go into Church.' In 1868 the *Jeune Joseph* was wrecked. Hawker wrote, 'I do indeed pray that I may be spared as much as possible the misery and indeed danger of proximity to the dead when far advanced in decay . . . If it were not for the fact that burial of the dead is one of the seven acts of mercy that God will surely requite, my heart would fail me.' After the wreck of the *Avonmore* in 1869, when those of the crew not cast ashore were devoured by sharks, Hawker 'gave way in the Churchyard from emotion and indeed from terror', as he added three more dead sailors to his group of forty already there. The fear of insanity, which had always dogged his mind, grew more acute and pervasive throughout his later years. In 1864 he referred to his 'terrible dread of losing power over my own mind. Like Dean Swift I have a horror of becoming "a spectacle to men".' In 1867 he wrote, 'How my mind has preserved its balance is to me a surprise. I do not recall one week for many years when my mind was free from a heavy and debasing terror.' Of course he was prone to exaggeration and self-dramatization. But there can be no doubt that he did suffer from a degree of mental derangement later in life and that the wrecks contributed to this. A man of less delicate sensitivity, having endured the lonely tribulations of his desolate shore, might have heard, as Hawker did, 'in every gust of the gale a dying sailor's cry'.

The constant threat of wrecks, and their occasional advent, meant that Hawker's life was spent in long periods of gnawing worry which culminated in moments of excruciating crisis. In the winter, when no one visited Morwenstow and Hawker was 'as lonely as Lundy', only the hostile elements invaded his seclusion. He felt himself to be at the mercy of the capricious, menacing power of the ocean, nowhere better conveyed than in the magnificent images at the end of *The Quest of the Sangraal*:

> There stood Dundagel, throned: and the great sea,
> Lay, a strong vassal at his master's gate,
> And, like a drunken giant, sobbed in sleep!

He listened to the wind 'howling over my chancel like a lion waiting for his prey', and heard in it terrible portents of future disasters. He declared, 'The sound of a driven leaf will I believe scare me to my dying day.' Over the years such 'weather of suicide' and the wrecks it brought in its wake had bizarre, eroding effects on Hawker's psychological topography. It helped to knead into strange conformations a character naturally given to eccentricity.

8

The Eccentric

The nineteenth-century Church attracted eccentrics. Or perhaps it would be truer to say that the Established Church, especially in rural areas, give men thus inclined unique opportunities to cultivate their eccentricities. This was particularly true in the diocese of Exeter which was so large that the bishop could not exert any real degree of control over his clergy. Hawker described the effects on earlier generations of West Country ministers of their being severed from London, 'the great metropolis of life and manners', and of having their 'abode in wilds that were almost inaccessible', in such terms as make it clear that he was also giving an account of his own predicament.

The Cornish clergyman, insulated within his own limited sphere, often without even the presence of a country squire (and unchecked by the influence of the fourth estate, for until the beginning of this nineteenth century, Flindell's Weekly Miscellany, distributed from house to house from the pannier of a mule, was the only light of the west), became developed about middle life into an original mind and man, sole and absolute within his parish boundary, eccentric when compared to his brethren in civilised regions, and yet, in German phrase 'a whole and seldom man' in his dominion of souls ... These men were not, however, smoothed down into a monotonous aspect of life and manners by this remote and secluded existence. They imbibed, each in his own peculiar circle, the hue of surrounding objects, and were tinged into distinctive colouring and character by many a contrast between scenery and people.

This too bland account may explain why country clergymen became eccentric. But it gives no indication of just how very odd they could become.

A few examples, all from the West Country, will illustrate the assertion, made by Lord Hugh Cecil to the Church Assembly, that 'The Church of England is rich in eccentrics.' One parson did not enter his church for fifty-three years and kennelled the local foxhounds in his vicarage. Another varied the colour of his communion wine, sometimes red, sometimes white. Another refused to take services but, 'clad in flowered dressing-gown and smoking a hookah', greeted his parishioners in the churchyard. Another drove away his congregations, replaced them by wooden and cardboard images in the pews and surrounded his vicarage with a barbed-wire fence behind which savage Alsatians patrolled. Another spent his life searching for the Number of the Beast. Yet another, the rector of Luffincott, to whom Hawker gave friendly advice on the subject, devoted his energies to calculating the date of the millennium. These pastimes, all relatively tame when set against the exploits of hunting, fighting, drunken or adulterous parsons, of whom many West Country instances could be given, demonstrate that in being eccentric Hawker was anything but unique. Indeed he might almost be regarded as run-of-the-mill, if stories from other parts of the land are to be believed – of the incumbent who 'equipped his stall in Church with its own sanitary arrangements', or the one who 'professed himself a neo-Platonist and sacrificed an ox to Jupiter', or the entire clerical complement of the diocese of Lincoln which, so the new bishop Edward King was informed, 'could be divided into three categories: those who had gone out of their minds; those who were about to go out of their minds; and those who had no minds to go out of'.

Still, there is no doubt that Hawker *was* eccentric, even by the standards of the nineteenth-century Church, and that he grew somewhat more than eccentric with age. The most obvious outward and visible sign of his eccentricity was the flamboyant clothes he wore. Observers were immediately struck by them. The Rev. W. Haslam, enough of an intimate of Hawker's to address him with the words, 'Arch-funny, Arch-priest, funny priest you are', reported the reaction of a friend who had glimpsed the vicar on one of his rare excursions from Morwenstow in 1850: 'I was so occupied in scanning his equipage that I lost the opportunity of any acumen [*sic*] that resides under the cassock he wears.' All sorts of reasons could be adduced to account for Hawker's dandyism. The psychologist might judge that, like Pitt the Elder, he concentrated on showy externals in order to banish the fear of attacks of 'gout in the head'. The local historian might remark that Hawker was not dissimilar to a whole class of Cornishmen, the miners, many of whom actually jeopardized their domestic comforts by 'their inordinate love of dress'. The moralist might say, with Carlyle, that Hawker was making a 'willing sacrifice of the Immortal to the Perishable'. Hawker himself sometimes explained his unusual garb in mystical or symbolic terms. He asserted that 'when the first priesthood was embodied God himself portrayed their garments as the primal source of their glory and their beauty.' Yet, though there may be elements of truth in all these explanations, one does not have to look much further than Hawker's simple vanity to account for his passion for sartorial extravagance.

Like many good-looking people he enjoyed adorning himself in a striking way. He liked to create a stir and he was always anxious to hear what kind of impression he had made on others. 'Tell us all the tittle about "the Appearance"', he instructed his brother in 1850, after he had visited Claud at Boscastle in full regalia of cap and cassock. Hawker must have looked an impressive figure. He was tall and well-built, and hardly tending by this time towards his subsequent stoutness. In 1848 he ordered a pair of trousers measuring exactly three feet round the waist. His later photographs reveal him as more corpulent than otherwise, though as late as 1865 he explained to Mrs Watson (whom he never met) that he had not grown fat because 'I take constant exercise and my mental worry I suppose keeps me down'. Hawker had blue eyes, long, fair hair which remained thick but turned white in later years, a loud, melodious voice, 'a peculiarly sensitive skin' and a ruddy complexion, 'what is called sanguineous or full of blood so that hot and bright weather is the worst that I can encounter or bear'. The jotted notes under the heading '*Face*', in one of his 'Thought Books', can only refer to himself: 'Broad full brow. Judgement and resolution in mouth and chin. Anti-sensual head. High nose. Aspiring outline. Magnanimity.' He was particularly proud of the fact that his ears had no lobes. He told Mrs Watson, 'The Duke of Wellington had ears of this shape, and, I hope I may say it without impropriety, although there are few to whom I would mention it – you of course the exception – you trace this feature in all the accurate pictures of our Lord from the Vera Effigies or exact likeness handed down from Ancient times.'

Hawker's usual attire in his early years was a cloth cassock of 'blushing brown', this being, he explained, 'the hue of Our Lady's hair'. His cassocks had velvet cuffs but he treated them as ordinary working-garb and did not look after them with any great care. He was prepared to scramble over the cliffs in a cassock, 'tucking up the full petticoat of his dress', in the words of a clerical visitor of 1853, 'and showing a pair of everyday-life grey trousers, which quite spoilt the effect. He crawled over hedges, jumped ditches and permeated tunnels with great agility.' With his cassock, Hawker wore a variety of headgear – a black-velvet cap or a pink, brimless hat not unlike a fez, such as was worn, he claimed, by priests of the Greek Church, or a thick, soft 'wide-awake' of reddish brown. He never put on a stiff clerical collar, preferring a soft white cravat, 'that very old-fashioned neck cover tied with a string of tape'. He hated black and reserved it almost exclusively to cover his feet. He had black socks made from the wool of his own ewe, locally spun and knitted by the schoolgirls of St Mark's.

And he wore big black (or brown) sea-boots which came up to his knees. He loathed the normal parsonical suits of black cloth. Seeing a waggonette full of neighbouring clergymen who were off to a visitation, he remarked, 'I congratulate you on the funereal appearance of your hearse.' When one of his colleagues remonstrated with him about his own appearance, Hawker replied that at least 'I don't make myself look like a waiter out-of-place, or an unemployed undertaker.' He had a horror, he said, of being 'the complete copy of my own Tailor in his gala suit'. It is not for nothing that a recent writer has described Hawker as 'the first hippie parson'.

In later years Hawker put aside his cassock in favour of a three-quarter-length coat, generally claret-coloured but sometimes purple. He usually left it unbuttoned so that underneath could be seen a blue fisherman's jersey, to indicate that he was a fisher of men. This had a small red cross woven into one side, to mark the entrance of 'the centurion's cruel spear'. In addition he sometimes donned scarlet gloves or gauntlets. For added warmth Hawker would swathe himself in a yellow poncho. His outdoor costume was completed by a variety of accoutrements which dangled from his person: a carpenter's pencil (a reference to Christ's trade), a bunch of seals to impress the wax on his letters with religious symbols (a fish, the pentacle of Solomon and so on), religious medallions (at least one of which, almost certainly, he had blessed by 'his Eminence', either Cardinal Wiseman or Manning). In his hand Hawker carried a walking-stick shaped like a sword but symbolizing the cross 'to enable him to keep off the Evil One', he used to say. He evidently encouraged his second wife to dress with a picturesqueness which complemented his own, reporting to a friend with delightful ingenuousness in 1865, 'I have bought a grey pony for Pauline, an admirable match for Carrow. We ride a great deal and with our red boots the effect is rather stunning than otherwise.' Indoors Hawker's peacock propensities were, if possible, even more unconstrained. He would wear, among other things, red slippers adorned with silver spangles, or a blue dressing-gown laced with gold braid and a vividly coloured biretta loaded with sequins.

Eccentricity in the matter of dress was not unknown in the Victorian period. W. J. Butler, who created a model Tractarian parish at Wantage, expected his clergy to appear in the curious costume of cassock and top hat. Bishops, many of whom still wore huge balloon-sleeves of lawn, and lavender kid gloves, hardly set a high standard of sartorial sobriety. But in general conventional proprieties were strictly observed and, though regarded as a natural phenomenon by his parishioners, Hawker appeared as something of a comic freak to outsiders. This annoyed him, for he preferred to be the object of awe rather than amusement, as the following vignette, penned in 1857, illustrates.

> Yesterday another visitation in its literal sense of Arch-deacon Bartholomew at Holsworthy, whither the curate of Welcombe appeared. Full medievally he rode, girt with belted cassock looped to the girdle on horseback and so revealing boots half way up the thigh in the very form where-in the Abbot rode out to Tavistock on his mule in the XIVth age. Red gauntlet gloves in the exact pattern of those pre-served in Oxford once worn by the founder of Magdalen – save that no patient nun had worked on the back of mine an embroidered Cross – a brown wide-brimmed hat and the Monk's cloak strapped before the saddle with the hood within. Said a smirking clerical idiot to me, 'How I wish, Mr H., I could have your photograph to shew how a clergy-man of the XIXth Century could dress.' 'Well,' said I, 'Luckily I don't want yours. A full length picture of a City Tailor on his gala day would do, except these bands.'

Like many wits, Hawker was not above repeating his *bons mots* and he was particularly apt to do so on the subject of his dress. He was given numerous opportunities.

Hawker's peculiarities extended further than clothes. His rela-tions with animals and the antics of his pets were a constant source of surprise to visitors. Hawker loved animals. His was more of a mystical than a sentimental devotion. His mind continually dwelt on the life and nature of animals and the mystery of their companionship with man. He explained their role, even after the publication of Darwin's *Origin of Species* in 1859, in spiritual and symbolic, not evolutionary, terms. Animals had 'a language of their own' and a life after death. They were 'the attributes of God visibly roaming the earth'. Birds especially preoccupied him.

> Of old it was wont to perplex me that whereas every created and material thing had a meaning and prophesied a doctrine, what could be the spiritual office of The Birds, those beautiful images that were born of water and came forth from their native element of ethereal moisture to cleave the air with a mission and a ministry of God ... Learn therefore that the angels demoniac or Divine announce their mysterious haunt by the votive vassalage of Birds, the clean and the unclean in the diverse augury of the air.

Hawker's explanations had no particular logical consistency or even coherence. They were attempts to gain an understanding of animals and man's relationship with them by a method which he considered to be reliable and which was, perhaps, the best available to him in his state of intellectual isolation – mystical intuition. In fact, it was not unreasonable to attempt to penetrate what even convinced modern rationalists, like Leonard Woolf, have admitted to be a mystery – the way in which, to use Hawker's words, 'animals somehow or other share in the destiny of men'.

Hawker was extraordinary for the literalness with which he followed his own (self-congratulatory) maxim: 'a fondness for [the] society of animals and pleasure in watching their familiar affections is a native and natural impulse with good and kind and holy men.' He kept a variety of pets, of which the most celebrated were his cats. He had nine of them at one point and they sometimes followed him to church, even 'into the pulpit', though whether it can be accepted, on the unsupported assertion of

Baring-Gould, that Hawker excommunicated one for catching a mouse on Sunday, must remain open to doubt. Certainly he doted on these cats. One of them, 'a noble cat called Kit', was as 'large as some dogs and so intelligent that he came to walk when I called him and would follow me a couple of miles'. As well as cats he kept a number of dogs and he did not object to their coming to services. Indeed, his church seems to have been an open house for animals. Once a big black retriever named Achille, belonging to Sir Thomas Acland's daughter, wandered in when Hawker was preaching. It was about to be removed when the vicar 'stopped his sermon. "Let him be, Mrs Mills, there were dogs in the ark." During the rest of the sermon Achille sat motionless on the pew apparently listening devoutly.' Hawker also kept a couple of deer called Robin Hood and Maid Marian. A visiting Low Church clergyman was once pinned to the ground between Robin's antlers and had to be rescued by Hawker. According to Baring-Gould, Robin also assaulted Bishop Phillpotts and tried to devour the episcopal apron. But this story bears the imprint of his (or Hawker's) inventive faculty. Hawker kept fewer pets as time went on, because 'we have suffered such grief and misery at their deaths'.

Animals in church were not unknown, nor were parsons with domestic pets – in the 1880s, for example, the rector of Hagworthingham tamed squirrels in his house. But Hawker's affinity for the brute creation, especially for birds, and his apparent ability to influence them, were unusual characteristics reminding one willy-nilly of St Francis of Assisi (though nobody, except perhaps A. L. Rowse, who described him as 'something of a Saint', would propose Hawker as a suitable case for canonization). Wild birds clustered round Hawker as he fed them crumbs in the mornings. He knew them by name, 'Jacky, Tommy, Robin', and they came when he called. A scarecrow, put up by one of Hawker's servants, was dressed in an old cassock and hat, had an effect quite opposite to what was intended. The birds fluttered round it hoping to be fed and, disappointed, wrought havoc with the vicar's peas and beans. Hawker encouraged rooks and jackdaws to congregate in the trees of his garden and the adjoining churchyard, and to build their nests in his chimney-tops. He claimed that they 'had come one night to build near his house just when he resolved the next day to endeavour to get some eggs in order to rear them'. Hawker had a knack with horses, seldom needing to guide them by touching the reins and thus being free to compose poetry as he rode. He invited rabbits to make their burrows close to his house. There are even stories of otters and seals coming to be fed by him, but these are unauthenticated. What is clear is that, lacking 'every human solace', Hawker found comfort and support in the company of dumb creatures. In 1858 he claimed that they meant even more to him than this: 'I do think if it were not for my birds and animals I should lose my mind.'

It is pleasant to visualize Hawker as his nephew did – 'I often picture you to myself calling to the jackdaws' – but obviously one must be cautious about crediting all the extravagant folk-tales that have accrued around him, especially on the subject of his association with animals. Apart from the errors and exaggerations that inevitably occurred in the repetition of such stories, Hawker himself was notoriously given to deception. The line he drew between fantasy and reality was blurred. For instance, he solemnly assured a rightly sceptical Sir Thomas Acland that the bees on his cliffs picked up pebbles for ballast in high winds, and dropped them at the entrance to their hive. Sometimes, of course, Hawker deliberately hoaxed visitors. He once said to a friend who called, 'Did you meet a waggonette full of people? I stuffed them up with all kinds of nonsense and they believed every word!' But it is not always clear when he was pulling wool over the eyes of the gullible. What is one to make of this report of Hawker by W. D. Macray, a visiting clergyman? 'He had seen spirits; one he gravely told me had once crossed his path just where we were walking, in the shape of a hare!' Macray's conclusion, from which it is difficult to dissent, was that Hawker 'got into a *habit* of nourishing eccentricities because they made him so noticeable, and

13 Pauline, née Kuczynski, Hawker's second wife, in about 1865

14, 15 Shipwrecks: though after Hawker's death, these suggest the
kind of scene with which he was forced to become familiar
(*above*) the *Capricorno*, sunk at Bude in 1900
(*below*) the *Crystal Springs*, wrecked just south of Bude in 1899

16, 17 Launching and (*below*) beaching the Bude lifeboat in 1900;
this display took place in calm weather, and shows the
difficulties involved in sending the lifeboat out under bad
conditions

18 Hawker in 1870, dressed as usual in a claret-coloured coat, a blue fisherman's jersey and sea-boots

they so developed ... in later life that he would have been quite out of place anywhere but in this remote Cornish home.'

In fact, even when the colourful stories about Hawker were true they were not always the expression of genuine idiosyncrasy. He undoubtedly cultivated some of his eccentricities in order to impress or dupe other people and to amuse himself. He was a consummate actor and possessed in modest degree two of the characteristics essential to those who aspire to thespian success – exhibitionism and narcissism. To make the vulgar tourists, those 'cads in lady's and gentleman's clothing', gawk, he loved to adopt the role of the hay-seed vicar, full of strange, vernacular wisdom. Or he would pose for more educated visitors as a minor prophet, explaining the secrets of his desert strand, and, as one clergyman put it (not without a touch of irony), 'pointing out symbolisms much too deep and dark for the uninitiated to perceive'. Or for his own parishioners he would play the part of witchdoctor-in-chief, having access to infinitely more powerful magic than was available to the cunningest of ancient men. Thus, for example, he read the exorcistic service in Latin over the farmers in the vestry, encouraged belief in 'Parson's Luck' in agricultural matters and sowed guano in one of his fields in the shape of a cross 'which stood out in verdant green, whilst the land around was comparatively barren'.

All this is not to suggest that Hawker was a complete charlatan. The masks were part of the man. Their increasingly important function was to protect his raw nerves from direct exposure to strangers, whose 'access' to his parish he grew 'to dread' over the years. Probably too, as his son-in-law claimed, Hawker was hardly able, later in life, 'to distinguish between jest and earnest, fact and fancy, belief and simulated belief'. Even so, it can hardly be denied that there was a distinct element of the mountebank in Hawker's character.

However, Hawker had less well-publicized fads and fancies which were intrinsic to his nature and had nothing to do with what is now known as 'projecting an image'. He abhorred beards.

He made a fetish of having very thick, woven paper ruled with faint red lines specially made for him (and, by his direction, for no one else) by the firm of De La Rue. On this he wrote with swan-quills (he hated steel-nibbed pens), using thick black ink, in what he obviously considered to be 'a leisurely exact hand'. Though it could be beautiful it was usually a monstrous scrawl, constantly slipping away from elegance. Hawker had a Johnsonian love of, and capacity for, tea. His idea of making a good cup was apparently to fill the pot with tea-leaves and then pour boiling water into the cracks. Even when suffering from his worst 'pecuniary terrors' Hawker insisted on spending money on tea. He told Mrs Watson, 'My sole luxury is tea. On great occasions the old souchong, 4/2 a lb., but for general use Pauline will only allow congou at 2/6, or now and then mixed. We have both from Twining [to whom he wrote personally] and certainly his congou is as good as other people's souchong.'

In fact, tea was not Hawker's 'sole luxury'. He also drank the 'best ground coffee'. He loved cream and, though he never lived off it exclusively (as Baring-Gould claimed), it is recorded that he was once discovered by a member of his household in the dairy at dead of night skimming off the beautiful thick cream from the previous day's milk with a spoon and devouring it as fast as he could. Hawker made a point of having the finest Latakia tobacco. Though he only took to smoking later in life it became a passion with him, as is indicated by the dramatic appeal he made to his friend Godwin, when he was running short. 'I must intreat you to send me by return of post another half pound of the same Latakia. Don't fail me.' Hawker smoked short-stemmed clay pipes with large bowls. He regarded tobacco as the 'weed of thought' and would often take a basket of ready-filled pipes out to the hut on his cliffs where he smoked and wrote. His desk at the vicarage was scarred with the burn-marks made by the hot bowls of his pipes which he set down while rapt in composition.

Hawker was the prey of other strange convictions and caprices, some of which dogged him with almost obsessional force. He seemed to believe, for example, that all false teeth were taken by dentists from the jaws of human corpses (some were, of course). Consequently he determined never to wear them after his own rotted away, which they had done completely by 1864. This in itself was a dreadful process, involving severe bouts of tooth-ache and trips to rural dentists who were little better than quacks. Their remedies for tooth-ache included the application of leeches and red-hot wires to the gums – before my own great-grandfather visited the Holsworthy dentist, who was also a farrier, he always drank, as the best available anodyne, half a bottle of brandy. But it was not fear of pain which inhibited Hawker from wearing false teeth. In spite of apprehensions that a 'toothless ministry' would be 'unintelligible' and that he would consequently have to resign from Morwenstow and face penury, Hawker could not endure human false teeth because he considered that they 'decayed sympathetically' with the bodies of their original hosts. What was worse, they betrayed the fact disgustingly. As he put it, 'a sickly and repulsive odour does proceed from the mouth of those who wear the teeth of dead men.' This idea was less odd than many others to which Hawker gave credence but it affords yet another indication of the peculiar quality of his mind. And it was this mind, permeated with queer beliefs and superstitions, much more than his superficial characteristics, that really fascinated the summer visitors. In increasing numbers they flocked to Morwenstow hoping to catch a glimpse of the vicar, whose reputation for eccentricity grew with the years. In 1864 Hawker wrote, 'Bude is in every sense a pest of us. The idlers come in droves. Their usual plea is to see the Church and I had from the servants their curiosity to see the Vicar.'

One thing those who came to Morwenstow were assured of was an unpredictable reception. Even Tennyson, who arrived in 1848, was greeted in the 'coldest manner' until the vicar was sure that it really was the poet whom he addressed – 'then all heartiness'. Often Hawker was not to be seen at all, as when eight people ('the very number who came out of the Ark', he remarked in a characteristically inconsequential parenthesis) made the cliff-top walk from Bude in July 1862. The vicar sent a servant to show them the church.

> Was Mr. H. at home? Yes, but he had company. Could a vehicle be borrowed to take them back again. No. Nobody had ever asked for one before. (This I thought a very happy answer). So at last they went on their way and we heard of them no more.

Hawker shared Charles Kingsley's snobbish disdain for the 'cockney excursionists and intrusive prigs' who came to north Cornwall. No doubt some visitors did merit his aloof unfriendliness. In 1863 Hawker reported furiously on the litter left near his hut by a group of trippers: 'Oh what a mess, lettuce leaves outside the door, on the path pieces of fat ham, the paper in which their lunch had been wrapped and a sediment which looked very much like what the woman had had for her dinner ... the day before.' Given the opportunity Hawker could meet forwardness with a devastating rebuff. When a visitor once asked him what his views and opinions were, he replied; 'There is Hennacliff, the highest cliff on this coast, on the right; the church on the left; the Atlantic Ocean in the middle. These are my views. My opinions I keep to myself.' Hawker was primarily concerned to guard his privacy against intrusion. 'It is worrying to be invaded by people you don't care about and to sacrifice that most precious thing, Time, to frivolous people and silly curiosity.' Yet, paradoxically, while he abhorred the psychological strains imposed on him by the violation of his solitude he *needed* new audiences and lamented their absence in winter – 'of all the summer birds that haunt us we incur in our wintry time not one'.

Very often Hawker was an ebullient host who dispensed open-handed hospitality, sometimes to large numbers of visitors at once. Like most Cornish parsons of his age he believed in setting a lavish table (over which was hung, incidentally, a sheaf of corn; this, Hawker said, was 'the harvest wave-offering, presented at the altar and waved before the Lord at the Harvest Festival' and then placed in its symbolic position 'through the following year'). One meal Hawker served guests in 1863 consisted of 'a haunch of Dartmoor mutton, the coin harricoted, three chicken and a tongue, junket and apple pie'. Nearly sixty years after the event, Margaret Martyn remembered how in 1870 Hawker had raced down the drive of Tonacombe Manor 'in a furious haste, in his little low phaeton he always drove, to ask my mother if she would possibly lend him a leg of mutton – some guests had suddenly arrived and he had nothing in the house'. One anonymous visitor records how Hawker galloped up behind him, inquired whether he was going to call at the vicarage and, on receiving a reply in the negative,

'You know the command', he loudly said, 'Be not forgetful to entertain strangers! I shall expect you there!' Slap went the spurs . . . I have the kindest remembrances of the hospitality of the dining room; the mutton was well hanged, the wine good, the fruit ripe and rich; but before the cheese was brought forth and cut my kind Entertainer said: 'Which hunk will you have Sir? This is Cheddar, this is American. My wife says it is good: I have never tasted it. I hate everything American.'

Visitors lucky enough to find Hawker in such expansive mood were guaranteed a conducted tour of his parish. It followed an almost ritual pattern – the vicarage, the church, the cliffs, the hut, the visitors' book, 'the little black mail he likes to levy'. As has been suggested, visitors were generally less struck by the features of interest pointed out than by the idiosyncrasies, whether voluntarily or involuntarily displayed, of the mind of their guide. One visitor's account may serve for many. A certain J. Hellia described a trip to Morwenstow which he made with his friends, the Aclands, in October 1853.

I reckon that day's excursion as one of the pleasantest I can remember. We didn't expect to see Hawker himself for he had been ill – quite out of his mind for some weeks – but to our surprise out he came to receive us, in full costume – brown cloth cassock with velvet cuffs, Greek hat, and long hair down his back. He took us into his church pointing out symbolisms ... and 'evermore' repeating legends of St. Morwenna and her brothers and sisters whose unpronounceable names I have forgotten. He told us calmly and soberly, that the Saint appeared to him in a vision this last July and gave him a text to preach upon the following Sunday and said he often had supernatural things happen to him. His Church is beautiful (chiefly from the way in which it is kept, for with the exception of a Norman arch or two its style is very poor perpendicular). We saw the sailors' graves with the figurehead [of the *Caledonia*] and oars tied in the shape of a cross fixed over them. Thence he acted as guide to the mighty cliffs close by... At Morwenstow there is a cliff of 454 [feet] perpendicular height from the level of the surf, the highest in England, for though others have greater height from the level of the water yet they slope more gradually down to its edge; and there you could drop a stone down at once. Up the sides of these heights he had clambered...still talking of legends from Adam downwards and evidently having as much faith in them as the soberest sense or most demonstrable facts ever written or told of. I suppose he is a born poet and his seclusion at Morwenstow helps to make his fancies realities to him.

This was a shrewd conclusion. Hawker did in fact make attempts to distinguish his own faith in the ubiquitous activities of supernatural forces from the superstitions of his Cornish parishioners, but not always successfully. To one visitor, for example, he talked about

the antiquarian lore of the neighbourhood. It was a subject to be reverently spoken of at that table, yet there was a tone in the Vicar's remarks as if he was desirous of being considered free from the superstitious beliefs of the ignorant. 'When I came here,' he said, 'I found much superstition among the common people, and I resolved to show how groundless were such idle fancies and I therefore determined to open a barrow and examine the relics of the dead. Of course it was said that the heavens would avenge such desecration: but I chose my day carefully when there was not a cloud in the sky, and cut a trench from South to North right in the centre of the mound where I found a stone grave with a cinerary urn, which I carried off in great triumph but on my way back the heavens grew black with clouds and storm, and before I reached home I was drenched to the skin.

Similarly Hawker wrote rather patronizingly of the conviction of his servant that the death of his sow's thirteen piglets in 1865 had occurred because 'they were overlooked i.e. bewitched. An ancient woman who lives near here is accused as the authoress of the misfortune. This notion is I believe universal in Cornwall among all classes of the agricultural people.' Yet he could also tell Mrs Watson that the cattle plague was 'manifestly a judgement inflicted by God for national sin,' that he had been 'assailed by the demons of the storm' who had blown off the roof of his barn, that 'half my poor people are kept alive and in health by herbs', that he had known warts to be 'charmed' away, that 'Stratton is under a doom since my poor father's death', and so on. And writing to his friend Godwin, he did in fact blame the 'Evil Eye' for the death of 'One of my Ewes'. Yet even to his own family Hawker felt it necessary to assert that he was immune to popular superstition. However, he did so in a comically revealing way when in 1864 he rebuked his niece Mary for sending him the superfluous gift of a pair of spectacles.

I told you that I had from Godwin a pair of Dollond's goggles, very good. Why did you think it necessary to get another pair? I will not affront you by sending them back but except old Sally Found the Witch, none of my acquaintances use spectacles, and if I give them to her it will be thought I do it from fear whereas I am not in the least afraid of her. So I must keep them to be carried off by someone when I am gone.

More will be said later on the subject of Hawker's superstitions and their mystic, poetic or perhaps even lunatic roots. The present point is that his beliefs in the all-pervasiveness of the supernatural were nourished, as they could have been nowhere else, in the fertile soil of far Cornwall, and that they were regarded by strangers from an increasingly urban and industrial England as expressions of the grossest eccentricity. To those of his contemporaries who lauded the achievements of technology and the virtues of self-help, Hawker's claim, constantly reiterated in one form or another, that 'my whole life has been a scene of miracles manifestly wrought by my unseen Master', was a perverse species of blasphemy. It spoke of a dark age when other-worldliness was synonymous with ignorance. Yet though the more extravagant of Hawker's beliefs, such as his conviction that he had seen mermaids in the bay below his hut, might be scorned as the figments of a disordered imagination, others, such as his opinion that each person had an active guardian angel, could not be dismissed out of hand. For notions of this kind were merely the logical conclusion of a faith to which nearly everyone (however optimistically committed to the doctrine of progress) paid lip-service. More than one visitor to Morwenstow explained Hawker's eccentricities in precisely these terms. For example, W. D. Macray wrote in 1862,

He was certainly a very remarkable man, of vivid poetical imagination but eccentric, as such a man often may be, to the verge of insanity. But many of his singularities arose I believe from his simple outspoken *faith*. He believed that God was continually present with his people and that this Presence was revealed in ordinary events of human life as we all profess to believe. But unlike most of us, Hawker was not ashamed openly and continually to acknowledge it, and to say of anything that happened unexpectedly or opportunely or strangely, that it was God's doing and that it was marvellous in his eyes.

For some, then, Hawker's eccentricities were less those of a demented crank than a holy fool. As such he actually exerted a positive influence over one or two of his brother clergy. From him the Rev. W. Haslam, vicar of Baldhu,

> learned many practical lessons. He was a man who prayed, and expected an answer; he had a wonderful perception for realizing unseen things, and took Scripture literally, with startling effect. He certainly was most eccentric in many of his ways; but there was a reality and straightforwardness about him which charmed me very much.

That so eccentric a figure as Hawker should have had any influence at all was only in part due to his being such a champion of faith in an epoch when unbelief was neither common nor respectable, (and when, incidentally, ghost-hunting, table-tapping and other forms of parapsychology were distinctly fashionable). In part, too, his impressiveness lay in the fact that he was a living embodiment of a peculiarly attractive alternative society, and that as such he was a challenge to his own age. He was an anachronism from the Middle Ages at a time when an intense nostalgia for a vanished medieval past was one of the central elements of the climate of ideas – as the Oxford Movement, the Gothic Revival, Young England, Pre-Raphaelitism, and the Guild of St George so clearly demonstrate. When so much of the wisdom of modern science seemed to express itself in the palpable foolishness of industrial squalor and crass materialism it was only natural that social critics should seek to resuscitate the spiritual values of an era of faith.

Thus Hawker's foolishness could be interpreted as wisdom by friends and admirers who saw in him reflections of a purer, simpler world. The Rev. W. West, for example, welcomed one of Hawker's missives in these terms: 'So in a happy hour comes a letter from Dreamland, and from him whom I always think of as our English Dante, born out of due time, some six hundred years behind "the progress of the age".' The popular novelist, Mortimer Collins, claimed that by his old-fashioned methods Hawker 'brought out original views of meaning which are lost to the disputatious theological pedants of the present day'. What, to the many, seemed the ravings of an eccentric seemed to the few the voice of one crying in the wilderness, or even the utterances of – in a phrase West actually applied to Hawker – 'a man of sorrows and acquainted with grief'. Understandably Hawker liked to see himself in the role of the inspired seer. And if his visions were scarcely very relevant (as in his view that pixies were 'the souls of unbaptized children') and were chiefly distinguished by the signs of his own inventiveness, there was an unmistakably vatic quality about Hawker's denunciations of the evils of the day. In 1862, for example, he chided Sir Thomas Acland for being

> absorbed in that great mart of the old pagan impulses of rivalry, envy, pride, jealousy, emulation, which is how the court of the Gentiles, ... London should be called. The Pelagian efforts are strong nowadays to accomplish vast results without God's grace, but they must always fail miserably.

Hawker wrote to F. G. Lee in similar vein: 'what is the Englishman or Scotchman of the nineteenth century but a dexterous Blacksmith to whom the Demons have surrendered their myths of Gas, Steam, and Electric force in requital for his strong hatred of God and his Church?' Such condemnations slid easily from the lips of a man who seldom mustered the will, the energy and the money to leave his own parish, though they were perhaps none the less apposite for that, and none the less telling on contemporaries.

Thus Hawker the eccentric, though by definition an anomaly, was not entirely out of tune with the spirit of the age. Indeed the whole tendency of one of the most famous works of that age,

John Stuart Mill's essay *On Liberty* (1859), was positively to encourage individual eccentricity. It was, Mill thought, a valuable counter to the deadening weight of mass conformity in an increasingly democratic society.

> Precisely because the tyranny of opinion is such as to make eccentricity a reproach, it is desirable, in order to break through that tyranny, that people should be eccentric. Eccentricity has always abounded when and where strength of character has abounded; and the amount of eccentricity in a society has generally been proportional to the amount of genius, mental vigour, and moral courage it contained.

Hawker would hardly have approved of Mill (and *vice versa*) but in these sentiments, especially as applied to his own case, he would have concurred. As he once wrote, 'There is a war to the knife between mediocrity and genius for all generations.' But though Hawker may have considered his eccentricities to be pure manifestations of 'genius' (and from the large number of suggestive snippets under that heading in his 'Thought Books' it seems that he did) his biographer must come to a more modest conclusion; and a less unequivocal one. For the complex aberrations of Hawker's character are not to be summed up in any glib formula. His eccentricities were in part the showy mannerisms of an accomplished *poseur*. In part they were fads which grew with time into manic obsessions. And in part (perhaps the largest part) they were the spontaneous overflow of a powerful imagination which had nothing to dwell on but the circumstances of its own isolation.

9

Neighbours

If Hawker's eccentricities were to some extent the product of
external stimuli, other factors besides shipwrecks contributed
to their development. These were, especially, farming and domestic problems, local disputes, financial worries, conflicts with
Dissenters and concern about his own and Charlotte's health. The
course of Hawker's life seldom ran smoothly and the years between
1843 and 1863 – the years of Hawker's middle age and his wife's
old age – were far from calm. Admittedly, to the superficial gaze
it appears that nothing much happened during these two decades
to disturb the regular round of the vicar's existence. But though
Hawker did not differ much from his ordinary clerical neighbours
outwardly, his response to his environment and his attempts to
make his mark on it were entirely extraordinary.

By great good fortune a number of original diaries written by
two clergymen who lived very near Hawker have been made
available to me for this book. They have never before been tapped
by historians or biographers of Hawker and their merit is that they
enable the vicar of Morwenstow to be viewed in his proper context – as one of a number of nineteenth-century parsons living in
north Cornwall. Only by measuring Hawker against similarly
placed contemporaries can one see him in true perspective and
estimate exactly wherein his uniqueness lay. The two clergymen
concerned are John Davis (1779–1857), who for the last fifty-three
years of his life was rector of Kilkhampton, a parish immediately
adjoining Morwenstow to the south, and Oliver Rouse, born in

1781, who was rector of Tetcott, just over the border in Devon, for thirty years until his death in 1846. Both men knew Hawker and there are occasional references to him in their diaries. Usually these are bare records of visits to or from Hawker for tea, supper or to take a service. But there are one or two more detailed entries. On 15 September 1840, for example, Rouse dropped in on Hawker, 'he being residing in his new House, a most beautiful romantic spot and house – I admire it much.' And on 9 August 1849 Davis makes a tantalizing allusion to Hawker's eccentric way of performing a baptism service at Morwenstow church – 'a curious scene took place there. Bobby, Bobby, thou art beside thyself!!!'

Generally Hawker's two neighbours seem to have been on polite calling terms with him. That they were not more intimate was probably due to the fact that they were both conventional men who looked askance at his various unorthodoxies, especially when these savoured of liberalism and Puseyism. Davis, who was an active political canvasser in the aristocratic Whig interest certainly fell out with Hawker's brother during the 1837 election. On 8 August he wrote, 'Claude Hawker and myself in collision at the Booths. He very impertinent and told me that I had asserted a falsehood, but the claptrap would not catch, and he got nothing by his impudence.' There was also some rivalry between the vicar of Morwenstow and the rector of Kilkhampton to assert their own brand of religious influence in the district. Davis probably resented the fact that Hawker, as rural dean, initiated the practice of holding ruridecanal synods in 1844 – a practice which, he successfully suggested to Phillpotts, should be repeated at diocesan level after 1850. Davis no doubt suspected that the vicar of Morwenstow would use the local meetings, the main function of which was to be a kind of clerical discussion group, to put forward his own brand of Anglo-Catholicism. In 1849 Davis referred disparagingly to Hawker's friend, the Rev. W. D. Anderson, as 'a pupil of the Morwenstow priest'. And Hawker wrote to Anderson in 1854 of a clergyman called Drake, 'you both have been in some degree my sons in the Church and are both right in the midst of a wrong generation. Poor Drake is one more of Davis's victims. Four curates utterly destroyed but for my rescue of two of them.'

The main interest of the Davis and Rouse diaries is that they afford a prosaically clear account of the daily round of two West Country parsons who may reasonably be regarded as typical. Both sets of diaries are straightforward records of events, embellished with few comments or lucubrations. In their lack of intellectual content they presumably give an accurate reflection of their writers, who in this respect afford a startling contrast to Hawker. His mind may have been excessively diffuse but it was incessantly active. All his spare time was spent mulling over theological books, Thomas Aquinas, Gretser or the Diatessaron, antiquarian tomes such as Hals's *History of Cornwall*, Leland's *Collectanea* and Whitaker's *Cathedral of Cornwall*. Or he wrote – poems, letters, occasional thoughts in his notebooks, 'fragments of his broken mind' as he called them with lofty humility, and 'legends which from the meagreness of the materials I almost entirely invented', whereas the sole intellectual activity of his neighbours seems to have been reading the newspapers or *Cruikshank's Almanack* in the evenings and playing cards with their ladies. Unlike Hawker they scarcely even made any references to their clerical calling, apart from formally recording their Sunday duties, Davis's weekly visit to the poor house and Rouse's frequent conclusion to the day, 'P & B' – Prayers and Bed.

The prime hobby of Davis and Rouse seems to have been eating and drinking. In this they were very different from the vicar of Morwenstow who, though a generous host, was personally quite abstemious, eating little meat in his later years and drinking no wine or spirits. He also habitually fasted, from a happy concatenation of religious and sanatory motives. In 1858 he told Mrs Watson,

For many long years I have eaten no flesh meat on Mondays, Wednesdays and Fridays throughout Lent. Our *Book of Common Prayer enjoins the fast.* Bishop Andrewes and Bishop Ken firmly kept and taught it and one phrase of our Lord's is to me a command ... I find also great personal benefit from the custom – clearness of mind. I fancy myself in better digestion all the year.

Elsewhere, Hawker wrote of fasting that 'the fatigue thereof made both body and soul serene.' Such an attitude was in every respect alien to that of his neighbours. Rouse ordered his alcohol by the cask. At the end of 1840, for example, he bought himself two gallons of natural brandy, two of gin and ten of port. He often drank deeply, mixing the grape and the grain indiscriminately, but he rarely admitted to over-indulgence; though, on 6 October 1840 he did record, 'drank a few glasses of wine too much'. Like Davis, Rouse was constantly dining on 'beautiful venison', 'a very fine goose', 'excellent lobster', 'a fowl and a pig's face', and both men enthused over meals of jugged hare, leg of mutton, rump of beef, pease soup and roast pork. Hawker detested this gormandizing and described one Kilkhampton curate as 'a brute' because his 'chief talk is about beef and beer'.

Of the other recreations of Hawker's neighbours shooting was by far the most important. Davis, especially, has interminable entries on the subject. Indeed he makes one early mention, in his 1826 diary, of 'shooting with R. Hawker in Stowe woods. Killed 2 cocks; lost 1'. This was a sport which Hawker soon gave up and he later deplored the fact that his clerical colleagues did not follow suit. 'It is indeed a pity when men like Clyde, Vicar of Bradworthy, the adjoining parish East of us, forget their profession so far as to hunt and shoot.' Hawker said that sport had led to Clyde's bankruptcy and continued, 'He is a marked man for evil – feels no remorse or shame.' Hawker was very free with puritanical jeremiads of this kind and to Mrs Watson especially (who seems to have been something of a strait-laced killjoy) he energetically denounced many of the seemingly innocent amusements of his neighbours. They occupied themselves with such entertainments as picnics, parties, balls, amateur dramatics, concerts, cricket matches, tea-drinking contests, games like Pope Joan, skittles, rummy, much 'chit-chat', many visits to shops, sales, fairs, exhibitions of wild animals and agricultural shows, and a good deal of 'sauntering about' the provincial towns of Devon and Cornwall. Hawker wrote to Mrs Watson, 'There is not to me a more pitiable sight than those scenes wherein your sex are wont to assemble for frivolous amusements or sinful and angry cards or idle words for every one of which our Judge declared we should give an account.' He deplored the fact that A. C. Thynne (rector of Kilkhampton 1859–1908) played cricket and performed at charity concerts, singing 'comic songs – the fox ran away with the parson's goose one!' He thought great exhibitions sinful as leading to competition, rivalry and envy and he told Mrs Watson, 'It may seem singular but I never was at a sale or a fair or at any one of such exhibitions in all my life.' He condemned the theatre (except Shakespeare) as 'frivolous and sinful' and he wrote indignantly in 1871 that he had been asked over to Welcombe to attend '*private* theatricals ... We of course declined instanter but that I should live to be invited is a climax in our history I never thought to witness.'

Such scowling censoriousness should be seen as an expression of Hawker's physical and psychological isolation as well as a product of his moral and religious convictions. He rejected society with one part of himself (a part which, as has been suggested, was in constant conflict with the companionable elements in his nature) not only because 'what is termed social ... I term selfish life', but also because he had become inured to loneliness. He instinctively tried to avoid any activity which brought him in contact with the outside world. Of course, he did not want to be distracted from his pastoral and poetic pursuits but as time passed he became conditioned to his seclusion. He wrote poignantly, 'I have read of prisoners shut up for long years and who, when the doors were at last unclosed, refused to leave the cell to which they had become habituated so long, and I can easily comprehend.'

The slightest threat to his solitary confinement upset him. In 1861, for example, he had to make a duty visit to Thynne and he told Mrs Watson, 'No one but yourself to whom I have confessed would imagine what a horror it is to me to emerge from my daily routine, even for so common a thing as a morning call.' When he remarked, as he did in 1852, 'a journey to Stratton is for me too great an undertaking', he was referring not just to bad roads, steep hills and the expense of taking his horses from the plough, but to the toll that the trip would take on his 'wretched nerves'. By 1867 he wrote, no doubt with some exaggeration, 'I have given up all visiting, go no-where, receive no one, but my safety is in quiet, secluded existence.' The attitudes of Hawker's neighbours were entirely antithetical to his. Their society was limited so they made the most of it. Calls and visits played a prominent part in their lives. So did journeys to Launceston, Bideford, Exeter, Taunton and Plymouth, where Rouse, especially, enjoyed 'toddling about the town', and acting as an escort to his mother-in-law and his wife, to whom he invariably referred by the attractive titles, 'the Dowager' and 'my Rib'. Morwenstow was, it is true, rather more geographically isolated than Kilkhampton or Tetcott, but the mobility and sociability of Hawker's neighbours indicates that his seclusion was to some extent self-imposed.

One preoccupation which Davis and Rouse did share with Hawker was their concern over the weather. Like George V, they both jotted down a meteorological summary every day and gave fuller details of anything out of the ordinary – as occurred for example, on 12 October 1836 when, Davis recorded, 'a complete gale, almost a hurricane of wind, came on which lasted till nearly the next morning – the depression of quicksilver in the barometer remarkably great, never but once greater during my recollection.' Of course the weather did not hold the peculiar terror for the incumbents of Kilkhampton and Tetcott that it did for the vicar of Morwenstow. They did not believe that storms were demoniacally inspired and they seem to have regarded shipwrecks with equanimity, giving brief, objective reports of them. They had no dark fears about the composition of flotsam or the propensities of wreckers, as is illustrated by Rouse's visit to Duckpool, on the southern boundary of Hawker's parish, in February 1840. He was, he wrote, hardly able to stand because of the 'tempestuous wind... sea grand beyond conception – 15 men there wrecking – and whilst we were there, a beam of the wreck by Bude washed in – to see the maneuvers [*sic*] of the men was entertaining.' Probably the main reason why Davis and Rouse were so watchful of the weather was that they were solicitous about their glebe farms (Rouse also owned land in Morwenstow).

In this worry Hawker resembled them. But glebe-farming was more vital to him than to his neighbours, and more of a trial, because of his dogged financial improvidence. As he remarked, 'I fully acknowledge the anxiety of farming but without the produce of my glebe I could not keep up my house nor carry on existence here.' Thus Hawker was driven into a vortex of agitation every harvest-time. On one occasion his crops were ruined twice in succession and he wrote despondently, 'Two years I have had to buy corn and the grief of this none but a farmer can understand.' Invariably he explained his success or failure in supernatural terms. When misfortune struck his farm he lamented, and blamed demons. In 1867 he wrote, 'In my whole life I never once suffered under such an accumulation of miseries and losses as assail me now. My sensation is that for some unknown cause the Demon is permitted to have power to try me to the uttermost. Yet I am not Job.' When he prospered he rejoiced and thanked God. 'I have remarked through life that of the two kinds of wealth, one, man's gold and coin, has been refused to me. The other, God's, the riches of the earth and air and water have been made over to me in kind and happy measure.'

In his concern for his farm and in his desire that it, together with his large vegetable garden, should make his remote parsonage virtually self-sufficient in food, Hawker differed only slightly from his neighbours. In his manner of running his 72-acre cliff-top glebe and the additional fields which he rented, he resembled them hardly at all. Whereas his neighbours used progressive methods and machinery which, he noticed critically, caused accidents and contributed to the depopulation of the district by causing unemployment, Hawker looked, in farming as in so much else, firmly to the past. He wrote in 1860, 'I do not farm as surrounding gentlemen and the clergy do. I have not one modern implement on my ground. I buy no scientific manure, my own plain dunghill must suffice ... I am the only person within twenty miles who threshes with the flail.' On the whole, Hawker's traditional methods paid dividends.

He did have certain advantages over his neighbours. What they gained in scientific expertise he made up for in native shrewdness. It is evidenced by the farming advice he gave to his friend Anderson.

> You are wrong about your poultry. You should have had Dorkings ... As a general rule hay is the most lucrative produce you can obtain from a grass field ... With regard to the calf, are you quite sure that the cow is her real mother? It is a very common practice here to put a newborn calf with an exhausted cow and to distend the udder by omitting to milk for a day or two.

What his neighbours had in wealth Hawker compensated for in the success of his mendicity. He wrote to Sir Thomas Acland with characteristic effrontery in 1864, 'You recognise the paper, the handwriting, and you already guess the Theme! "Some favour to be sought, some entreaty to be urged," say you, as you read – and you are right.' Hawker asked for, and apparently received, 'a young Exmoor Ram of your fine Holnicote Breed'. By means of such shameless expedients, by spending his wife's money on new buildings, and spurred on by an intense interest in agricultural matters – he liked nothing better than to dilate, for the benefit of the uninitiated, on different varieties of 'taties' – Hawker made his farm a prosperous one. As he wrote complacently in 1863, 'One thing is clear, nothing can exceed the success of my farm.' Like his neighbours Hawker had a patriarchial involvement in rural affairs. Unlike them he restricted himself to fewer secular pursuits – for motives which they could hardly have shared. Echoing the conclusion of *Candide*, Hawker wrote, 'The most innocent of pleasures is the care of the land.'

To a great extent Hawker resembled his clerical neighbours in his relations with his social inferiors, especially servants. He might properly have been described in the terms applied to the Rev. J. S. Avery, who served St Michael's, Bude, for most of the time Hawker was at Morwenstow, as 'an old-fashioned autocratic parson'. Though not, like Davis, a magistrate, Hawker was quite as ready to intervene, arbitrate and dictate in local matters – as the rector of Kilkhampton did, for example, on 15 June 1841: 'A prize fight at Collaton Hill between Wilbur Stone of Bideford and Jonathan Vanstone of Poughill – went and put a stop to it.' Hawker was even capable of acting with the kind of high-handedness displayed by Rouse in 1846 – 'paid off Jack Abbott, and he left my service, he refusing to learn the collect for yesterday.' Hawker kept his maids 'under discipline'. He considered that 'the English servant of the 19th century is tinged strongly with Americanism and would fain make every house a republic', and he made sure that his own remained unequivocally a patriarchate. Though he could be capriciously generous, parting with bottles of gin or brandy here and half-crowns or shillings there, Hawker kept his servants' wages low, rebuked them when they haggled for perks like free beer, and resented any erosion of the deference which he considered his due. He was an inveterate *laudator temporis acti*, often complaining bitterly, as he did in 1862,

The world of twenty years agone exists no longer. I have long seen it. The vices of our kitchen are a part of the great national crime – *Pride*, the first sin of our mother Eve and of Adam her husband, an unseemly pride, discontent with the station which God allotted and an insane attempt to *go up higher*. It is the cancer at the heart of England and instead of checking it, every law, every usage is actually adapted now to foster this low vile vanity, the alloy of every virtue, the fuel of every sin.

Hawker was less severe with his servants in practice than he was in theory. His behaviour towards one of his thirteen-year-old maids, as retailed in a letter to his niece in 1863, affords an instance of how the strictness of his paternalism was tempered by a rather intimidating kind of benevolence. It shows that, in spite of the contractual nature of his servants' employment, Hawker clung to the traditional idea that domestics were part of the family and that it was his duty as head of that family to give firm moral guidance. Indeed he claimed that he was, in the eyes of his maid, 'more a father to her than her own'.

Mary is one of the most docile and dutiful maids I ever saw. She was naturally desirous of a beau, seeing Jane's boy here, so yesterday week, I found William Olde, Jane's brother (about 16), sitting behind the door and although I asked him twice what he wanted, he stuck on. I scolded. Next day ... You may conceive my storm. 'A Ploughboy! ... Half idiot father unable to maintain himself or children, married a second time to a disreputable bitch etc. etc.' Result: 'I forbid you to think of such a thing. If you do a Merry Christmas and Happy New Year', and the fate I meditate for him, it is improper to relate. She cried and promised solemnly that he should not come here again. I like her very much. Quite idiotic but desirous to do her best.

In his aversion to 'followers', Hawker was a typical member of his age and class. However, he seems to have been judicious in not banning them altogether. In 1868 the Rev. A. J. Plow of Todmorden was murdered by a furious parishioner whom he had forbidden to court his sixteen-year-old serving maid, and, to Hawker's disgust, the Cornish sympathized with the murderer. Hawker had an obsessive dread that his house would be 'disgraced' by an illegitimate birth and he complained latterly that 'so immodest and evil are [women-servants] that our only chance for safety is to hire only those who are too old or, as I have now, too young to be mothers.' Hawker's precautions were successful for he recorded that, 'Our servants are ignorant and rough, entire country bred, but I believe them thoroughly honest and those sins so common in the houses of our acquaintance have not harassed us.'

Hawker's letters are full of dire tales of the harassments of neighbouring clergy. In 1859, for example, an unmarried servant at Poughill rectory gave birth to a child, whom she then murdered. Carnsew, the rector, grumbled to Hawker that 'the hussey ... must have taken service here with the intention of making our house a lying-in hospital.' Hawker reported the outcome: 'Police, custody, inquest. She imprisoned, verdict concealment.' In 1862 the distemper spread to Kilkhampton rectory. Hawker wrote,

> We have realized a mournful winter of indoor gloom and if we look, like Noah from the door of the Ark, we witness nothing but misery and judgement. The latest blotch is the birth of a Mormon child at Penstowe. The sire (one Arscott Harris [the coachman]) is dismissed and the dame not having been confined a week is supposed by lenient critics not to be enceinte again.

But, though he was disingenuous about the fact to Mrs Watson, there had been at least one occasion when Hawker was similarly embarrassed. In 1856 he told Anderson that his farm manager, John,

> has now carried his pranks so far that I have given him notice to quit and so he shall whatsoever the cost. Last Wednesday night the Martyns at Tidnacombe [i.e. Tonacombe Manor] discovered, on getting up to pacify the child who cried, that their maid-servant had not been in bed for the night, and on further search she was found to have passed it in an outhouse

with John. This being the third maid of theirs that he had corrupted – how far no one knows ...

There is no doubt that Hawker was more preoccupied than his neighbours with sexual immorality. They took it in their stride. Thynne soon reinstated his coachman, Arscott Harris, much to Hawker's disgust. Carnsew seemed less concerned with the sin of his maid-servant than with the inconvenience it caused him. Rouse mentioned that he passed through 'Whore's Alley' in Taunton, but his disapproval appears to have been more aesthetic than moral – 'both right hand and left inhabited by Nymphs of the place, having faces like brass and tongues like cymbals.' Hawker never came to terms with the fact that, as one contemporary commentator put it, 'sexual intercourse was almost universal prior to marriage in the agricultural district.' For it is generally true to say that just as the urban proletariat have never been religious, so the rural poor have never been chaste. (It would be interesting to know how long the common north Cornish joke has been extant – that the only virgin in Morwenstow is the figurehead of the *Caledonia* in the churchyard.) Anyway the situation was as clear to Hawker as it was to all but the most blinkered observers, though this did not prevent Victorians from giving vent to horror at the fact that farm workers 'seem hardly to comprehend or value [chastity] as a virtue'. Hawker's expressions of shock were not simply those of moral outrage, or offended delicacy, though what he took to be the violation of female purity did disturb him, for he not only respected women in a conventional way, he actually liked them. Nor, as far as one can tell, did Hawker denounce promiscuity with such fervour because, like so many members of the frightened, frustrated bourgeoisie, he was a victim of sexual envy. The motives behind his frequent comminations were signal.

It has already been seen that Hawker blamed unchastity on 'that father of English fornication', John Wesley. What is clear from his unpublished writings is that Hawker considered that there was a direct relationship, indeed, a correspondence, between Methodism and sexual feeling. It was not just that he thought that Methodists were pre-eminently lascivious – though he did. His letters are studded with assertions like 'In Cornwall and in Wales, the thick places of Methodism, not one woman in 500 (and I speak from statistics verified from official authority) ever marries without disgrace ... It is so general as to be no longer a reproach among themselves.' Or such announcements as 'On Saturday I marry Eliza Close, class-leader, pregnant and near child-birth, to Daniel Venning, class-leader and fornicator.' Nor was it simply that there was a strong association in Hawker's mind between servants, Methodists and sexual licence, as is illustrated in these three sentences which are linked by a logic apparent to no one but him:

> In former times Methodist preachers expelled from their society any person of evil life. But they have long given up that discipline; one half or more of the depraved females are of that sect. But if I were asked what was the great grievance and sorrow of England I should answer at once, the servants.

No, Hawker's most visceral conviction about Methodism was that it was a nearly overt expression of sexual feeling and in particular the central, dramatic Evangelical experience – the conversion – was akin to an orgasm.

Hawker often described Methodism as a 'Spasm of the ganglions' and he declared that its central fallacy was the belief that conversion, a spiritual transformation, could be physically experienced. 'It is untruth that our forgiveness is made known to us sensuously – *i.e.*, by a touch, or stroke, upon the ganglions.' Hawker, no physiologist, defined ganglions as 'the fibres of the diaphragm', 'a nervous centre [where] ... Soul and Body as it were meet'. But there is a resonance about the word which, when juxtaposed with Hawker's many explicit remarks, such as his accusation that Methodism was 'the mother of the brothel ... of modern England', suggests that in certain contexts he was actually thinking of the genitals. The following vituperative lines, addressed to the Methodist convert, are full of unmistakable sexual imagery.

Deem as thou wilt,
That filthy heart of thine is not the Vale
Of Armageddon: nor may thy ganglions
Thrill with the doom which He, the Son of Man,
Holds for the rapture of that utterance
Reserved, and for his own reward requited.
Lo! When thy carcase of foul flesh shall writhe
Fierce with its renal heat and wild with spasm
It is not He, the Paraclete, whose course [illegible]
Is like dove's and whose unconscious touch
Falls as the Dew's upon the fleece of wool,
Pure, soft and soundless.

It is difficult to avoid the conclusion that Hawker believed Methodist conversions, particularly when accompanied by ejaculations and ecstatic convulsions, by the quakings, shakings and holy rollings so often mentioned by Wesley and his followers, to be a form of sexual release. The psychology of conversion is a large and complex subject and it is not to be pretended that Hawker plumbed its depths with this single insight. Nevertheless it was an insight, a modern one, reminiscent of E. P. Thompson's celebrated account of Methodism as 'a ritualised form of psychic masturbation', and Hawker deserves credit for it. Of course, William James's warning that 'few conceptions are less instructive than this re-interpretation of religion as perverted sexuality' should also be heeded. But it is clear, according to an authoritative student of the psychology of the Methodist revival, that in some cases conversion did involve the sudden resolution of the unconscious conflicts which had been caused by repression of the sex instinct. What Freud called the sublimation of these potentially disruptive urges, their idealization in religious form, led to an abrupt release of tension and corresponding emotional satisfaction.

The sect of Methodism which was most vigorous in north Cornwall was that founded by William O'Bryan in 1815, known as the Bible Christians or Bryanites. Hawker was certainly right in thinking that Bryanite worship was characterized by a great deal of 'wildness and excitability'. Typically, he exaggerated this in his account of the way in which the Bible Christians 'hunted the Devil out' at their meetings.

> The preacher having worked the people up into a great state of excitement, they are provided with sticks, and the lights are extinguished. A general *mêlée* ensues. Every one who hits thinks he is dealing the Devil his death-blow; and every one who receives a blow believes it is a butt from the Devil's horns.

This travesty was rebutted in the *Bible Christian Magazine* under the heading 'Clerical Slander'. Nevertheless, historians of Methodism admit that there were frequent 'corybantic sessions' in Bryanite worship and that men and women often 'behaved as if under demoniacal possession. Relief was obtained as they yielded themselves to the claims of Christ.' Among Methodists generally Hawker claimed that there were no less than four deaths at local meeting-houses in the decade after 1850, which he attributed to the fact that congregations were 'worked up to a pitch of excitement, almost frenzy'. Whatever the truth of this it was certainly usual for large meetings to be so drowned by 'cries for mercy' that nothing else could receive attention. Such hysteria was all grist to Hawker's mill and he was not inhibited from grinding out malediction by the fact that the Bible Christians were distinguished by characteristics which he might have been expected to find sympathetic. These were especially other-worldliness and political quietism.

Oddly enough, O'Bryan resembled Hawker personally in many ways, most strikingly in his intense awareness of the ubiquity of the supernatural world. O'Bryan sensed the presence of Satan following him 'like a great bear on his hind legs'. Like Hawker, he 'believed himself the subject of particular providences in the smallest things, and was vividly conscious of the opposition of the powers of evil'. Partly as a consequence of this, partly because superstition was integral to the life of the Celtic west, 'Bible Christians were greatly affected by dreams, mysterious voices, signs and tokens.' Perhaps Hawker saw all this as a sacrilegious parody of his own spirituality. At any rate his hostility to the Bryanites was not diminished by it or its corollary, the tacit support which they gave to the existing order. The eyes of the Bible Christians were fixed on heavenly rewards, not on the earthly ameliorations promised by radicals or Chartists. The latter were a particular bugbear in the West Country, probably because they were such an unknown threat. On 29 January 1840, for example, Oliver Rouse recorded in his diary, 'Dowager frightened about the Chartists'. But although in general the Bible Christians did not agitate for political or social change, Hawker regarded their very presence as a grievous affront. In the 1830s, according to two distinguished modern historians, 'A nonconformist congregation in a village is a clear indication of some group which wishes to assert its independence of squire and parson.' For Hawker the particular horror of the Bryanites was that they constituted a force which was subversive alike to conventional morality, to orthodox religion and to traditional society. In short, 'A Sectarian is a Mutineer.'

It is not surprising, in view of all this, that Hawker felt a more violent antipathy to Dissenters than did neighbouring clergymen. Admittedly he never allowed his dislike to interfere with his charitable endeavours, as some did. '"Starve you we will," said a clerical guardian to [a certain] Widow Lock, "unless you forsake these meetings."' Moreover, Hawker remained on good enough terms with his churchwarden, W. G. Harris, who was a prominent Dissenting preacher and a large farmer, to be offered and to accept help from him with the harvest although, Hawker added, 'I never spare heresy or schism ministerially.' But generally Hawker did not consort with those of his parishioners who were

Methodists. Rouse and Davis did. The latter certainly had a low enough opinion of the Bible Christians. In 1821 he reported to the bishop of Exeter that there were about fifty of them in Kilkhampton, that these 'are very fanatical and they consist almost without exception of the lowest Classes of Society'. It was evidently the social inferiority of the Bryanites as much as their zealotry which alienated Davis, for his diaries are full of references to agreeable fraternization with wealthy local Dissenters, as are Rouse's.

By contrast, Hawker indulged in a series of rows and feuds. The simple visit of a Nonconformist minister could evoke a furious response. 'He the schismatic leader of a conventicle in Barnstaple. What an audacious intrusion. I must put an end to this.' For Dissenters who dwelt permanently in his parish Hawker cherished a more lasting rancour, especially when they managed to thwart him over church rates. Among the many who roused his ire was a prosperous Methodist farmer, John Brimacombe of Marsland, with whom Davis and Rouse were on good terms. Brimacombe was a Morwenstow churchwarden in 1854 and Hawker described him as 'the most bitter, the vilest' of his opponents. Hawker particularly resented the fact that an earlier vicar of Morwenstow had rescued the Brimacombe family 'from poverty and perdition' and yet they had soon after succumbed to the 'emissaries of . . . John Wesley' who

crept into Marsland. He and his became victims and the heresy rampant. Moody madness has raged ever since within his walls. Wife and daughter insane from the failure of that spasm in the ganglions which the Methodist calls the witness of the Spirit, or assurance of the sensual perception of the forgiveness of sin, the badge and shibboleth of the Wesleyan all over the world and here in Cornwall the solitary doctrine of this vile sect. But more than all the parish does not contain a more venomous adversary of the Church than this John Brimacombe, the clergyman's almsman of former time. He is one of the Churchwardens chosen by his brother Dissenters and is red hot with vengeance towards that Church.

No doubt this bitterness was partly caused by the fact that Hawker could not hold forth as he wished directly for he owed his parishioner money. 'I dare not rebuke Brimacombe, the sinful warden, as I should if I were not in fear of him.' His indebtedness quite frequently prevented Hawker from speaking out against his enemies. But when unconstrained by such considerations he used every weapon in his rhetorical arsenal to attack Dissent publicly. Often he resorted to humour, once preaching a sermon about a Nonconformist missioner with the text, 'Abide ye here with the ass, while I and the lad go yonder and worship.' He wrote verses.

> I've no respect for Calvin's Face,
> Nor Whitfield's locks of gray,
> John Wesley's Picture hath no Place
> Where I kneel down to pray!

> There is no 'Blessed' Man, nor 'Sweet',
> No popular Divine,
> Whose graven Image others greet,
> Can bend these limbs of mine!

But Hawker's main stand-by was straightforward denunciation. He *'horse-whipped the Dissenters out of the Temple'*, as he claimed Christ had done.

Religious prejudice was hardly a rare phenomenon in Hawker's day, though it was most often directed towards Popery. Many examples spring to mind – the young Browning sitting at the feet of a preacher who earnestly assured his congregation that 'Roman Catholic and midnight assassin are synonymous terms'; Ruskin's early supposition that the malaria in the Campagna was 'the consequence of the Papacy'; Edmund Gosse's mother, whose conviction that Rome was doomed in 1857 '"irradiated her dying hours with an assurance that was like the light of the Morning Star, the harbinger of the rising sun"'. Still, the hatred that

Hawker felt for Dissenters was different both in degree and in kind from the religious intolerance of his contemporaries. The malignity of his language did not simply reflect his belief in the corrupt nature and corrupting effects of Methodism. There can be no doubt that it was to some extent pathologically inspired.

The state of Hawker's mental health and the effects of opium on his nervous system will be discussed in the following chapters. This one may be concluded by remarking that even in the common matter of physical illness and its concomitants Hawker differed from his neighbours. Of course, he was subjected to the same barbarous medical treatment. Had he been woken, as Davis was on 27 February 1837, by an attack of asthma, he would doubtless have been 'bled in both arms till I fainted after losing nearly a quart of blood'. Davis suffered from no unpleasant after-effects – indeed he found 'instant relief in the head – breathing somewhat relieved' – and it seems that his maladies were accompanied by no psychological disorders. Hawker's were. He often blamed physical debilitation on mental stress and *vice versa*. 'The truth is that all my life the least worry has immediately acted on my system. A painful event or a harassing letter at once produces a gnawing pain under the diaphragm, the region of the stomach, and visceral action ensues.' Physiological ailments, such as the ulcerated sore throats and sciatica to which he was prone, brought on nervous attacks. Body and mind were afflicted together during his many bouts of 'neuralgic diarrhoea', especially when they occurred during church services and Hawker had to make an undignified dash for the vicarage. In his response to ill-health, as to so many of the external circumstances of his existence in Morwenstow, Hawker was a world away from the matter-of-fact attitudes and humdrum lives of his clerical neighbours. His psychological isolation and physical remoteness reinforced one another.

10

Paranoia

If Hawker's life has been illustrated by measuring him against
contemporary neighbours, his character may perhaps be
further illuminated by comparing him with a literary figure who
shared many of his psychological peculiarities – Frederick Rolfe,
otherwise known as Baron Corvo. Hawker cannot, of course, be
explained. The claims of 'psychohistorians', biographers like Leon
Edel and Erik Erikson, to have plumbed the depths of their
subjects' minds by means of Freudian techniques are, by the very
fact of their retrospective character, not susceptible to proof. They
are doomed to remain speculations. The kind of analysis (especially when conducted by an amateur) which reduces some intricate
psyche to an Oedipus complex or an identity crisis carries with it a
built-in guarantee of implausibility. This is not to say that all
psychological insights should be eschewed by the (to use Joyce's
attractive word) 'biografiend'. It is merely to suggest that the
emphasis should be placed on concrete description rather than
abstract hypothesis – as will occur in this dissection of Hawker's
paranoid personality.

Compare this,

I have been provoked, abused, calumniated, traduced,
assailed with insinuation, innuendo, misrepresentation, lies
... my life has been held up to ridicule, and to most
inferior contempt ... the most preposterous stories to my
detriment have been invented, hawked about, believed.

175

with this:

Our history may be soon told. Each day brings on some fresh insult from some wretched brute of a parishioner in the shape of an insolent letter or some fierce bad lie, refuted as soon as told, and some attempt to injure us in the Church or out of it ... I cannot tell you in one letter a week's malignity and every week is the same.

The second quotation is of course from Hawker's pen and is part of a letter addressed to his clerical friend W. D. Anderson. The first comes from Fr. Rolfe's semi-autobiographical fantasy, *Hadrian the Seventh*. Both passages betray unmistakable signs of paranoia. The causes of this derangement are obscure and it is not even known whether the wide 'variety of paranoid syndromes ... are forms of human existence or diseases'. The definition of paranoia is confused by the fact that most people exhibit paranoid traits of one kind or another in the course of their lives. However, the truly paranoid personality is characterized by long-lasting delusions of persecution and/or grandeur. These are not generally accompanied by hallucinations but are systematized logically and result in behaviour in which suspicion, hostility, irascibility and seclusiveness figure largely. But a generalized account of the nature of paranoia is less helpful to an understanding of Hawker than a specific comparison. Rousseau apart (and excluding what one might call the partially paranoid, such as Landor, Haydon and Rossetti), Fr. Rolfe (1860–1913) is perhaps the best-documented example of a gifted literary man who suffered from paranoia; he provides a yardstick by which to estimate the nature and degree of Hawker's own disorder.

The curious resemblances between Rolfe and Hawker make the comparison more interesting. Both were writers with (in words which Pamela Hansford Johnson applied to Rolfe) 'no talent but a little genius'. Both created quasi-historical romances. Both were medievalists who believed that the world was out of joint. Both were unrepentant sciolists. Both became Roman Catholics and were especially drawn to the picturesque side of the Church. Both were intensely superstitious, went in for elaborate self-adornment, practised exquisite calligraphy, coined neologisms, enjoyed shrouding themselves in mystery, were improvident about money, relished large quantities of cream, had a passion for Latakia tobacco and claimed to understand the language of cats. Both men showed themselves capable of great goodness and great malignity. Rolfe often compared himself to a crab, sometimes of the hermit variety – behind his nipping claws and beneath his hard shell he was 'soft as butter, and just one labyrinthine mass of the most sensitive of nerves'. It is a good description of the eremitical Hawker who, under his formidable exterior, was, as he often said, 'a mass of thrilling nerves and fibres'.

The two men differed in certain respects, of course. Rolfe was a homosexual, never held down a regular job and alienated nearly every friend he had. Hawker often seemed to forget his successive spouses in the frequent lamentations over his loneliness but there is no doubting his devotion to them, nor theirs to him. Though, unlike Rolfe, he took opium, he worked hard and successfully in his parish and managed to retain most of his friends. But it is symptomatic of their common disorder that just as Rolfe denounced 'all of you professing and non-practising friends of mine', Hawker referred to 'one of those people called by the courtesy of England "friends". But there are few to whom I through life have applied that sacred name.'

It was in his persecution mania and the consequent rancour that Hawker resembled Rolfe most closely. The former wrote, 'What I go through does surpass human conception – to be baited as I am by the base and the vile transcends the endurance of man.' The latter echoed both sentiments and language: 'The sneers and insults I endure are indescribable.' The paranoiac often has some initial germ of real grievance which gradually infects his whole mind and expresses itself in truculence and vituperation. Rolfe's wrong was his unjustified (so he claimed) exclusion from the Roman Catholic priesthood. Hawker's spleen probably had more diffuse causes – the prevalence of Dissent in Morwenstow plus all the evils, examined in the previous chapter, which he associated with it, and the lack of what he regarded as due recognition and reward for his pastoral and literary work. Certainly the Methodists provoked his shrillest cries of martyrdom, producing, for example, this McGonagallesque rhyme and the subsequent malevolence.

> The hunters are upon me with their cry,
> And the dogs harass me with frequent fang.
> This is not to be borne so I must die
> And rush away to God with one strong pang ...

Never man's degrading griefs were like mine. A part of my return for their conduct is Anathema at the Altar. I uttered it. It works. Brimacombe's wife is raving mad. Bethuel Adams in Australia shot himself and died lockjawed in the self-same hour his brother and his father were blaspheming the Church and me here in England.

Just as Rolfe fantasized about becoming Pope, Hawker imagined himself precipitating divine vengeance on his enemies. He was always on the look-out for signs that his comminations were having practical results.

I said to Patteson – 'I am now 50 years old. I have undergone a great deal of anguish and loss. But I have always seen that howsoever my enemies may triumph over me for a time God always [fulfils] the prophecy, "When thine enemies perish thou shalt see it". God has a thousand times rewarded those who dealt kindly with me and requited those who have wronged me,' said I. I feel sure I shall see this man smitten and cut down for his guilt towards poor Mrs Hawker and me. But I did not think it would have been so soon. The crimes committed by that wretched man are more than twenty gaols can atone for.

Hawker invariably interpreted the deaths and illnesses of local Wesleyans as the product of his urgent imprecations to, and intimate relationship with, the jealous, vengeful God of the Old Testament. But the vindictiveness of some of his expressions (which closely parallel many of Rolfe's) obviously owes more to a pathological than a religious incentive.

> Bartlett's daughter is dead. I buried her last week. Church full of venom. Bartlett himself is said to be ill but reptiles are tenacious of life. Still I have no fear but that I shall be able to 'handle serpents', and I hope to shake him off. Sherman's disease was a great blessing.

Hawker in middle age increasingly came to feel that every man's hand was against him. Like Rolfe he elevated the slightest incident into an elaborate plot to do him down. Both men, for example, imagined that their friends were deliberately stealing their books. Rolfe, dramatizing himself in the role of a 'friendless, stripped, penniless' Prospero, attributed to 'Caliban' (his literary collaborator H. Pirie-Gordon) the words, 'Remember, first to possess his books, for (without them) He's but a sot, as I am.' Hawker wrote in 1858,

> I am despoiled by others of *every* University book. Adams, the farmer's son of Morwenstow whom I educated and brought into the Church and whose bite has been to me like a serpent's tooth, he began the deprivation and my nephew R. Kingdon completed the rest . . . When I look back and recall my departed years one clear destiny runs through them. I have been everybody's victim ... a sufferer for others' good.

In his ineradicable conviction that he was the whipping-boy of the world, that his friends were in league against him, Hawker, like Rolfe, conjured insults out of the air. Witness his suspicious quizzing of Anderson in 1854.

Will you tell me candidly what passed involving my name
or poor Nectan's [Hawker's tame colt, which ate from his
hand and 'calls me "Daddie"'] in conversation at your house
when you had the Reynoldses there. That something occurred harmless enough in itself but still sufficient to supply
that venemous little miscreant James Reynolds with means of
slander I am quite sure. A friend of ours, between us and you,
has a nasty habit of sneering at his betters under the semblance
of jest but with the reality of envious ill-nature. So he too
may have helped to work the poison. It does seem hard that I
cannot even rear a pet without exciting deep malignity. The
cause of this inquiry is a letter which has reached me from the
neighbourhood of James the dwarf which betrays his slaver
in every line ... I never cross the boundary of my parish to
meddle with anyone. I try to do everyone as much good as I
can. I gave that scamp his first idea. And what follows. Hardly
a day without some foul abuse.

To Hawker's unbalanced mind it was apparent that even his
farm-manager John, whom he dismissed for sexual promiscuity in
1856, had become involved in the diabolical freemasonry of his
persecutors. 'What I have endured from one sole cause. Insults
enow to have beaten a man's brain ... Often I have said that with
such a man as John strutting about my fields every Angel must
glide away disgusted. Nor could God's blessing descend. When he
went away my evil luck went too.'
   Hawker the writer was particularly the victim of a hostile conspiracy. His work was systematically plagiarized and others
'assumed the putative paternity of my literary offspring, without
leave'. What was more galling, they profited, whereas his best
endeavours reaped a poor financial reward. He wrote to Godwin
in 1862, 'Failure again. So be it. I acquiesce in my conscious doom.
And a very singular one. Of all that I have written I hardly saw an
adverse criticism. All that I ever printed sold immediately until

question arose of probable profit to me. And then descended instant doom.' Hawker suffered from what Rolfe, describing his own symptoms, called 'acute barabbitis' – the reference is to the old joke that 'Barabbas was a publisher'. Hawker complained that he was regularly cheated of the fruits of his labours and that 'friends I have none but instead of them Booksellers'. Admittedly this is a paranoid fancy to which all authors are more or less prone. One remembers the approving laughter which greeted Thomas Campbell's justification of his initially unpopular toast to Bonaparte at a literary dinner during the Napoleonic war.

'Gentlemen,' he said, 'You must not mistake me. I admit that the French Emperor is a tyrant. I admit that he is a monster. I admit that he is the sworn foe of our own nation, and, if you will, of the whole human race. But, gentlemen, we must be just to our great enemy. We must not forget that he once shot a bookseller.'

The vitriolic indictments hurled at their publishers and editors by Hawker and Rolfe had little in common with this ghoulishly good-humoured joke. Hawker wrote, for example, 'It is mortifying to be compelled to submit to the caprice and vulgar taste of an uneducated captious prig like Wills the Editor [of *All the Year Round*]. I ought to have known that if he did not habitually admit the low and mean and reject the great and good his periodical would not be what it is.' Both Hawker and Rolfe were intensely desirous of what the latter called '*commercial success*' as writers. Hawker claimed, 'my single solitary motive in this search for a publisher is a strong undissembled desire for coin – that and no other.' Like Rolfe, Hawker avidly sought to advertise his books, and he even realized that bad publicity was good publicity. He wrote to a West Country bookseller about *Cornish Ballads* in 1869,

I am personally unknown to all the public people in the county and from my very secluded life my very existence is to most Cornishmen an unknown fact. If by your own advertisements you have established a connexion with any serial or newspaper would you have the kindness to give my sorry book notoriety. I don't care what is said about the book. It may be abused with advantage to me.

Unpaid and unacclaimed, yet conscious of outstanding literary gifts, Hawker and Rolfe sought, found and denounced the proliferating intrigues which they believed to be at the root of their troubles.

Embattled, they lashed out in all directions. Hawker quarrelled with nearly everyone in his family apart from his wives. He blamed his brother, Claud, for not subsidizing him financially, and continued bitterly, 'I regret that your sympathy with me is not extensive enough to enable you to receive "such dreadful letters" without repulsion . . . Still I have always said that the craftiest thing and the most selfish thing that the family could have done would have been to keep me on my legs. On the same principle feed a bullock on barley meal.' His brother's wife was not immune from attack, perhaps with some justification. 'Of all the hard, covetous, treacherous and selfish women that I ever knew Claud's wife is the most transcendent. She turned out of the house as soon as her father was dead all the old faithful servants.' Hawker told Mrs Watson that the faces of his 'two selfish sisters', Caroline Dinham and Jane Kingdon, were 'images to recall past unkindness or to suggest stony neglect'. He particularly disliked Jane's husband, describing him as 'a very coarse and hard man ... But he is a Kingdon and I know not a word so expressive of what I call brutishness of mind. There are I believe, seventy persons of that name now in this neighbourhood and not one of them fit to associate with a Christian man's swine.' When his Dinham brother-in-law died in 1858 Hawker wrote to Anderson,

As usual in these family catastrophes I am a marked sufferer and as usual it is unacknowledged, unnoted and unknown. 'O if it's only Robert never mind.' I had lent my name continually to bills of accommodation for D. to get money on at the banks and two of these acceptances are now coming due for me to pay, one for £20, the other for £17.10.0. With regard to what has been done for the widow and children I assent as I *am bound to do* to every arrangement ... Those who conduct these affairs well know that they may *command* from me my attestation of goodwill on all occasions and at all times.

To give Hawker his due, this was not an entirely idle boast. He did occasionally bail out members of his family when they got into financial difficulties. Like Rolfe he was capable of spontaneous acts of great generosity and altruism. In 1830 he sent his brother Stephen 'at my own expense fitted out as a medical assistant to the Swan River and it crippled me for some years to do it. But he soon spent all and became a wanderer.' In 1839 Hawker helped his brother Tom emigrate to Australia. Tom was 'a superior man', a doctor in Stratton who went bankrupt, perhaps because of his preference, approved of by his eldest brother, for prescribing 'nine times out of ten for all internal inflammatory complaints infusion of elder blossom instead of medicines'. Hawker wrote an extremely overbearing letter to one of Tom's creditors inquiring why he was insisting on immediate payment instead of concurring in a plan for 'a complete though gradual adjustment of every claim. I regard my responsibility as identified with his [i.e. Tom's] and any rejection of the proposal as much a distrust of my responsibility as of his own.'

No less than his relations, Hawker's friends were abused on the slightest pretext, or on none at all. That so many of them remained loyal to him is a tribute not only to the charm of his personality, a characteristic he shared with Rolfe, but also to the dissimulation which caused him to revile them more often behind their backs than to their faces. In this he did not resemble Rolfe, whose insulting letters were frequently sandwiched between salutations like 'Quite cretinous creature', and valedictions such as

'Bitterest execrations'. Hawker's most aggressive (extant) letter to a friend was addressed to Anderson and is tame by comparison. Containing no greeting or signature it reads starkly,

> You neither come nor write nor send. Yet from the day when you came into the country as strangers no one has taken more sincere interest in your welfare, no one been more glad to see you at their house than the Vicar of Morwenstow and his wife. When they are gone and you arrive to visit their successors in this place remember this.

Hawker also crossed swords openly with his oldest college friend, Arthur Kelly of Kelly in Devon. Kelly refused him a loan of £100 with 'such bitterness' that Hawker severed all communication with him for ten years. When they met again in 1862 Hawker described Kelly as being worth seven to eight thousand pounds a year but 'a mere frame of bones'. He gleefully recounted how he scored off his friend with this sally: 'He said to me, "You have been wonderfully carried through all your trials". I said, "So I have. God has taught me that man does not live by bread alone."'

Other friends received shorter shrift. Godwin, who lent Hawker money and was 'my only confidential friend', was depicted to Mrs Watson as 'always what I must call mercenary'. Hawker wrote of his friend Jeune's 'exceeding shallowness ... I know that he disgusted and repelled his Angel by his laxity of speech and silly efforts to be witty on sacred themes.' In 1872 Hawker complained that A. C. Thynne, who had acted with great kindness towards him when Charlotte died and at other times, had behaved badly to him 'on all occasions'. Of J. T. Blight, whom he had helped with his literary work, Hawker wrote that he was 'a singular embodiment of those Brain-suckers who have surrounded my life', though he assured Mrs Watson: 'Pray do not think I could feel anger with a man like Blight. He is of low origin.' The way in which the Waddon Martyns were reviled has already been indicated, yet they gave to his charities and N. H. Lawrence Martyn considered that though 'Hawker was a person with *very few* intimate friends ... he was as friendly with us as with anybody'. Of one of his most sympathetic benefactors Hawker wrote,

> Sir T. Acland is an old friend of both of us but the last man I should like to solicit pecuniary aid from or be under obligation to. He is a very low Church man and Lady Acland, one of the Hoare family, was a Protestant Dissenter ... He is of that heartless school the great world where people have little feeling.

It is not easy to resolve the question of how much of an excuse paranoia affords for these libels on friends or for the much more violent abuse which Hawker flung at his enemies. The element of malicious relish which was so often present in his remarks, as it was in Rolfe's, makes it difficult to regard either of them as being entirely determined by over-mastering impulses. Both men, for instance, clearly delighted in inventing scabrous nicknames for their antagonists. Just as Rolfe dedicated *Don Renato* to 'Apistophilos Echis' (i.e. 'untruth-loving viper', the name he coined for his erstwhile friend, Trevor Haddon) so Hawker called the Stratton barber 'Naked-Nose', the Treasurer of the Stratton Union 'Mumbo-Jumbo' and another enemy 'Master Blackmuzzle alias Snuffle-Lie'. Fretting over his opponents in a dispute about church rate he described them as 'Chaw Bacons. Their very veins run with liquid lard instead of man's blood.' However, the very extravagance of Hawker's animadversions does seem to indicate that he was the prey of a compulsion which he found hard to control. Examples are legion. Charles Kingsley was 'a mere nosey babbler'. Sir Page Wood was a 'vulgar low dissenter'. Lord John Thynne was 'a Tractarian strong in common vulgarism'. Boscastle, in 'the clutch of the Belial Avery', seemed 'to be a kind of shadow and rehearsal of the future regions of misery and pain'. Hawker complained of the 'vile calumnies' of a 'Plymouth fiend' and remarked, 'As a general principle no Plymouth person can speak a true word. Epilepsy would ensue.' Referring to a local political opponent Hawker told Claud, 'that bestial miscreant at Stratton might have been by this time strangled had your men only done their bounden duty. Mercy to such as he is cruelty to better men.' And another local man, apparently a lawyer at Flexbury, was called by Hawker a 'eunuch: cf. his metallic voice. Witness his baboon grimaces in parody of a gentleman, encounter the sour smell of the office and hear the history.'

Whether Hawker is to be pitied as the unwitting victim of paranoia or blamed as the conscious author of malevolence (or perhaps both), it is clear that he did not enjoy discord in Rolfe's spirited manner. Rolfe admitted frankly, 'I bathe in a row.' Hawker was not being wholly disingenuous when he reassured Mrs Watson, 'Do not fear my quarrelling with anyone. My mode of life forbids it ... No, my fault is not readiness to take offence but the reverse – I put up with insult and injury all my days.' Of course, he did pursue numerous altercations, some of them with gusto. However, unlike Rolfe, Hawker was not naturally litigious. He did, it is true, become involved in a celebrated lawsuit with Sir John Buller in 1843 (which he won, with costs) over the Church's right to the ownership of St John's well, on the eastern boundary of his parish. But he fainted during the trial and afterwards went to great lengths never to appeal to the law again. In 1858, for example, he dismissed a dishonest maid instead of prosecuting her, 'from the dread I have of the Assizes and standing in the witness box'. Rolfe himself broke down under cross-examination during a legal case which he had precipitated. But evidently disputes did not take such a serious toll on his nervous system as they did on Hawker's.

Rolfe, indeed, did suffer from what he described as 'congestion of the nerve-centres' and at least once he was in danger of a nervous breakdown. But Hawker's case was more serious – even when allowance is made for his exaggerations and for contemporary medical men, the main function of whose diagnoses seems to have been (as Heine suggested) to qualify their patients to give lectures in heaven on the ignorance of doctors on earth. In 1853,

Hawker recorded, 'I lost consciousness of passing events for . . .
nearly six weeks!! and the only medical opinion was pressure of
thought, and so indeed it was.' Hawker's doctor pronounced that
'he had never encountered in all his practice so excitable a tissue
that which held my Brain. He hinted that any great trial or sorrow
would in all likelihood overwhelm my mind.' Many of the trials
and sorrows by which Hawker's 'wretched nerves are shaken'
have been discussed, but several more which had particularly
serious effects on him must be mentioned. For they are the primary features of what is known to psychiatrists as 'involutional
paranoia', which tends to develop in middle age, and they suggest
that it was to this variety of the disorder that Hawker succumbed.

Involutional paranoia has been defined in the following way.
'Characteristically, such depressions manifest a triad of symptoms,
consisting of delusions of sin and guilt and/or of poverty, an
obsession with death, and a delusional fixation on the gastro-
intestinal tract, all in a setting of agitation and dejection.' Hawker
conforms to this description in all but one feature – he had no
delusions of sin and guilt. He was often acutely depressed in his
middle and later years. To Godwin he remarked on 'my ancient
malady, depression of spirits', and complained of 'the millstone of
thought which drags me down into the earth'. To Anderson he
exclaimed, 'Will no one ever understand the complete and total
prostration of every thought, desire and plan of all my days to one
horizon – the dawn of the next day.' To Mrs Watson he wrote,
'Railways and accidents, illness, influenza and the humdrum ills
that flesh is heir to made a sad grumble in my always morbid
mind ... Can you wonder that I am depressed? My own astonishment is how ... I command courage and calmness for the daily
duties of my public life.' To Claud he mourned 'the downhearted-
ness which deadens my days. I have not a smile left. I drag myself
through the weekly routine of duty done, and count every week
as so much nearer a sad and inevitable end.'

In some moods of depression Hawker claimed to 'yearn for
death', but there is no doubt that his later years were dogged by

dark fears of extinction. The 'total transit of time', which he regarded as 'a fearful mystery', filled him with apprehension. At the beginning of 1862 he wrote to Mrs Watson.

The date has yet hardly lost the thrill with which I first wrote 62. What can be more awful than the question which every thoughtful mind must ask in silence as the figures gain upon the page? What griefs, how many terrors, what sickness, whose deaths shall date from this new and another year of measured time? Will this poor hand of mine ever write upon a page 1863?

Later in the same year he carried the theme to its grim conclusion.

The earth has many trials, sorrows, anxieties, pains, but what are all these and the worst of them compared with the severance and gulph of death? Life under any penalty is best and may be borne. But that departure which divides for ever in this world, that awful dread which overwhelms and paralyses all of woman born, anything but that. The wretch in in the dungeon would rather inhabit his chains than go forth to die. We must not think of any surviving trouble while we can look on each other's faces in the light of life. I think of my own terror.

Perhaps it was the fear of dying rather than death itself which most daunted Hawker. For increasingly he came to be obsessed by the conviction that he was doomed to die of cancer of the stomach, as several of his family had done. He often suffered from severe gastric pains, and as early as 1848 he claimed that he was 'never free' of a 'dull, deadly, dragging weight on the diaphragm'. Sometimes 'nervous dyspepsia' induced sudden, convulsive starts: 'While I have been reading or sitting in thought I have sometimes well nigh bounded from my chair and I well remember how I used to frighten my wife by that quick cry.' Interestingly, Hawker associated his stomach pains with that other main symptom of involutional paranoia – what he once called the 'worst of horrors, money terror, money shame – the perpetual dread of debt and its penalties.' He wrote,

> When you add to all a degrading and debasing lack of L.S.D. it does indeed drag down the mind like a dull, heavy, filthy weight. Never one moment without a sense of actual pain upon the pit of the stomach night and day. Yet after all why should I relate this or look for sympathy from man. Only God's angels can soothe and they for inscrutable reasons do not.

More than on any other subject Hawker harped, during the latter part of his life, on the theme of his incipient bankruptcy and its dire consequences for him and his family. 'Pecuniary terrors' were, he assured Mrs Watson, 'the most difficult of all for a sensitive mind to endure.' And again, 'time and misfortune have made money money money the theme and terror of my daily and nightly thoughts'. It would be interesting to know whether Hawker's financial fears were based on genuine needs or on paranoid delusions.

At least one of his friends, Anderson, suspected that they were considerably exaggerated. But when he unwarily suggested this to Hawker he was roundly rebuked. But Hawker, like Rolfe when he vaunted his 'astonishing adherence to truth', surely protests too much to carry entire conviction.

> When you say that you 'cannot think I am not well off' you do not pay a very high compliment to my veracity. I have repeatedly told you the truth that I am harassed and perplexed very often from scarcity of money – the natural result of my outlay of a large share of my wife's fortune in Morwenstow in buildings for which I could obtain no aidance from the usual sources because of my own unpopularity. I have told you moreover the truth that so universally has the public prejudice been envenomed against me that my pecuniary credit in all the district is gone. Since the circulation of the

last lie, which was coined at Combe, that I had an execution in my house I have never been able to get my draft discounted at a bank for £20 and so successful has the conspiracy of my enemies become that we cannot even sell our lands at a sacrifice of half their value. These facts you must either believe or account me a base deceiver. I have repeatedly related the wretched events and what reason have you to doubt my assertions?

It is impossible to discover the truth about Hawker's financial affairs at this distance of time, especially as he had every motive for exaggerating to his correspondents, nearly all of them actual or potential benefactors, the seriousness of his plight. What can be said with certainty is, first, that he never did go bankrupt but, secondly, that money and his lack of it became the endless, obsessional refrain of his letters during his final years.

Hawker was, like Rolfe, somewhat unscrupulous, if not downright dishonest, in money matters. Writing to Hawker's widow in 1876, his friend Maskell tried to put the best face on the facts, but without much success. One of Hawker's creditors, John Adams,

> charges Hawker with having destroyed (somewhere about 1856) a note of hand for 100£ which Adams had sent him for renewal: but not a shred of evidence except Adams's assertion [exists] ... Unhappily, however, there is a letter of Hawker's [referring to money] which (although it *may* admit of an explanation not altogether unsatisfactory) would be most injurious to his character [if published].

Certainly Hawker's begging letters, even when allowance is made for their obvious neurotic features, do not exhibit him in an attractive light. They tended to follow a set pattern. Hawker would give an account of his history, emphasizing his Oxford education, the fact that he had won the Newdigate, his various expenditures and endeavours at Morwenstow. He would refer to his 'worn and broken mind', his isolated and 'friendless' condition, his dependent wife, his misfortunes and his present financial emergency.

This letter to Gladstone, written in 1854, may serve as a typical example.

I found my parish an ecclesiastical wilderness but full of youth and hope and zeal I girded myself to my work and began. I built this Vicarage with its offices and restored to cultivation a desolate glebe. I erected a national school house and rooms at a very large personal cost in addition to a government grant. I have restored single-handed, with the exception of a chancel window, the gift of Lord Clinton, my Church. The outlay by which these preparations for future vicars has been accomplished has utterly exhausted the only pecuniary resource I ever possessed, my wife's portion of £4,000 ... I find myself at the age of 51 in a position of extreme anguish and impending shame. A demand for £100, such as I am at this very moment imperilled by, will if unaverted drive me from my home. But for one, and the only one for whom in all the world I live, my own dear wife, I should readily relinquish my roof and seek in some distant place shelter from rebuke. I thank God that, saving her, I am utterly alone. Friends I have not one on earth: my life has been always one of solitude: except when sickness has hindered me I have not failed to say the morning and evening service in my Church every day ... There does not exist in your vast patronage a position I would take. I have survived here alone by the sea every earthly desire ... [But] it has occurred to me that it may possibly be in your power to employ my pen so that I may earn a sum for rescue or that there may be resources within your reach whereby you may be able to deliver me from that disgrace and ruin to which my existing exigency might, indeed if unalleviated, will, lead.

Gladstone, who never met Hawker, replied but without, apparently, alleviating his exigency. In 1880, however, he compensated for this by securing a civil list pension of £80 a year for Hawker's widow, assuring her that the grant 'was not the result of any solicitation, nor even of sympathy, however just that may have been, but was awarded on the ground of true poetical merit'.

Both Rolfe and Hawker were blatantly disingenuous about their begging. Rolfe claimed to one of his benefactors that he was 'by no means an expert in the art and mystery of mendicity'. Hawker wrote to Mrs Watson with transparent lack of consistency in 1855, 'I am not successful as a suppliant. Indeed this is the very first time in all my professional life that I ever resorted to the staff of extraneous succour.' Actually, both men were adepts at the art of extracting contributions from grudging patrons. They gauged their various approaches with superlative skill. Hawker's appeals ranged from dignified, if snobbish, cajolery ('I have to sustain the aspect of a clergyman with means hardly above the earnings of a subordinate farmer'), via elaborate self-vindication ('I have banished from this seaboard the reproach and existence of the wrecker'), to frantic importunity ('I am nearly crushed into the earth with the continual worry of my bitter existence'). Interestingly enough, it is their expert and ubiquitous mendicancy which marks the one (indirect) point of historical contact between Rolfe and Hawker. Both men requested and received help from the charitable, Roman Catholic third marquis of Bute. Hawker told Godwin that he had 'grown quite callous as to humiliation and shame' and that he was absolutely desperate for Lord Bute's 'signature to a cheque for my rescue which would ring through the Halls of Hades like a trumpet to invoke and win the applause of Angels and the requital of God'. Hawker's application to Lord Bute, whom he congratulated on his recent marriage, was written in his most ingratiating manner. He alluded to

the goading pecuniary terror of my harassed existence. An adverse balance at my bank of upwards of £200 has long been a millstone around my neck. While it drags me down to the earth I am utterly unequal to those mental labours which might, if successful, augment my future resources and assuage my daily dread. It did occur to me as a way to add one happy remembrance more to your Lordship's after life if at this seed-time of joy you might be induced to cast upon the waters a deed of generous kindness towards me to spring up in your path as a memorial of recompense for future days. It is, however, a generosity for which I have no right to plead or pray. It could only proceed from the spontaneous impulse of such a soul as I know you have the happiness to possess.

Perhaps the best that may be said of this letter is that Rolfe himself could not have penned a more perfect one as far as calligraphy goes.

Hawker's paranoia was less severe than Rolfe's, just as his literary gifts were more modest. But this protracted comparison between the two men has perhaps demonstrated that Hawker shared to a remarkable degree Rolfe's psychological peculiarities. Outwardly Hawker lived a more sedate and orthodox life but his interior existence was, if anything, more anguished and turbulent than Rolfe's. He wrote, 'When associations arise of a certain sort I am obliged to rise up and drive them from me like scorpions or I should grow maddened and die.' It seems likely that, in spite of the aggressively confident faces they presented to the world, both men were mortifyingly conscious of their internal disorders. This would certainly explain the powerfully ambivalent feeling they shared about, as Rolfe put it, 'communion with my fellow creatures. I loathe it and I crave it.' Rolfe, hermit-crab-like, retreated inside his shell when threatened. Hawker's less substantial but more commodious carapace was his isolated situation. Here he protected himself not only against intruders from outside but also against more intrinsic ills. Here he discovered what Coleridge called 'A spot of enchantment, a green spot of fountain and flowers and trees in the very heart of a waste of sands'. For here he was transported into the ultimate seclusion – the visionary world of opium.

Opium

The vicar of Morwenstow's opium addiction (or dependence, as some modern experts prefer to call it) is shrouded in obscurity. Hawker's isolation enabled him to keep it a secret from all but his closest relations and he seems never to have mentioned it in letters to friends. However, after his death, his brother, Claud, revealed the truth to Baring-Gould who promptly published it. Hawker's widow was horrified at Baring-Gould's 'cruelty and bad taste' and she was presumably referring to the disclosures about opium when she complained that 'there are things revealed' in the biography 'which I had kept secret from my own mother, brought to light by *the brother*'. Claud's is the only direct contemporary testimony about Hawker's opium addiction and it deserves to be quoted in full.

> Towards the close of his life, my brother (I am grieved to state it) renewed a habit he had contracted on the death of his first wife, but had abandoned – of taking opium. This had a most injurious effect on his nerves: it violently excited him for a while, and then cast him into fits of the most profound depression. When under this influence he wrote and spoke in the wildest and most unreasonable manner, and said things which in moments of calmer judgement, I am sure, he bitterly deplored. He would at times work himself into the geatest excitement about the most trivial matters, over which he would laugh in his more serene moments.

Hawker's son-in-law confirmed this account though he was less definite about the date at which Hawker's addiction began, which suggests (as does other evidence) that it may have had its origins earlier than Claud either knew or reported. Byles said that Hawker first took opium 'as a medicine, afterwards from habit and there can be little doubt that this explained a great deal in his character and mental attitude. Under its influence, perhaps, much of his finest work in poetry was written.'

Byles's caution about explaining the effects of opium on Hawker's personality and poetry was well judged. For even today there is no agreement among students of the subject as to the impact of opium on the life and work of nineteenth-century writers. Take Coleridge, for example. It is the thesis of a very recent book that 'his whole nature, intellectual and moral, was eroded by ... morphine-reliance, and that his lies, his plagiarism, his treatment of his family and friends, cannot be judged as though he were a fully responsible agent.' In direct opposition to this view, another Coleridge scholar claims that 'The most careful and full studies of the subject tend to show that in lives which we might have supposed were ruined by opium the actual primary cause of ruin was the original psychological makeup of the individual.' What was cause and what effect? Which came first, the demoralized neurotic or the opium addict? Did the narcotic itself produce mystical visions or was it the recourse of those who wished to counterfeit them? Where lay the real creative force, in the native inspiration of the poet or in the artificial afflatus of the poppy?

These questions cannot be resolved with certainty in Hawker's case, particularly as sure knowledge is lacking about when his addiction started. Still, given the reasonable assumption that he did not take opium regularly until at least the 1850s, there is a good deal of evidence (as the previous chapter has indicated) to show that Hawker's psyche was in a disordered state before he became addicted. Indeed, his character conforms with remarkable fidelity to the archetypal figure – delineated in Alethea Hayter's excellent book, *Opium and the Romantic Imagination* – who is classically predisposed to addiction. First, he had a restless 'curiosity about strange and novel mental experiences'. The entire texture of his thought demonstrates that Hawker was a mystic *manqué*, a man who so longed to have his 'soul blended in trance with God' that he was probably not averse to taking what Aldous Huxley once called 'toxic short cuts to self-transcendence', via drugs. De Quincey, whom Hawker had certainly read by 1854, and whom he resembled in so many ways (in his fascination with murders, for example), may have led him in this direction, as he led others. Secondly, Hawker shared 'the longing for peace and freedom from anxiety' which is the common trait of people predisposed to take opium. Like them he tended to exaggerate his sufferings and his inability to bear them. He yearned, as they did, 'for relief from tension, from the failures and disappointments of their everyday life, [and] for something which will annihilate the gap between their idea of themselves and their actual selves'. Finally, Hawker, like others liable to succumb to opium, delighted 'in being an initiate'. As Miss Hayter says, 'Those who cannot make a place and a relationship for themselves in the daylight world of humanity persuade themselves that their isolation is a distinction, a setting-apart of the chosen ones.' Hawker's beautiful lines, obviously referring to himself, in *The Quest of the Sangraal*, perfectly illustrate this last characteristic. He wrote of

> One of the choir, whose life is Orison!
> They had their lodges in the wilderness, –
> Or built them cells beside the shadowy sea,
> And there they dwelt with Angels, like a dream:
> So they unrolled the volume of the Book,
> And filled the fields of the Evangelist
> With antique thoughts, that breathed of Paradise.

None of this proves that Hawker deliberately plunged into what De Quincey called the 'abyss of divine enjoyment', that he took opium as a voluptuous escape from the troubles that multiplied around him in late middle age. It does not show that

Hawker's psychological instability caused his addiction – merely that it preceded it and was conducive to it. The *post hoc ergo propter hoc* argument may seem an obvious way of unravelling this web of causation, but it is by no means conclusive. In fact, there is no reason to doubt Byles's statement that Hawker originally took opium as an anodyne. Probably he began to drink it in the form of the easily, cheaply and legally obtainable laudanum during the 1850s to anaesthetize himself against acute neuralgic pains in the stomach, the hip and perhaps also in the throat and gums. Probably, too, he experimented. In 1857 he sent Mrs Watson some morphine tablets, insisting that she should not take more than one every six hours, and said that he had used them with good effect. It is also possible that Hawker initially took laudanum as a soporific. He had 'always been wakeful at night. The thick coming fancies or rather remembrances and anticipations have so flocked around me whensoever I close my lids that sleep is very very difficult to win.' In 1860 he certainly tried to banish his insomnia by means of drugs, 'with the penalty of the headache which always results with me from anodynes'. In spite of having read De Quincey, Hawker was probably not sharply conscious of the dangers of addiction, the use of opiates as painkillers being so commonly accepted in his time. Even as pleasure-givers they were taken by such eminently respectable people as Hawker's neighbour Oliver Rouse, one of whose favourite tipples was 'gin and paregoric', i.e. camphorated tincture of opium.

Perhaps Hawker also valued opium for its initial property of dispelling his nervous depressions and replacing them by feelings of serene well-being. At any rate, he reached an unprecedented peak of mental distress during his wife's final months. This was accompanied by physical exhaustion, for he nursed Charlotte himself. He also continued the practice, begun when she had become blind, of reading aloud to her a series of popular novels which he borrowed from Mudie's circulating library and which left no trace on his preoccupied mind, so that he could afterwards remember nothing of plot or characters. He claimed that during her last illness he did not go to bed at all – from Christmas 1862 until her death on 2 February 1863. This letter to William Waddon Martyn confirms that he did not leave her side and gives indication of his hysterical wretchedness.

> I *implore* you by every thought of human *agony* and earthly *anguish* to take off my broken heart the burthen of my services at my Churches on Sunday. I adjure you to arrange with what-soever sacrifice of yourself for that day to take my morning service here at Morwenstow at eleven and Wellcombe Church in the afternoon at half past two . . . Poor Cann will explain to you my awful awful grief. She grows a bit weak[er] every hour.

When Charlotte died Hawker was convulsed by a prolonged paroxysm of grief.

To say that he indulged his feelings is not to doubt their gen-uineness so much as to suggest that he was something of an *afficionado* of self-pity, a connoisseur of woe. 'Grief' had been a frequent heading in his 'Thought Books' years before this time. He once called it 'The Twin of Genius, the inseparable com-panion of God's Goodwill'. Hawker justified his lamentations thus:

> It is not rebellion against God's decree nor is it any morbid indulgence of grief that overwhelms me so, but it is the helpless outburst of nature that so rushes on heart and eyes when I begin any custom or usage, such as this letter to you, as to hurry me away like a storm . . . All my ways and deeds and thoughts are broken-hearted.

Some of the details of Hawker's grief-stricken state are truly pathetic. He broke down both in church and, when he went to visit the sick, 'at sight of the dying bed'. During the night he would find himself 'talking of her in a half-sleep and wake up every now and then uttering an exceeding bitter cry of her name', until his young nieces, Mary Hawker and Jane Kingdon, who looked after him for some time after his bereavement, ran to his bedroom door in alarm. His home felt like a mere house to him now that he no longer shared it – 'happiness was born a twin'. He determined to keep no more company. He asked Mrs Watson poignantly, 'What can heal my broken heart? It is not, I do assure you, mere severance of husband and wife but every fibre of life was so unconsciously blended with her that all is jangled and rent and desolate.'

It is clear that Hawker had every incentive at this period for trying to dull his pains and elevate his spirits by means of laudanum. Perhaps grief educated him, as it did De Quincey, through opium. But in the gradual rebuilding of his life which occurred over the next few months there is little or nothing that bears obvious witness to his addiction. He seems to have sought consolation in a mechanical performance of his old routines. On 12 July he sent Mrs Watson an account of his daily timetable. He only slept for three and a half hours a night on average and was up long before his eight o'clock breakfast. He said morning prayers at nine and then visited the sick. He ate chiefly eggs, bread and ham for

Dinner at one. Books and MSS till teatime. Then if fine a walk on the cliffs alone and happiest now. When night sets in and my lamp is lit, reading and writing again till I feel resolved to go to bed – often a very late hour. And thus I look forward to pass my future time.

Mrs Watson had made him a present of the oil lamp in 1858 and his enthusiasm for its 'radiance' – 'it is to me like an added sense' – witnesses to the dimness of his candle-lit evenings before its arrival. He read and wrote by it upstairs in what he called his 'snuggery', his 'bed and reading room, very small, built for a dressing room, looking towards the sea'. Soon he was entirely alone, apart from his servants, for his nieces deserted him, not being 'able to bear the habitual solitude of this house'.

In August, Hawker remarked that 'it does seem so fatal that this year of 1863 should be to me one long grim history of anguish and trial'. It was, indeed, a bad year for him, with his wife's death at the beginning, a fire at the vicarage in the summer which damaged part of the roof, and the wreck of the *Margaret Quayle* in December. But it was also the year of Hawker's greatest poetic achievement. For between spring and autumn he wrote *The Quest of the Sangraal*, judged by both Longfellow and Tennyson to be superior to the latter's treatment of the same subject.

It cannot be definitely ascertained whether opium stimulated Hawker to produce his masterpiece. The legendary theme and the supernatural imagery of the poem had been the warp and woof of his thought from his earliest years, and some of *The Quest's* phrases he had already written down piecemeal in his 'Thought Books'. But *The Quest* is unique among Hawker's poems in being written in blank verse. It is his most sustained work, and in many ways it represents the imaginative crystallization of the 'fragments of his broken mind', what one would call in a more systematic thinker, his philosophical synthesis. As Byles hinted, it was perhaps opium which gave him the sudden power to bring his ideas together, to transmute his diffuse meditations into a significant whole. If the verdict of one good modern critic is correct, that *The Quest* is 'the most successful poem directly inspired by the Arthurian legend in English since the Middle Ages, and one of the most interesting poems of its period', it is worth examining the separate elements in Hawker's thought and attempting to assess the degree to which opium contributed to their artistic fusion in his greatest work.

Hawker saw himself as a thinker grappling with what he often called 'Vast Themes'. He considered that his 'Thought Books' contained 'sentences of great value to future Scribes and Students of the Oracles of God'. He maintained that 'There are materials in MSS in this house that if they could be arranged and printed would be of enormous money value.' He believed he had a 'power of grasping a whole from its fragments . . . a power to generalize i.e. to embrace in a glance a severed and scattered whole'. And in some moods he claimed that his insights were buttressed by scholarship, as when he commented on an article he had written, 'To my knowledge there is more learning in it than English literature has embraced for 300 years.' In fact, however, until *The Quest* Hawker's thought is chiefly characterized by its disconnectedness and lack of intellectual stamina. It has been rightly described as 'a collection of scraps'. Hawker's 'Thought Books' contain an extraordinary mélange of Biblical, poetical and philosophical quotations, snippets of semi-metaphysical, semi-poetical thought, germs of ideas for sermons and poems, symbolic images, ruminations on mesmerism, current affairs, foreign countries, church history, clothes, and a huge miscellany of aphorisms, proverbs, visions, jokes, charms, superstitions, farming notes and so on. Occasionally there is a remark of particular interest to the biographer, as when Hawker recorded, 'I listen to Lolia with delight. Women retain old words longer than men. They hear fewer new ones. I listen to her and think thus her father spake and thus her ancestors.' But generally Hawker's thoughts are a sprawling muddle.

Those spiritual speculations which have been printed present a misleading impression of coherence and homogeneity. To give the true flavour of Hawker's mind they would have to be interspersed, as they are in the 'Thought Books', with such notes (picked out here and there from a mass of material written between 1844 and 1858) as the following.

Hades. Joyless, sunless, loveless, where hope and memory are extinguished and one long, vague remorse replaceth time and eternity.

Thou scarest me with dreams.

Grace. Weakness is the true misery. The secret of peace is fire-eyed defiance.

Vigil. Counsel of the night.

Fat and heavy men are usually affable.

Unicorn. Will never approach any woman but a pure maid.

Reliques. The silent eloquence of some ruined tower or some deserted court shadowed by the mossy trees that have out-lived the eagle.

Jews. The presence of one with certain men will produce a cold chill. Cf. snake.

AntiChrist. There have been giants in each generation which were successive emanations of the Great Enemy which is yet to appear.

Herbert said a country parson should be sad. 1846 all worth a cent are ???

Charms. There be herbs of grace.

Poet. His pen he dipped in mind demi-divine.

The sea. Nothing save the majestic swoop of the snowy albatross.

Dante. Too proud and sensitive to be happy.

Works. We want not talent but purpose. Not power to achieve but resolve to toil.

Love the dash of the waves, the song of the winds.

Genius. Great minds are all self-centred.

A black cow will give white milk.

A tree the earliest rune. A garden first picture of Heaven.

Witch. Her feet always turn inwards.

Wit. A very verdant state of mind.

Chloroform ... is a sign how medical discoveries may avert moral doom.

Life. Its aim. Not L.S.D., rank, success, but soul safe.

Fish. Report of a cannon makes a lobster shed his left claw.

Charm. For consumption. Bake a mole alive in a slow oven.

Cambridge. Their hearts hardened by mathematics.

Church. In human bodies beware faeces. The tail tries to sting the head evermore.

Apocalypse. Write at the head of this book: it is *not* for you to know the signs and the seasons.

Resurrection. Dead rise naked or clad?

Souls. Not in divers places at once but glide so swiftly on their own wishes that by desire . . . they might traverse seas, may girdle the orb during an Ave.

Symbols. The sheep and the lamb were made to be perpetual emblems in the field and on the altar.

War. A scourge of God. How can it be a glory? How justify such myriads of sudden deaths?

Evil Eye. Salt over him thrice then cast into fire.

Demons. Cf. De Quincey's sham men etc. Those who had been dead and came back. Appearances not real. Grasp hands to find nothing. Shadowy fingers. Cf. yearn for bodies as the demons did at Gadara . . . Can use the natural powers latent in matter to produce wonders e.g. hasten the fermentation of a dunghill, to hatch snakes and frogs.

BVM. There was a feminine as well as a masculine element evolved from the Godhead.

Angels enlighten men, their lower link. Persuade but not compel – only God can give a will. Act on the imagery in dreams and in frenzy.

As we eat so we are. Lamb and rice: mild blood. Hog-fed: Porcine.

Hawker lived in a twilight zone between the blinding illumina-
tion of mysticism and the dark night of superstition. He constantly endeavoured to attune his spiritual antennae to the reception of images from the ethereal world which existed, he believed,
immediately behind the veil of the visible world. Alone in his
chancel or in his cliff-top hut he tried to 'think of God and melt
away', thus achieving the 'climax of all bliss' which was to 'understand substance separated from matter'. It was by closing up his
'bodily senses' and sending out 'a Spiracle of Research from every
pore' that Hawker discovered the 'Atmosphere of God', which he
called 'Numyne' – 'Remember I claim the Word'.This was 'An
Element so rarified, so thin, elastic, pure, that it forms the Medium
or Woof wherein Solar Light undulates, glances and glides: so
holy and divine, that it is the native Atmosphere of Angels and
Spiritual Things, and so replete with Godhead that therewithal
The Celestial Persons can become tangible to the Senses'. It was
while alone in church, deep in metaphysical meditation, that
Hawker had the other mystical experience to which he often
referred. He saw 'a grave calm noble Form in White' which
breathed the oracular message, 'Ephphatha is not so good for thee
as Amen', and later went on to explain 'the meaning of St. Lucia
with her eyeballs in a dish'. From the same source Hawker was
subsequently vouchsafed less equivocal information about dis-
puted points of doctrine 'in clear and beautiful Words as the
lightning leaps from the dark cloud suddenly'.

A biographer should resist the temptation to be ironical at his
subject's expense, but this is not always easy in Hawker's case.
Even flippant speculations about whether or not his 'Form' spoke
with a Cornish accent are difficult to suppress. For so much of
Hawker's mysticism smacks of a juvenile conjuring trick. Though,
obviously, he was intensely serious about his aspirations to be a
mystic, Hawker hardly seemed able in practice to differentiate
between mysticism and magic. He appeared to take a schoolboy's
delight in the former's jack-in-the-box inconsequentiality, its
harlequin anomalousness. He hardly distinguished mysticism, as a

means of providing him with insight or information, from super-stition, myth, poetry, tradition, folklore, all of which, as has been seen, are mixed indiscriminately together in his 'Thought Books'. Even astrology was incorporated into Hawker's world-view, the only consistency in which was its resistance to mundane criteria of validation.

> 'They greatly wrong the skies' said St. Augustine, 'who impute to planetary influences the guilty deeds of men.' Cf. Napoleon's star. Yet God *decrees*. Why not by stars as well as by *words*? An orb may be filled with sorrow like an urn for a man to drink a cup of stars [*sic*].

It was not surprising that Hawker believed that the 1857 comet might collide with the earth, thus fulfilling the prophecy that its end would occur 6,000 years after its creation.

If Hawker's 'Thought Books' reveal his otherworldliness they also demonstrate that his supernatural ideas were a kind of intellec-tual crazy paving without cement. Eloquent and beautiful mysti-cal reflections jostled brokenly with banal and absurd superstitions. Yet Hawker betrayed little sign that he recognized the anarchic incongruity of his reflections. Even his more prolonged lucubra-tions, often strange, empyrean reveries, have a naïve, factitious quality about them. This waking vision of Charlemagne's amulet is clearly fictional, like Hawker's extraordinary account of the journey of Prince Albert's soul to the judgment seat, and his history of the ass on which Christ rode into Jerusalem. But it, too, is related with such circumstantial detail that it seems to be designed to carry the conviction of fact.

> The Emperor Charlemagne had an amulet, a fragment of the actual Cross which, enclosed in a golden case, he wore around his neck hanging from a massive chain of gold! This relique, trailing numyne, repelled the Demons. So the Emperor commanded that when according to his own ritual he should be placed in his vault seated in his chair of state,

robed, with his orb and sceptre on the table before him, this talisman should be fastened, as in life, to his breast.

When in 18— the first Napoleon caused the vault to be disclosed and went down into it, followed by his staff, he stood face to face with his imperial predecessor! He saw and understood the chained casket and he said, 'He wore it, I take it'.

Evermore the Corsican Emperor had it on, save twice, when he went to Moscow and at Waterloo. Both these times he delivered it to Hortense. At his death she [gave it] to her son from whom it is not severed, no, not in sleep.

Still it trails the gossamer, the fibre of Mary's silk, the Numyne. You understand the halo around a saint is expressive not of holiness but power woven into that numyniferous woof.

However one categorizes conceits of this kind, whether as fairy stories, manufactured myths, mystical visions, opium dreams, or just as the vagaries of a lonely imagination, they do give an indication of both the content and the characteristic bent of Hawker's mind before he wrote *The Quest*.

Even in Hawker's more disciplined imaginative exercises, his poetry, there was, until 1863, a distinct lack of stamina. This biography is not the place to mount a detailed criticism of Hawker's poetry, about which much has been written elsewhere. All that need be said is that before he wrote *The Quest* Hawker had devoted himself almost exclusively to the writing of ballads. Most of these took for their subjects Cornish legends, Christian myths or incidents of Hawker's own time, and embroidered on them elaborately. They cannot claim to be poetry of the very first order but they are virile and honest and they have a fine, authentic ring to them. At their best they are simply and vigorously expressed in the traditional rhythmic idiom of the ballad-monger. This can be most succinctly exemplified in Hawker's evocative account of 'Featherstone's Doom'. Featherstone was a wrecker whose soul was said to be imprisoned under the huge black rock in Wide-mouth Bay. His sisyphean punishment, for refusing to throw a rescue line to the sailors whose ship he had lured ashore, was to weave a rope of sand.

> Twist thou and twine! in light and gloom
> A spell is on thine hand;
> The wind shall be thy changeful loom,
> Thy web the shifting sand.
>
> Twine from this hour, in ceaseless toil,
> On Blackrock's sullen shore;
> Till cordage of the sand shall coil
> Where crested surges roar.
>
> 'Tis for that hour, when, from the wave,
> Near voices wildly cried;
> When thy stern hand no succour gave,
> The cable at thy side.

Hawker's other verse consisted mainly of brief lyrics, many of them sombre celebrations of the stark beauties of his native scenery. But none of his poems, in terms either of quantity or quality, matched his great blank-verse epic, *The Quest of the Sangraal*.

It thus seems possible, even likely, that opium provided Hawker with the motive power to write *The Quest*. It did not give him the imaginative ingredients which had for so many years per-meated his mind. As he told Mrs Watson, 'it is of course a remote, abstruse and medieval subject but there are themes in [it] which I have gathered up from singular sources and which I shall thus record before I die.' In any case, opium cannot put into the addict's head thoughts which were not there in some shape or form in the first place, as De Quincey's famous maxim indicates: 'He whose talk is of oxen will probably dream of oxen.' But it can remove inhibitions to creativity, it can inspire for short, euphoric periods and it can stimulate a poet to create (though probably not to complete) a synthesis out of a mass of disparate materials. Miss Hayter believes Baudelaire's judgment, that opium can be in certain limited ways a 'machine à penser', to be 'decisive'. Of course, opium quickly takes away more than it originally gave. It impairs creativity, makes sustained work impossible and produces intellectual listlessness and stagnation. It subjects the addict to the torture of withdrawal symptoms which can occur, if the dosage is not maintained, during addiction as well as at its end. While he continues to take opium, he is progressively cut off from the society of other human beings, he 'feels he is an outcast, a pariah, and he cherishes his solitude and isolation, hating to be interrupted and ready to tell any lie if his drug habit is endangered'.

There are, indeed, passages in *The Quest* which look as though they could have been drug-inspired. Hawker encapsulated the opium addict's familiar experience of bewildering temporal elasticity in a beautiful line: 'Whole ages glided in that blink of time.' His vision of the fabulous regions of the earth in which the Holy Grail was to be sought – the East where 'the great cone of space was sown with stars', or the North, 'the lair of demons' – might easily have been precipitated by the 'fierce chemistry' of opium. There are even hints in Hawker's letters that during this uniquely creative period he experienced states, such as opium might induce, of hyperaesthetic visualization, 'for my usage is to *see* what I *think* of', he explained. However, all this is essentially speculation and it becomes less, rather than more, convincing when *The Quest* is compared to the many other nineteenth-century treatments of the Arthurian legend. Just as Ronald Knox managed to prove, in his famous spoof, that Queen Victoria was the author of *In Memoriam*, so a clever commentator could cull 'evidence' from the texts of Wordsworth, Scott, Bulwer Lytton, Morris, Tennyson, Swinburne, and even Peacock (who wrote in prose) that each was drunk on laudanum when he went down to Camelot. The biographer is on more certain ground when he dwells on *The Quest's* achievement of winning for its author the attention of succeeding generations. Hawker was consciously writing with fame in view. He was determined that his poem should not be open to the Voltairean scoff which had greeted Rousseau's *Ode to Posterity* – that it would not reach its destination.

> I have no son, no daughter of my loins,
> To breathe, 'mid future men, their father's name:
> My blood will perish when these veins are dry
> Yet am I fain some deeds of mine should live –
> I would not be forgotten in this land.

The Quest can be seen most clearly as the poetic epitome of Hawker's life. For it gave expression to his fundamental criticisms of the age he had rejected, and it advocated the alternative ideals of medievalism, which he had attempted to put into practice during his long sojourn by 'the cruel sea . . . 'Mid all things fierce, and wild, and strange, alone!' In the voice of 'the lonely one', King Arthur, Hawker anathematized Victorian England for its materialistic preoccupations, for committing sacrilege against those natural beauties which were so eloquent of God.

> Ah! native Cornwall! throned upon the hills:
> Thy moorland pathways worn by Angel feet,
> Thy streams that march in music to the sea
> 'Mid Ocean's merry noise, his billowy laugh!
> Ah me! a gloom falls heavy on my soul –
> The birds that sung to me in youth are dead;
> I think, in dreamy vigils of the night,
> It may be God is angry with my land –
> Too much athirst for fame: too fond of blood;
> And all for earth, for shadows, and the dream
> To glean an echo from the winds of song.

In the figure of Merlin, Hawker prophesied that England's punishment for the rejection of spiritual values would be wars in which chivalry would have no place. Instead men would 'wing with flame the metal of the mine' and 'hurl a distant death from some deep den'. However, there was a chance of salvation if the Sangraal, emblem of God's grace, could be recovered. Merlin's vision of this apocalyptic event is one of Hawker's finest passages, full of burning faith and solemn music. Sir Galahad returns:

> A vase he held on high; one molten gem,
> Like massive ruby or the chrysolite:
> Thence gushed the light in flakes; and flowing, fell
> As though the pavement of the sky brake up,
> And stars were shed to sojourn on the hills,
> From grey Morwenna's stone to Michael's tor,
> Until the rocky land was like a heaven.
> Then saw they that the mighty quest was won:
> The Sangraal swooned along the golden air:
> The sea breathed balsam, like Gennesaret:
> The streams were touched with supernatural light:
> And fonts of Saxon rock, stood, full of God!

Possibly opium provided Hawker with the power, or perhaps it even directly inspired him, to distil lines like these from the galli-maufry of ideas fermenting in his head. Certainly *The Quest*, flawed and fragmentary though it is, deservedly achieved its author's object – the perpetuation of the name of Hawker.

Before leaving the subject of opium, it is worth giving one final illustration of the difficulty of assessing the drug's effect on Hawker. As has been said, one of the invariable characteristics of the addict is that he becomes a compulsive liar. Hawker con-formed to type. He frequently wrote less than the truth on financial and literary matters, and shortly before Charlotte's death he told two flagrant lies to Mrs Watson. He said that 'I utterly disapprove of collections in Churches'; also that he abhorred the idea that 'the holiness of God's house' should be polluted by the presence of animals. The motive for such falsehoods is open to question. Perhaps they were a means of ingratiating himself with a benefactor. Possibly, like Emerson, Hawker regarded consistency as the hobgoblin of little minds. He certainly regarded it as boring:

'I agree with O'Connell, that no man can be called [inconsistent] unless he adopts Two conflicting opinions at the same time; if he allows five minutes to intervene ... then he is only contrasting his sentiments to avoid monotony, which is always vapid and tiresome.' That Hawker reckoned consistency to be the last refuge of the unimaginative is partially confirmed by one of the best contemporary sketches of the vicar in middle life. This was penned by Francis Jeune's prim wife, Margaret, and it dwells with fascination on Hawker's comic duplicity. After describing his looks (she found his 'fine head', 'full expressive' eyes and 'very taking' countenance spoilt by the vulgar 'mahogany colour' of his weather-beaten skin) and dress (she was amused to be 'charioteered by a figure representing en tableau vivant a Popish Priest'), she continued,

Nor is his character less of an anomaly than his appearance. He has a fund of drollery which never fails him, and furnishes him with a series of stories and jokes, which he attributes to others, and tells inimitably – as opposed to this most merry nature he is suddenly overcome by such fits of depression that one is startled by his sighs and groans, one's compassion for which, however, is considerably blunted from the conviction that they proceed – not from wholesome sorrow, nor from mental travail – but from a most childish love for tarts and clotted cream. Alas! that a Poet should be so unrefined in his tastes! Another drawback to the effect of his powers of amusement is that he exerts them at the expense of truth – a fact which I was very unwilling to credit but it was forced upon me. So that while his striking countenance, his rich voice, his vivid fancy, charm – his eccentric appearance tinged with coarseness, his *power* and tendency to palm off falsehood for the dear honest truth (I don't like to say his want of truthfulness) and his childish fitful temper, keep one from giving one's *approval* hand in hand with occasional admiration.

Perhaps the explanation of Byles's censor, Prebendary

Hingeston-Randolph, is the correct one; he doubted that Hawker was 'a mean, lying sneak' and argued, 'we all know that Mr Hawker was highly poetical and not a little romantick, and that strict accuracy was not to be expected of him in consequence.' Alternatively it could be argued that opium was to blame for weakening Hawker's moral fibre.

As with Hawker's physical ailments, his ulcerated sore throats, his sciatica, his abdominal and neuralgic pains, his diarrhoea and so on, it is almost impossible to break into the vicious circle of cause and effect. It cannot be proved that Hawker's moods of intense melancholia and irritation were pre- or post-opium symptoms, or even that they had anything to do with opium at all. His vehement intolerance of opposition, described by him as a strong yearning 'for sympathy' was a characteristic (and euphemism) he shared with many eminent Victorians. Even the best indication of his opium addiction is not conclusive. He suffered from an attack of what was described as 'brain fever' in March 1864, just as he was beginning to take an interest in Pauline Kuczynski, who was to be his second wife. It seems highly probable that this was the result of a sudden determined attempt to shake off his addiction, to 'go cold turkey' in the expressive idiom of the modern junkie, in order to marry her. There may have been some pressure from her, for Hawker later recorded that Pauline herself, though applying laudanum to an aching tooth, would not swallow it because 'her dread of that drug is so intense'. Hawker's 'congestion of the brain' sounds very much like the physical and psychological cataclysm of withdrawal symptoms, the 'writhing, throbbing, palpitating, shattered' feelings which afflicted De Quincey, the 'species of madness' experienced by Coleridge, the 'typhoid-like convalescence' undergone by Cocteau. At any rate Hawker, who had since the 1840s been increasingly apt to lament that he was finished, was suddenly presented with the prospect of a new lease of existence in 1864. He embraced it avidly, gladly repudiating, though only for a time, the lonely half-life of opium.

12

Rebirth and Death

The last few chapters have dwelt, perhaps too exclusively, on the darker side of Hawker's nature. It is important, before considering his second marriage, not to lose sight of the fact that in spite of all his faults he was an extremely attractive person. The verdict of one of his flock deserves to be treated with respect: 'Lovely gentleman he was ... say what you like he was a good man.' His friends, neighbours and colleagues must have been aware, to a greater or less extent, of his uncongenial characteristics, yet few of them were permanently alienated. They revered his faith, respected his good works and especially, in the words of a local woman, 'appreciated Mr Hawker's tenderness for those thrown up on our shores'. They admired his poetry, enjoyed his hospitality and above all they laughed at his jokes. Hawker always remained a practical joker. Once, near the end of his life, he slipped behind the counter of an empty confectioner's in Barnstaple, donned an apron and, to the horror of his wife, started to serve customers who came into the shop. But Hawker had a sense of humour as well as a sense of fun. He could coin a good sharp epigram: 'Conceit is the compensation afforded by benignant Nature for mental deficiency.' He could be humorous about small domestic incidents. He wrote to Claud of their sister's child, 'I suppose you know that Caroline's infant has turned out a decided Protestant and won't suck. Someone has let the children into the right of private judgement and they demand liberty to choose their own mess of meat. Caroline is rather horrified. Pap not

Puseyism is the cry.' Hawker could even laugh at himself, once reporting, 'A stiff neck (an unclerical ailment) has fastened me in one posture for nearly a week.'

Hawker was especially quick at repartee, the most testing form of wit. Asked at an inquest whether its subject had died a natural death, he replied, 'Certainly ... there was not a doctor near him.' When a politician thundered from the Stratton hustings that he would never be priest-ridden, Hawker immediately riposted with this stanza.

> Thou ridden! no! that shall not be,
> By prophet or by priest!
> Balaam is dead, and none but he
> Could choose *thee* for his beast.

Hawker stood no nonsense from a sentimental young lady who inscribed the following lines on the sand with her parasol.

> On this soft sand thy name I trace,
> Which ocean's tide will soon efface;
> But vain the power of ocean's art
> To wash thine image from my heart.

Hawker's reply, also written in the sand so that the young lady who was coyly watching from a distance could read it, went thus:

> On these soft sands we just have read
> The effusion of thy softer head:
> Old Ocean's power indeed is vain
> To wash the nonsense from thy brain.

No doubt the victims of Hawker's jocular malice resented it but such lively local entertainment was a delight to his friends. Like Macaulay, Hawker could fabricate doggerel as fast as he could recite it and one witness cherished long the memory of a picnic on Morwenstow cliffs at which the vicar 'with us all congregated round ... composed poetry on the enjoyments of the day'.

When in jovial mood Hawker was obviously very good company. The affability of his manner is evidenced by this letter to Kelly, written in 1862, in which there is no hint that there had ever been a coolness between them. Having explained the difficulties of visiting his friend, Hawker continued,

> the first feasible hour will find me in the driving seat with the window behind me closed and the female passenger made fast within. We cannot well fix the day amid these fearful changes of the sky but when there is a lull, [we shall] make our plunge into your midst. Forgotten you! Why we have talked of, thought of, nobody else these many days.

When Hawker was not charming his friends he was intriguing them. Whether tracing 'as distinct a difference between the two Persons of the Trinity, the second and the third, as I discover between any two writers of genius and intellect among men' for the benefit of Sir Thomas Acland's daughter, Agnes, or explaining to a parishioner the methods by which demons inhabit the human frames of unbaptized and sinful men – 'they lift the limbs and use the lungs and the voice, the touch, motion and sight, so that each evil spirit becomes to the man as it were a second and a stronger soul' – Hawker clearly exerted a mesmeric fascination on those with whom he came in contact. His stern didacticism, whether on the subject of, say, angels' wings having no feathers or gargoyles being intended to represent evil spirits 'disgorging the superfluous Water of the Ch[urch], which nevertheless cannot cool their actual Tongue', was only to be expected from one who spoke from another age. Like his other faults, it was excused by his friends on that account. This assessment of Hawker, by John Skelton, who reviewed his 'very good poetry, indeed' in *Fraser's Magazine*, best sums up contemporary feelings of romantic attraction towards the vicar of Morwenstow.

> He lives in an enchanted world, – the world of Arthur and of early Christian romance. He loves the sea and the saints, and

names his daughters out of the Saxon calendar. He knows all
the legends of his district by heart, as he knows all its people
by head-mark. For he is a pleasant, cultivated, popular
parson, of the high-bred, hard-working, High Church
type.

Or, in the more concise estimation of a shrewd clerical visitor,
Hawker was 'picturesque, kind, clever, imaginative, but as I
thought, very peculiar'.

It is necessary to stress the fact of Hawker's attractiveness, even
glamour, in order to explain why he was able to woo and win an
intelligent, personable, high-spirited girl, forty years his junior,
whose initial impression of him was that, though 'a very clever old
soul', he was subject to 'the most absurd delusions' and was
'slightly cracked'. Pauline Kuczynski was twenty years old in
1864. She was the daughter of an Englishwoman and an exiled
Pole. When Hawker met her she was employed to look after the
children of the Rev. W. Valentine, vicar of Whixley in Yorkshire,
who had come to convalesce in the sea air of Morwenstow.
Hawker was soon on good terms with Valentine, of whom he
wrote, 'I don't think his wisdom or his judgement strong but he is
well-meaning, credulous to a fault and remarkably self-subdued
and lowly.' But Hawker at first reciprocated Pauline's slight antipathy, for the characteristically snobbish reason that she was 'not
very exalted ... in grade'. 'I should have termed [her] an upper
servant but she is termed a nursery governess.' By the beginning of
1864, however, they began to be drawn to each other. There were
sound practical reasons for this, of course. Hawker needed someone to share and mitigate his loneliness, and to manage his house.
Pauline's father, a nobleman, had not destined her to occupy the
equivocal social role of governess. But he had died and her mother
had married a merchant called Henry Stevens who promptly lost
most of his money as a result of the American Civil War. Consequently she had been forced to enter the ranks of what was
probably the second most over-crowded female profession in

Victorian England. So from every point of view, even the economic one, becoming a vicar's wife was a marked step up for Pauline.

There is no need to make much of these considerations, however, for Hawker's second marriage, like his first, was primarily motivated not by mutual convenience but by mutual love. Hawker, in fact, said that the spirit of his first wife rested upon Pauline. There is even a suggestion that she usurped Charlotte's place in his heart as well as in his house. For when, subsequently, Hawker presented people with copies of *The Quest* he cut out the page dedicating it to his first wife – 'To: a vacant Chair: and an added Stone: I chant these solitary sounds.' At any rate, Hawker doted on Pauline quite passionately. He extolled her in verse:

> The violet eyes! The violet eyes
> That gleam'd, a glimpse of Paradise.

He idolized her in prose: 'a young woman with a Face and Form to win an Emperor, a mind to comprehend the Universe, and a taste and judgement congenial with all that is great and good among men'. He scrawled incoherent phrases of love in his notebooks: 'My own darling ... my own, my own ... If a time should be coming when she is to awake and be averted let me first before it comes die. Pauline the music of this name.' On the few occasions after marriage when they were apart, Hawker wrote her adoring letters.

Home after great trouble but to an empty Place. No dear foot nor voice to hear on the stairs ... How I miss my darling, my darling and little Morry's [Morwenna, his eldest daughter] murmuring voice ... Without my blessed face before me it is hard my darling, my darling. Take little Morry into your arms for me and make her say Dadda. I did not know how much I loved her and her *too* dear mother. I cannot bear it to think that the most blessed creature on God's earth is my own, own Pauline.

Pauline's claim, after her husband's death, that Hawker 'would rather have gone to Hell than cause me trouble' was perhaps a pardonable hyperbole.

Pauline certainly returned Hawker's devotion in equal measure. The pathetic way in which she cherished his memory and her selfless concern for his posthumous reputation is sufficient testimony of this. Though so much in need of money by 1878 that she was having to take in lodgers, she told Godwin that she was willing 'to reap *no benefit*' from a collected edition of her husband's poems, which she wanted published so that 'a tribute may be offered to the memory of Robert Stephen Hawker'. There is no reason to doubt Hawker's assertion that one reason for the haste with which they married was 'that severance from myself would have been, strange as it may appear, a deep and abiding anguish to Pauline'. There was, of course, considerable opposition to the match from Pauline's family. Hawker wrote that her mother, 'a cool, callous woman of the world who has twice married in utter defiance of the dictates of prudence and advice of *her* friends, now comes forward to forbid her own daughter from marrying the man of her choice'. Pauline, asserting that she would rather spend ten years with Hawker than a lifetime with any other man, was 'unchanged and unchangeable'. But in order to gain her mother's consent the vicar of Morwenstow had to go to London to plead his suit in person.

Many colourful stories, probably not altogether apocryphal, are told about what was only the second journey he had ever made by train. They perhaps help to explain his conviction that 'the railway life of England' was 'one great cause' of the fact that 'heart disease is well-nigh the predominant malady of England'. Hawker is supposed to have lost his brown beaver hat while looking out of the carriage window, to have pulled the communication cord and demanded of the guard that the train should return so that he could fetch it. Thwarted in this enterprise and, indeed, threatened with prosecution, he next interrogated the station-master at Salisbury about where he could buy a hat. On being told that they did not sell hats on Salisbury station he apparently replied, 'Bless my soul

... what a benighted place this is!' Finally, it is said, he arrived in
the metropolis dressed in his usual garb of claret-coloured coat,
fisherman's jersey and long boots, with the addition of a red hand-
kerchief which he had tied around his head. In spite of, or perhaps
because of, this unconventional outfit he was successful in his
mission. With the blessings of Pauline's family they were married
at Holy Trinity Church, Paddington, on 21 December 1864.
Hawker was anxious to spend his honeymoon at Oxford, which
among its other attractions contained, lodged, he believed, in the
Library of All Souls, a holograph copy of the Devil's signature.
There is no record that he fulfilled his ambition to see it and after a
brief stay in the city the couple returned to spend the first of the
ten Christmases they were to enjoy together at Morwenstow.
They were given a jubilant reception by the villagers, some of
whom had apparently suggested the match in an effort to rescue
their vicar from his mournful state of depression, and all of whom
were no doubt anxious to have a slice of the 'large and very good
Wedding Cake' which Hawker had ordered.

Most of Hawker's friends and relations seemed equally pleased
about his marriage. The Thynnes were very friendly, Kelly congratulated him and so did his Kingdon brother-in-law, who wrote
somewhat ambiguously, 'I often think of you in the night-watches;
my thoughts in future will be less oppressed.' Only his benefactor
Mrs Watson seemed to consider the match unsatisfactory, perhaps
from jealousy or perhaps because Hawker had always maintained
that 'no man should' marry twice. He had broken the news of his
intentions shufflingly, writing to her on 4 September 1864, 'No
one is to be had to take the "vacant chair" nor do I wish it.' On
13 November he hinted more strongly, 'I receive daily kindness
from the Valentines. Mrs Valentine always asks me the names of
the sick and poor and sends the governess, a very good, religious
person, to carry wine and soup and to employ those who work
with the needle.' Mrs Watson guessed what was in the wind, but
to gain her full 'approval and sympathy' Hawker had to justify
himself in his most persuasive tones.

I do not expect what is usually called love nor deep feeling but only that companionship which in my dreary desolate house I cannot live without. Now I will confess to you that I have often feared and so have others also that my brain would give way. If you could see me in my lonely house shut in by cliffs and Sea, with the Church and graves the only objects visible from my door and windows, with no relief beyond the bedsides of the sick and poor, only some casual visitor by day and the winds howling over the roof all night, you would discern that to a man of my impulsive temperament and studious habits only a kind voice would soothe me and a kind hand satisfy and relieve.

Mrs Watson was won round and then immediately offended again by the speed with which the nuptials were concluded. Hawker had to write another long vindication, cajoling her back into her usual 'kindness of language', promising that marriage would not interrupt their correspondence and explaining that 'with the contrast of a happier future before me it was not well that I should wait'.

Hawker's optimistic hopes were fulfilled for a time. He shook off the unprecedented 'kind of apathy' which had crippled him early in 1864. He went on gay horse-riding expeditions with Pauline. He mixed more freely in society, often visiting the Thynnes at their newly-built parsonage, Penstowe Manor. Mrs Thynne, whom Hawker had earlier criticized as being 'utterly ignorant of good breeding and high manners', having 'only a fine shewy figure and a good face' to recommend her, was especially kind to Pauline. Hawker said that without her they 'should indeed feel desolate, but to have a friend near who is like an actual sister to my wife is a great comfort'. There were snags to staying at Penstowe, however. Hawker could not accustom himself to the 'highly seasoned meat', their numerous indoor servants, the absence of his familiar desk, chair and curtained four-poster bed. Hawker's new-born vigour also expressed itself in his writing. It had previously been his practice to wait until he was moved by fitful gusts of inspiration: 'I never could in my life write as it were on compulsion, that is with subject and measure chosen and fixed for me before.' Now he made a determined (though unsuccessful) attempt to earn money from prose as he had never been able to from poetry. He wrote most of the antiquarian essays which eventually comprised *Footprints of Former Men in Far Cornwall*. This was a particularly creditable effort, for after his 'brain fever' of March 1864 he had written despairingly, 'My *memory* is *shaken*', and it remained unreliable for the rest of his life. However, he had now every incentive to succeed financially. 'My anxieties multiply', he told Godwin, as the time approached when Pauline was to give birth to their first child.

Hawker was understandably nervous when the baby was late. He told Mrs Watson that 'every day and indeed hour may bring the crisis when as you may well suppose my fears and hopes will well-nigh overwhelm my always excited mind'. Just before the birth he was harassed by another domestic worry. He heard 'a Parish rumour' that their new cook had visited 'a Conventicle. If this is verified we must of course dismiss her, a sad loss because she is a very good servant and a time is at hand when it will not do to have a bad one.' Luckily, though, Hawker was soon able to report that 'the cook has not manifested any more of that treachery called Methodism'. One of the few surviving leaves of Hawker's desk diary records the birth of his daughter, Morwenna Pauline, named after the patron saint of his church, and his wife.

27 November [1865]: Pauline ill all night. At ½ past 2 sent Frederick to Stratton. By 4 a.m. Mr Braund came. In labour all day – preliminary pains. Thynne came. Braund stayed here. Baby born ¼ before midnight. *28 November*: My darling in bed. Safe but suffering all day. My blessed baby and lovely gentle child.

Hawker received many 'letters full of kind feeling'. He wrote in his diary on 1 December: 'Baby happy and well. What can God give more?' Actually, he was bitterly disappointed, for he had desperately wanted 'a Manchild' to perpetuate his name.

This ambition was to be thwarted. Pauline gave birth to two more girls, Rosalind ('an ancestral name in my family') in 1867 and two years later Juliot (so called after the Church near Boscastle, which Hardy helped to restore in 1870). Hawker was devoted to his children but there is no doubt that they imposed a great additional strain on his body and mind. He wrote, 'the usual maladies of children beset ours', and these illnesses so preoccupied Pauline that she was prevented from fulfilling the Baconian function of being a nurse to her husband in old age. Indeed, when her resistance was sapped, Pauline herself was subject to attacks of anaemia and hereditary rheumatic gout, and Hawker sometimes found himself looking after her. In 1868 he recorded, 'My poor wife is worn to mere bone. How can she be otherwise? Not one full night's rest since baby was born now five months ago, and now teething makes her more restless.' Illness at home or the danger of transmitting to his children the 'epidemic diseases so common around us', especially smallpox and scarlet fever, kept Hawker a prisoner in his own house as often as did his recurring nervous depressions. This letter to his sister, Caroline, written in 1871, gives a characteristic impression of Hawker's domestic situation.

> We cannot go out any where. My spirits are much too broken. And Pauline is so absorbed in the children that they occupy her total time. We went to the beach at Combe last week. The children all got sopping wet playing about in the pools and have been laid up all three in coughs and colds ever since.

As Hawker contemplated his daughters, 'three lovely little girls whose faces I cannot look at without a shudder as to their future life', he knew that he 'ought to trust them to [God's] hands and our lady's care'. In fact, he made increasingly frantic efforts to provide for them himself. He continued his literary work, stepped up his begging letters, sold his farm produce more profitably and advertised, unsuccessfully, for pupils. He also mustered his friends, again without success, 'to bring their influence to bear upon [Mr Gladstone] for the exercize of his patronage' in the direction of a canonry, a literary pension, or, best of all, a suitable post at Oxford. But his attitude to leaving Morwenstow was, not unreasonably, ambivalent. He told Mrs Watson.

Of course I should rejoice to increase my income in the Church if it could be done, and at whatsoever sacrifice I would gladly exchange this for a better living. But I feel that my day and my chance are gone ... Notwithstanding what I have just said about leaving Morwenstow I feel that to move my residence now would assuredly kill me.

Meeting failure at almost every turn, Hawker's last resort was to sell off some of his furniture and Charlotte's family silver, which to his disgust turned out to be plated. Hawker may have complained interminably but he never capitulated. Not every clergyman possessed his fortitude – the rector of Great Rollright in Oxfordshire, for example, who, having overspent himself by building too large a parsonage, announced his text one Sunday in 1851, 'Forgive us our debts as we forgive our debtors', whereupon 'he disappeared into the vestry and was seen no more'.

Apart from his domestic circumstances much conspired to trouble Hawker during his last decade. As he put it, 'evil multiplies on every side'. There was a widespread potato blight and a serious outbreak of cattle plague. In 1869, 'after a long lapse of years without molestation from such a source' he found himself 'assailed by an unlooked for an undeserved [tax] assessment for "Armorial Bearings!"'. Several times demons of the storm attacked and damaged his barn. He was 'badly shaken' by a number of horrid accidents. In 1866 his churchwarden, Cann, drank some paraffin oil by mistake and Hawker, quickly forcing him to swallow a mustard drink, made him vomit and thus probably saved his life. In 1871 part of the roof of his church fell in while he was preaching and although no one was hurt he had to face all the problems of another restoration. In 1875 he had 'a fearful fright. Screams from the kitchen . . . On rushing out we found Mary the cook swathed in fire. She had poured benzoline oil into a lighted paraffin lamp and was blazing. My man James just came in by chance, grasped her and folded her garments round her and saved *her life*. She was however terribly burnt although Braund says not dangerously yet.' As Hawker became increasingly incapacitated by illness, old age and opium (which he began to take again about 1870) he had to employ a number of curates, none of whom stayed very long and all of whom joined in the conspiracy to persecute him. Of one, named Abrahall, Hawker expostulated, 'Anything more abominable than his whole conduct cannot be conceived.' Another, the Rev. J. A. Rawlins, was more effective and among other reforming activities succeeded in removing no less than two wheelbarrow-loads of dirt from the church. Nevertheless Hawker complained jealously that he 'was a far more advanced Ritualist than I am but because of his youth and his black beard every womb in Morwenstow yearned after him'.

More distant events also afflicted Hawker. The increasing number (as he supposed) of murders horrified him, and he was unable 'to sleep from the thought of the wretched woman' Constance Kent, the child-murderer, who was hanged at Exeter in 1865. He looked to the police – ' I confess to a liking for the surveillance and espionage of that body' – but in vain as far as prevention was concerned. Nor could they shield him in 1868 from 'the Fenian worry' which 'continues even here'. The 1867 Reform Bill appalled Hawker: 'What sorrows are to be soothed or what evils lessened by enabling the working classes to vote I cannot understand.' Irish Church disestablishment was more than irrelevant, it was dangerous. It would 'produce an actual Revolution ... without bloodshed I hope'. Both political actions were grim portents for the future. Hawker prophesied,

We shall not behold it but in the next generation I for one

believe no Queen or King will reign in England unless the
lower orders vote for it. No Church will exist but multitudes
of sects even more than now. And the peers will be banished
from the House of Lords. The land will be divided among
the people and a state of rebellion against all authority will
exist throughout the land.

Even in his remote eyrie Hawker could not ostracize the world
entirely but, though only tangentially affected by the materialistic
panaceas being advanced in his own day, he became more and
more perturbed by them. He alluded to the fact with unwonted
humility, in a letter to Mrs Watson: 'Pray remember that there
are many topics on which from my very lonely life and distance
from the living world I think so differently from the current
notions of the day that I could not give my own private judgement
without umbrage or assumption.' Assumption or no, Hawker was
not generally backward in putting his views forward, especially
when advocating the spiritual solutions of the past. 'Who are these
idiots,' he asked indignantly in 1867, 'who take upon them to
deny what the wise and the learned and the good of all generations have searched and found true and consoling?'
    Hawker was increasingly out of temper not only with his time
but also with his Church. By the 1860s there was growing pressure from many of its intellectual leaders to jettison those scrip-
tural tenets such as the Creation story and the Flood (not to
mention Balaam's talking ass and Jonah's accommodating whale)
which new scientific studies had shown to be no longer credible.
This pressure expressed itself in various ways, most notably in the
publication of *Essays and Reviews*, the aim of which was to bring
Anglicanism into conformity with new geological, biological and
philological knowledge. Significantly this controversial book
appeared in 1860, just a year after Darwin's *Origin of Species*.
Hawker considered that *Essays and Reviews* would 'foam infidelity
over the land', and he regarded it as a direct assault on everything
he cherished. This was to be expected. Benjamin Jowett, perhaps

the most powerful of the essayists, might have had Hawker speci-
fically in mind when he condemned 'mystical interpretation' of
Scripture, and those who 'have read the Bible crosswise, or deci-
phered it as a book of symbols'. Hawker's response to the
attempts to rationalize his faith was the familiar Tractarian one of
insisting yet more vigorously on the impalpable mystery of the
cosmos. Like St Augustine and Tertullian, he believed because he
did not understand, he was certain because it was impossible. His
own emphatic axiom was, 'No mystery – No God.' Evolutionary
arguments could not be expected to impress one who considered,
as Hawker did, that time was merely 'the clock of Adam', which
had nothing in common with the chronology of everlasting God.
Natural laws accounted only initially and superficially for all
mundane phenomena, whose ultimate authorship and motive
force was the divine creator. It was the

> young men in white garments . . . the Battalions of the
> Lord of Hosts . . . [who] each with delegated office fulfil what
> their 'King Invisible' decrees; not with the dull, inert
> mechanism of fixed and Natural Law, but with the unslum-
> bering energy and the rational obedience of Spiritual Life.
> They mould the atom; they wield the force; and, as Newton
> rightly guessed, they rule the World of matter beneath the
> silent Omnipotence of God.

Many doubters existed before Darwin, of course, but J. M.
Keynes's conjecture that the late 1860s 'will be regarded by
historians of opinion as the critical moment at which Christian
dogma fell away from the serious philosophical world of England'
was a shrewd one. Inevitably the vicar of Morwenstow was
unhappy surrounded by a climate of opinion in which the old
certainties were in danger of being swept away. Even he had to
admit that there were 'errors in the translation of the Bible',
though he naturally considered them 'not enough to impair that
Book as a code of salvation'. But Hawker could not feel comfortable in a Church which was bound to tolerate Colenso's denial

of the historical accuracy of the Pentateuch; which had to accept
the appointment of Frederick Temple, one of the contributors to
Essays and Reviews, to the bishopric of Exeter in 1869; which
protested only ineffectually at the crucial loss of its privileged
educational position in 1870; and which objected hardly at all to
the elevation to the primacy in 1868 of A. C. Tait, whose baptism
(in the eyes of some, Hawker included) was suspect, who seemed
to agree with Matthew Arnold's opinion that the Athanasian
Creed was an 'insane licence of affirmation', and who was the
main advocate of the Public Worship Regulation Act, passed in
1874 to suppress extreme manifestations of ritualism. Of course,
Hawker did not have to struggle with doubts about the truth of
the Christian revelation as did so many eminent Victorians,
Tennyson, Ruskin, Froude, Arnold and Clough who opined that
the First Cause would probably turn out to be a 'smudgy person
with a sub-intelligent look about the eyes'. But he did come to
doubt whether it was any longer possible for him to believe that
what so many regarded as the Protestant Church of England
could really be the Catholic Church in England. Like others who
had come under Tractarian influence he increasingly looked
towards 'the obvious Ark' – the Church of Rome.

Far from reconciling itself with what the *Syllabus of Errors*
called, in a famous phrase, 'progress, liberalism and modern
civilization', the Roman Catholic Church was vigorously
repudiating it in the 1850s and '60s. Hawker was delighted by
Pius IX's Bull on the Immaculate Conception. He found it very
striking that 'the Old Man at the Tomb of the Apostles utterly
forgets "the things that are seen", and seeks to satisfy and soothe
the Dwellers in the invisible World by Confession of a dogma
fraught with personal Danger.' Of the doctrine itself Hawker
wrote, 'You don't invent the gem: it was in the casket but nothing
hinders you may set it.' Other Roman Catholic doctrines also
seem to have won his assent as early as the 1850s. He wrote that
sacramental confession was 'the safeguard of female chastity ...
both in Italy and Ireland. Compare Morwenstow and its brothels

with Ireland and its confessional and Cf. the vast bridgeless gulph.'
Hawker also believed in purgatory, transubstantiation and Papal
supremacy.

What attracted him to Roman Catholicism was that it constantly asserted. It made positive demands on the faith instead of
being, like Protestantism, 'a gigantic sneer of religious negation'.
Hawker wrote in 1864, 'Only a Catholic can deal with such men
as wrote Essays and Reviews. To any Denomination of Protestantism they reply "you deny – I deny – My denial is as valid as
yours". The total Denier is but a boundless Protestant after all.'
By 1870 he recorded, 'my Breviary is the only book I can bear to
read.' None of this, of course, proves anything about Hawker's
deathbed conversion, though when added to the evidence printed
below it may be deemed all but conclusive. However, like so
much else about this paradoxical man, certainty is elusive. Also,
two provisos must always be made about Hawker's theological
views. First, they were apt to become subsidiary to more pressing
considerations. He wrote to Mrs Watson in 1867, 'What are
Reform and Ritualism and High Church and Low Church to one
oppressed with a personal anguish like you and, I must add, myself
almost always?' Secondly, in theology, as in almost everything
else, Hawker was often inconsistent. For example, when asserting
his right to perform his own brand of ritualism he put forward an
argument which totally contradicted his oft-expressed respect for
traditional authority.

How can a decision of courts and bishops override individual
practice. The cornerstone of the Establishment is private
judgement, that is personal opinion. Whatsoever tenet or
usage an Englishman thinks is right *is* right.

It may just have been invincible inconsistency which kept
Hawker an Anglican parson while he privately professed doctrines
indistinguishable from Roman Catholicism. But in the judgment
of his wife Pauline, the person who best knew his mind, more
powerful motives delayed his secession until the last moment.

Pauline, who became a convert after her husband's death, was convinced that Hawker had been for many years 'at heart a Roman Catholic'. She stated her view categorically: 'If I had not believed that for all the years I knew Mr Hawker his mind was made up without the least shadow of a doubt as to the Catholic Church – I should not have dared to send for Canon Mansfield.' Pauline quoted some impressive evidence to support her opinion and to explain why Hawker remained vicar of Morwenstow despite his convictions. She told Maskell that in his copy of a book by Newman, Hawker had marked a certain passage. It said that although there was no salvation out of the Roman Catholic Church the rule did not hold in the case of good men who are in invincible '"ignorance"': this last word is underlined and a foot-note in my husband's handwriting says "or poverty or entangle-ment".' Pauline's verdict that Hawker remained outside the One True Fold since to enter it would have involved his own and his family's financial ruin carries a good deal of weight – because only an overriding conviction that the truth had to be told could have caused her to impute calculated hypocrisy and systematic double-dealing to the one whom above all others she adored.

Alone among those who took sides in the prolonged and acri-monious debate which raged after Hawker's death about whether or not he had been capable of taking the decision to secede, Pauline was not pleading a partisan case. Maskell's anxiety that she should not broadcast her view tells its own story: 'I think it would do great harm, holding the opinion which you do of Mr. Hawk-er's state of mind for some time before his death if you were to make it public.' Maskell himself asserted the orthodox Roman Catholic view of the vicar of Morwenstow's conversion 'viz: that until within a day of his death, Mr Hawker's course of duty was not plain before him'. To have agreed with Pauline and branded Hawker as a man who refused to sacrifice his benefice for his (and their) principles, would have been a great propaganda blow to the Roman Catholics. But, like all the others who were more interested in polemics than in truth, Maskell did not know all the facts. What is more, he elsewhere admitted it: 'For more than twenty years, Mr Hawker and myself never discussed or spoke of religious questions in a controversial way.' Claud Hawker, cited together with *all* the vicar of Morwenstow's nearest relations in support of Baring-Gould's belief that it was not Hawker's 'intention to leave the Church of England before he died', similarly disqualified himself. He wrote in 1877, 'I am not in a position to think, still less to enlarge on, the views which it is alleged my Brother held with regard to the faith. I never exchanged a word with him on the subject.' Apart from herself, Pauline implied, only Godwin had known of Hawker's clandestine Roman Catholicism – 'from the first he made no secret of *HIS GREAT SECRET* to you'. Godwin was not in the least surprised by Hawker's final step.

The step does not perhaps seem so momentous today as it did then. Moreover it is tempting to take the anachronistic line that any moral deficit incurred by Hawker's ultimate theological change is vastly outweighed by the credit he earned in a life-time of dedicated parochial work. But if, as is proper, the vicar of Morwenstow is judged by the dogmatic canons of his own age it is almost impossible to avoid the conclusion that he was blameworthy. On the other hand, those who claimed that Hawker was not in his right mind when he became a Roman Catholic are certainly supported by the fact that his final months were marked by a sad demoralization. He had made a last desperate journey to London in 1874 to seek medical help for himself and Pauline (who had just undergone a very serious illness), and to raise money for the Morwenstow church restoration. In spite of having preached several well-received sermons he reaped little financial reward and was actually rebuffed in some quarters. He told Godwin, 'my journey has revealed to me the utter narrowness and selfishness of the Ritualist clergy'. Nor were metropolitan doctors of much avail. On his return to Morwenstow, Hawker referred to Pauline as an 'invalid' and said that she 'continues to be a source of unrelaxing anxiety and fear ... My life of vigil by night and anxiety by day is a state very hard to bear.'

Hawker struggled on through the freezing winter of 1874-5, weakened by ill-health, persecuted by his curate who had 'brought everything Roman' to his church that was there, loathing the growing Erastianism of the Church and the callousness of local landlords, terrified by money worries, by the prospect of more wrecks, by an epidemic of scarlet fever in the parish, by a murder at Bude. He wrote, 'Never was a man so harassed by a diversity of dooms as I am. What shall I do? Those faces, those blessed faces downstairs! How can I brook to see them?' In spite of (or because of) taking 'copious doses of arsenic unbeknown' to his doctor, he was tormented by attacks of eczema. Though regularly drinking laudanum he was dogged by insomnia. His final letters are filled with remarks like, 'up from 3 to 5 ... with frenzied thoughts', or 'pacing the passages like a troubled ghost'. In January 1875 Hawker warned Godwin that his state of disease admonished him to prepare for the end. Throughout the spring, his condition deteriorated. In June, leaving the parish in the care of a new curate, Hawker made a last health-seeking pilgrimage to Boscastle where he stayed with his brother. Then he went on to Plymouth, probably in pursuit of more expert medical help. Here, in rented lodgings, Hawker's mind more and more gave way and he recognized people only intermittently. There is some evidence that in spite of his fatal debilitation he planned to return to Morwenstow, whether in the hope of living or resigned to dying it is impossible to say.

However, on 13 August a blood clot settled in the artery of his left arm, paralysing it. 'About twenty four hours before the end came,' Pauline later recorded, 'my husband looked upon three who stood around his bed and said, "Can this be death?"' Hawker had latterly considered death 'terrible': 'At all times and in every rank ... the last journey of a separated soul is a very awful path.' He had meditated with Johnsonian trepidation on

The Shadow cloak'd from head to foot,
Who keeps the keys of all the creeds.

But in the event he approached death calmly. Pauline wrote to
Godwin on 15 August, 'My darling Husband went to his rest
most peacefully at 8.20 a.m. today. He was at his earnest desire
Baptized and Received into the Catholic Church not 12 hours
before his death.' Respecting Hawker's aversion to the colour
black, the mourners at his funeral wore purple. He was buried in
Plymouth Cemetery and in addition to details of his birth and death
(to which Pauline's, who only survived him for eighteen years,
were subsequently added) his tomb was inscribed with a line from
The Quest of the Sangraal:

I would not be forgotten in this land.

Though he has been dead for a hundred years Hawker is remembered still. Such fame as he now possesses is based less on his
achievements as pastor and poet than on his life itself, on the
totality of his strange, lonely, passionate existence by the sea.
Of course, he dramatized himself and his situation with every arti-
fice. He compared himself to Alexander Selkirk; he pronounced,
'My motto has long been the verse from Moses" song, "The
people shall dwell alone and shall not be reckoned among the
nations"'; he lamented, 'One line describes my life. "Remote,
unfriended, solitary, slow."' Yet Hawker's existence really was
extraordinarily isolated, distant both in space and time from that
of his increasingly urbanized contemporaries. And there was no
pretence about the struggle raging within him between pride,
vanity, dogmatism, irascibility, malice, superstition, and courage,
charitableness, humour, affection, humaneness, piety. Those who
know Morwenstow will always associate the grandeur of its
scenery in differing atmospheric moods with the personality of its
sometime vicar.

Bibliographical Note

In view of the bibliographical nature of the first chapter and the fairly comprehensive character of the Notes it seems otiose to compile in addition either a select book-list or a full bibliography. What may be useful, however, is a brief description of the manuscript sources on which this book is based.

Bodleian Library: Nicholas Ross Collection – 27 volumes of letters, 'Thought Books', sermons, poems, press cuttings, photographs, etc. Microfilm of approximately 350 letters from Hawker to Mrs Watson – originals in the Humanities Research Centre, University of Texas.

British Museum: Maskell MSS. 'The Book of Wrecks at Bude'. One letter from Hawker in the Gladstone Papers.

Cornwall County Record Office: a number of letters from Hawker to J. T. Blight. Morwenstow Church Rate Book.

Exeter Public Library Record Office: a few miscellaneous letters from Hawker. A large bundle of letters from R. Hawker D.D. to Richard and Jemima Croft.

Hartnoll MSS, in possession of Mrs Morwenna Hartnoll: 7 diaries of John Davis and 5 of Oliver Rouse.

Kelly MSS, in possession of Mr Michael Kelly: a number of Hawker's letters, poems and miscellanea.

Morwenstow Church: parish registers.

Pembroke College, Oxford: Hawker's letters to W. D. Anderson.

St Mark's School, Morwenstow: miscellaneous papers and School Log.

Tonacombe Manor MSS, in possession of Mr William Waddon-Martyn: a number of letters from Hawker to William Waddon Martyn.

Truro Library: two letters and some poems in Hawker's hand.

Truro Museum: one letter from Hawker to Davies Gilbert.

I have also received copies of one letter belonging to Professor Nathan Starr and another lodged in the University of Iowa Libraries. I own several Hawker letters myself.

For the complete bibliography of Hawker's own works, see Cecil Woolf, 'Some Uncollected Authors XXXIX: Hawker of Morwenstow', *Book Collector* (Spring/Summer 1965).

Notes

Chapter 1

page 23, line 19 See, e.g., Edith Sitwell, *The English Eccentrics* (1933), *passim*.

page 24, line 13 R. S. Hawker, *Footprints of Former Men in Far Cornwall* (1870), 184.

page 25, line 19 S. Baring-Gould, *The Vicar of Morwenstow* (1949 edn), 217.

page 25, line 28 B. H. Dickinson, *Sabine Baring-Gould, Squarson, Writer and Folklorist 1834–1924* (Bristol, 1970), 59.

page 25, line 31 Ibid., 153.

page 26, line 14 Baring-Gould, 63.

page 26, line 23 *Athenaeum* (25 Mar. 1876), 418.

page 26, line 24 B[ritish] M[useum] Add. MSS 37825, f.4.

page 26, line 28 *Athenaeum* (17 June 1876), 825–6.

page 27, line 7 Encouraged by journalists, e.g. E. Kerr, *The Western Morning News* (2 Aug. 1962), and E. J. Dunstan, ibid. (11 May 1973).

page 27, line 18 Dickinson, *Baring-Gould*, 149–50. J. Heath-Stubbs, *The Darkling Plain* (1950), 78.

page 27, line 33 H. R. T. Brandreth, *Dr Lee of Lambeth* (1951), 124.

page 28, line 11 F. G. Lee, *Memorials of the Rev. R. S. Hawker* (1876), 64.

page 28, line 11 Ibid., 4–5.

page 28, line 19 M. Donovan, *After the Tractarians* (1933), 44.

page 28, line 33 Bodleian MS Eng. Lett. e. 96, f. 57.

page 29, line 6 M. F. Burrows, *Robert Stephen Hawker: A Study of his Thought and Poetry* (Oxford, 1926).

page 29, line 7 E.g. P. E. More, 'The Vicar of Morwenstow', in *Shelburne Essays* (*fourth series*, 1906); E. W. Martin, *The Secret People: English Village Life after 1750* (1954), 97–100; A. L. Rowse, 'Robert Stephen Hawker of Morwenstow: A Belated Medieval', *Essays and Studies*, XII (1959); D. M. Hopkinson, 'Parson Hawker of Morwenstow', *History Today* (Jan. 1968).

page 29, line 18 H. H. Breton, *Hawker of Morwenstow* (1927 edn), 41. Breton was a subsequent vicar of Morwenstow.

page 29, line 25   Bodleian MS Eng. Misc. e. 595, f. 26. In order to avoid confusion I have often, when quoting from Hawker's MSS, altered his idiosyncratic punctuation, capitalization and spelling.

page 29, line 34   C. E. Byles, *The Life and Letters of R. S. Hawker* (1905), 361.

page 30, line 13   Watson [Hawker's letters to Mrs Watson, originals in the Humanities Research Centre, University of Texas], 27 Aug. 1858.

page 30, line 35   Bodleian MS Eng. Misc. e. 592, f. 158.

page 31, line 1   From *The Quest of the Sangraal*, quoted by P. D. Martyn, *Morwenstowe Church* (Bude, n.d.), 20.

page 31, line 4   Byles, p. iii.

Chapter 2

page 32, line 1   Bodleian MS Eng. Misc. b. 73, f. 5.

page 32, line 19   J. Williams (ed.), *The Works of the Rev. Robert Hawker D.D.* (1831), I, 5 and 9.

page 33, line 7   Byles, 3.

page 33, line 14   Williams, *Works of Robert Hawker*, I, 69.

page 33, line 18   Bodleian MS Eng. Misc. b. 93, f. 24.

page 33, line 23   Ibid., e. 592, f. 138.

page 33, line 30   G. S. Faber, *A Dissertation on the Prophecies* (1814), II, 492.

page 34, line 4   R. Hawker, *The Best of Remedies for the Worst of Times* (n.d.), 9.

page 34, line 12   Byles, 606.

page 34, line 16   Williams, *Works of Robert Hawker*, II, 537.

page 34, line 21   Ibid., I, 28.

page 34, line 35   Ibid., I, 106.

page 35, line 2   Ibid., I, 52.

page 35, line 8   Ibid., I, 11–12.

page 35, line 28   Ibid., I, 24.

page 35, line 32   Bodleian MS Eng. Misc. d. 649, f. 213.

page 37, line 2   Byles, 2–3.

page 37, line 6   *A View of Plymouth Dock* (Plymouth, 1812), 30.

page 37, line 8   *Reminiscences of the Ministry of the Late Rev. John Hawker B.A.*, by one of his Congregation (1851), p. xv.

page 37, line 2   Ibid., p. xix. Ironically enough, 'Eldad' was subsequently bought by the Church of England, renamed St Peter's and given a Tractarian incumbent – with riotous consequences.

page 37, line 35   Byles, 2.

page 38, line 8   Watson, 8 Dec. 1867.

page 38, line 17   Bodleian MS Eng. Lett. d. 225, f. 27.

page 38, line 19   R. S. Hawker, *The Cornish Ballads and Other Poems*, ed. C. E. Byles (1904), 243.

page 38, line 23   Ibid., 242.

page 38, line 26   Ibid., 243.

page 38, line 32   Bodleian MS Eng. Misc. d. 649, f. 67.

page 39, line 15   Hawker, *Cornish Ballads*, 257. Bodleian MS Eng. Misc. d. 649, f. 174.

page 39, line 19   Watson, 22 May 1864.

page 39, line 24   Bodleian MS Eng. Misc. e. 591, f. 128, and e. 594, f. 3.

page 40, line 10   A. L. Rowse, *A Cornish Childhood* (1942), 37.

page 40, line 10   Ibid., 51.

page 40, line 12   For other examples of rural practical jokes, see, e.g., J. Galt, *Annals of the Parish*, ed. J. Kinsley (1967), 30 and 77.

page 41, line 5   R. Friedenthal, *Goethe: His Life and Times* (1965), 174–5.

page 41, line 8   Bodleian MS Eng. Lett. d. 224, f. 103.

page 41, line 28   Byles, 7.

page 42, line 1   Ibid., 8.

page 43, line 6   A. Harper (ed.), *History of the Cheltenham Grammar School* (Cheltenham, 1856), 4.

page 43, line 18   Watson, 27 July 1862.

page 43, line 28   Ibid., 20 Sept. 1863.

page 43, line 32   Ibid., 18 Apr. 1856.

page 44, line 16   Hawker, *Cornish Ballads*, 270.

page 44, line 24   Watson, 14 Oct. 1860.

page 44, line 28   Byles, 11.

Chapter 3

page 45, line 8   Baring-Gould, 8.

page 45, line 22   Watson, 17 Apr. 1856.

page 46, line 1   Ibid., 2 July 1860.

page 46, line 26   B.M. Add. MSS 37826, ff. 39 and 9.

page 46, line 30   *John Bull* (15 Apr. 1876).

page 46, line 32   *Athenaeum* (25 Mar. 1876), 418.

page 46, line 34   Byles, 484.

page 47, line 5   Watson, 22 May 1864.

page 47, line 11   Bodleian MS Eng. Misc. d. 650/3, f. 35.

page 47, line 28   Ibid., d. 224, f.22.

page 47, line 32   Watson, 13 Jan. 1861.

page 48, line 1   Ibid., 24 Sept. 1864.
page 48, line 7   Ibid., 21 Feb. 1858.
page 48, line 11   Ibid., Cowie to Hawker, 6 Feb. 1863.
page 48, line 28   *John Bull* (15 Apr. 1876).
page 49, line 13   Byles, 20.
page 49, line 15   Watson, 25 Apr. 1857.
page 49, line 19   Tonacombe Manor MSS, Hawker to W. Waddon Martyn, 7 Feb. 1852.
page 49, line 32   Hawker, *Footprints*, 229.
page 50, line 8   Ibid., 226–8.
page 51, line 18   G. V. Cox, *Recollections of Oxford* (1868), 103.
page 51, line 26   W. Tuckwell, *Reminiscences of Oxford* (1900), 4.
page 52, line 9   E. Gibbon, *Autobiography* (1907 edn), 40.
page 52, line 21   T. Mozley, *Reminiscences, chiefly of Oriel College and the Oxford Movement* (1882 edn), 1, 179.
page 52, line 24   Tuckwell, *Reminiscences*, 46.
page 52, line 33   Ibid., 129.
page 53, line 8   W. Tuckwell, *Pre-Tractarian Oxford* (1909), 34.
page 53, line 9   Watson, 18 Apr. 1856
page 53, line 14   D. W. Rannie, *Oriel College* (1900), 176.
page 53, line 19   Bodleian MS Eng. Misc. b. 73, f. 48.
page 53, line 22   Ibid., e. 590, f. 100.
page 53, line 28   Ibid., d. 649, f. 156. This was Nicholas Ross, who described himself as 'A walking fire for the cause of Hawker of Morwenstow'. Ibid., f. 169.
page 54, line 2   Ibid., e. 590–95, *passim*.
page 54, line 9   Watson, 3 Nov. 1861.
page 54, line 23   Ibid., 28 Mar. 1858.
page 54, line 27   His testimony about whether he had known the leaders of the Oxford Movement is contradictory. Compare Byles, 19, where Hawker claims to remember 'the faces and words' of Newman, Pusey, Ward and Marriott, who were 'in the common room every evening discussing, talking, reading', with Watson, 18 Mar. 1860, where Hawker says, 'I never read more than two sermons by Dr Pusey and only know him and his comates by repute.' Newman recorded that he had never seen Hawker, though they later corresponded briefly. Hawker could not have seen Ward, since he went up to Oxford after Hawker had left.
page 55, line 4   Watson, 19 Oct. 1855.
page 55, line 18   G. Murray, 'The Oxford Ars Poetica: or, How to Write a Newdigate', in G. Gordon (ed.), *Three Oxford Ironies* (1927), 135.
page 55, line 22   Ibid., 171.

page 55, line 29   T. B. Macaulay, 'Pompeii', in *Cambridge Prize Poems* (1828), 109.

page 55, line 32   Hawker, *Cornish Ballads*, 8.

page 56, line 6   E. Bulwer Lytton (trans.), *The Poems and Ballads of Schiller* (1844), I, 77ff.

page 56, line 11   Byles, 420.

page 56, line 29   *Athenaeum* (21 Nov. 1891), 686–7.

page 56, line 33   Byles, 33ff.

page 57, line 1   Hawker, *Cornish Ballads*, 1.

page 57, line 27   Byles, 24.

page 58, line 10   Hawker, *Footprints*, 244.

page 58, line 18   Bodleian MS Eng. Misc. e. 591, f. 105.

page 58, line 22   Ibid., f. 77. The phrase comes from Wordsworth, 'Airey-force Valley', line 14. Some of the notes in Hawker's 'Thought Books' are quotation and these are rarely acknowledged. I have generally tried to avoid reproducing thoughts which I know or suspect are not Hawker's own. Where this practice has not been followed, I have attributed quotations to their original authors – some, of course, I may have missed.

page 58, line 23   Ibid., f. 85.

page 58, line 24   Byles, 21.

page 59, line 1   Ibid., 39.

page 59, line 5   Bodleian MS Eng. Misc. e. 595, f. 76.

page 59, line 10   Ibid., e. 591, f. 59. The lines are taken, slightly misquoted and without acknowledgment, from Wordsworth's 'Ode to a Skylark'.

Chapter 4

page 60, line 4   G. C. B. Davies, *Henry Phillpotts Bishop of Exeter, 1778–1869* (1954), 121–2.

page 60, line 9   Watson, 3 Nov. 1861.

page 60, line 12   L. Dimier, 'Quelques Traits Inédits de Hawker Vicaire de Morwenstow', *Times Literary Supplement* (17 Feb. 1921), 108.

page 60, line 16   Byles, 34.

page 61, line 3   Watson, 19 Mar. 1865.

page 61, line 10   Byles, 35.

page 61, line 20   Ibid., 40.

page 61, line 28   Watson, 24 Mar. 1856.

page 62, line 18   Ibid., 24 Dec. 1856.

page 62, line 25   Byles, 440.

page 63, line 14   W. G. V. Balchin, *The Making of the English Landscape: Cornwall* (1954), 54.

page 63, line 20   J. E. B. Gover, 'Placenames of Cornwall' II, 18, in Cornwall County Record Office, Davies Gilbert suggested 'St. Morwen' in *The Parochial History of Cornwall* (1838), III, 254.

page 63, line 23   See F. E. Halliday, *A History of Cornwall* (1959), 93.

page 63, line 33   Hawker, *Footprints*, 6–8.

page 64, line 2   A. Wallis (ed.), *The Poetical Works of Robert Stephen Hawker M.A.* (1899), 47. For its subsequent history see Martyn, *Morwenstowe Church*.

page 64, line 8   E. G. Sandford (ed.), *Memoirs of Archbishop Temple* (1906), I, 262.

page 64, line 14   Halliday, *History of Cornwall*, 98.

page 64, line 21   P. Penn (ed.), *Cornish Notes and Queries* (1906), 103–4.

page 64, line 22   *Chambers's Edinburgh Journal* (13 Nov. 1852), 317.

page 64, line 25   W. J. Townsend, H. B. Workman and G. Eayrs (eds), *A New History of Methodism* (1909), I, 513.

page 65, line 1   W. Marshall, *The Review and Abstracts of the County Reports to the Board of Agriculture* (1818), v, 525.

page 65, line 9   A. Gibson (ed.), *Early Tours in Devon and Cornwall* (Newton Abbot, 1967), originally edited in 1918 by R. Pearse Chope, 170.

page 65, line 10   Balchin, *Cornwall*, 13.

page 65, line 20   E. B. Ellman, *Recollections of a Sussex Parson* (1912), 167.

page 65, line 23   Hawker, *Footprints*, 163.

page 65, line 26   A. P. Stanley, *Life and Correspondence of Thomas Arnold D.D.* (1846 edn), 204.

page 65, line 30   W. G. Hoskins, *Devon* (Newton Abbot, 1972 edn), 152.

page 66, line 13   See H. Harris and M. Ellis, *The Bude Canal* (Newton Abbot, 1972).

page 66, line 14   Bodleian MS Eng. Lett. d. 224, f. 141.

page 66, line 17   Watson, 19 June 1864. For another complaint of the same kind see ibid., 23 Apr. 1865.

page 66, line 25   Byles, 233–4.

page 66, line 29   Watson, 30 Mar. 1862.

page 66, line 30   Ibid., 6 Apr. 1862.

page 67, line 4   Ibid., 26 July 1863.

page 67, line 20   Hawker, *Footprints*, 184–5.

page 67, line 30   A. K. Hamilton Jenkin, *Cornwall and its People* (1970 edn), 66.

page 68, line 3   Hawker, *Footprints*, 184.

page 68, line 11   Watson, 19 Mar. 1865.

page 68, line 18   J. Lawson and H. Silver, *A Social History of Education in England* (1973), 278.

page 68, line 27   Tonacombe Manor MSS, 21 Feb. 1861.

page 68, line 34   Watson, 17 May 1863.

page 68, line 34   Bodleian MS Eng. Lett. d. 224, f. 175.

page 69, line 3   Pembroke College MSS, 15 Feb. 1855.

page 69, line 7   Watson, 7 Dec. 1862.

page 69, line 9   Byles, 72.

page 69, line 10   Watson, 28 Aug. 1864.

page 69, line 20   Bodleian MS Eng. Lett. d. 226, f. 36.

page 69, line 22   Ibid., Misc. d. 650/3, f. 40. and Pembroke College MSS, 20 Mar. 1852.

page 69, line 27   See R. Polwhele, *The History of Cornwall* (1803), III, 49; R. M. Barton (ed.), *Life in Cornwall in the Early Nineteenth Century* (1970), 11 and *passim*; and R. Dew, *A History of the Parish and Church of Kilkhampton* (1926), 61.

page 69, line 29   Watson, 15 Nov. 1857.

page 69, line 34   Ibid., 23 June 1861.

page 70, line 1   Bodleian MS Eng. Lett. d. 226, f. 50.

page 70, line 3   Watson, n.d.

page 70, line 5   Ibid., 31 May 1863.

page 70, line 6   Ibid., 23 June 1863.

page 70, line 13   Ibid., 13 Aug. 1865.

page 70, line 17   Ibid., 29 Sept. 1861.

page 70, line 19   Ibid., 22 May 1864.

page 70, line 29   F. C. Hamlyn, *A History of Morwenstowe after the Restoration* (1930), 60–62.

page 70, line 31   Watson, 25 Aug. 1861.

page 71, line 5   See e.g., P. Mathias, *The First Industrial Nation* (1969), 213–26.

page 71, line 6   Watson, 15 May 1864. As far as the pig, 'Cobbett's test of labouring felicity', and the potato patch were concerned, Morwenstow was going against the national trend. See J. H. Clapham, *An Economic History of Modern Britain* (Cambridge, 1926 and 1932), I, 473 and II, 287.

page 71, line 16   Watson, 21 Aug. 1864.

page 71, line 26   Ibid., 3 Nov. 1861.

page 72, line 2   Ibid., 28 July 1861.

page 72, line 8   F. E. Halliday (ed.), *Richard Carew of Antony* (1953), 187.

page 72, line 12   See, e.g., Watson, 8 Nov. 1863, where Hawker records the death of a man 'worn out and exhausted by hard work'.

page 72, line 12   Ibid., 20 Dec. 1863. Hawker was never an entirely reliable witness but his remarks about the diet and other features of local impoverishment are interestingly confirmed in a detailed, scholarly study of a parish only fifteen miles from Morwenstow: J. S. Taylor, 'Poverty in a West

Devon parish (Bradford)', *Report and Transactions of the Devonshire Association*, CI (Torquay, 1969), 173–5.

page 72, line 18 See C. Singer and E. A. Underwood, *A Short History of Medicine* (Oxford, 1962 edn), 193.

page 72, line 21 F. G. Heath, *Peasant Life in the West of England* (1880), 276–7.

page 73, line 14 Watson, 25 Feb. 1866.

page 73, line 21 Bodleian MS Eng. Lett. d. 225, f. 158.

page 73, line 31 Ibid., f. 64.

page 74, line 6 Watson, 1 Dec. 1861.

page 74, line 11 Bodleian MS Eng. Misc. e. 592, f. 228.

page 74, line 14 Watson, 16 Oct. 1863.

page 74, line 19 [C. F. Crofton], *Bencoolen to Capricorno: A Record of Wrecks at Bude 1862–1900* (Manchester, 1902), 5.

page 74, line 26 Watson, 14 Oct. 1860.

page 75, line 19 Ibid., 4 Nov. 1857.

page 75, line 24 K. Thomas, *Religion and the Decline of Magic* (1971), 14 and 658.

page 75, line 33 Watson, 31 Aug. 1863.

page 76, line 3 Ibid., 4 Sept. 1864.

page 76, line 13 Ibid., 16 Aug. 1863.

page 76, line 33 Ibid., 27 July 1862.

page 77, line 3 Ibid., 31 July 1856.

page 77, line 7 See O. Chadwick, *The Victorian Church* (1966), I, 517.

page 77, line 13 Watson, 22 May 1864.

page 77, line 21 Ibid., 29 Dec. 1861.

page 78, line 17 J. L. and B. Hammond, *The Village Labourer* (Guild Books, 1948), II, 39.

page 78, line 18 Watson, 3 June 1860.

page 78, line 23 Bodleian MS Eng. Lett. d. 223, f. 132.

page 79, line 6 M. K. Ashby, *Joseph Ashby of Tysoe* (Cambridge, 1961), 46.

page 79, line 9 J. Arch, *The Story of his life* (1898), 16–17.

page 79, line 10 G. Kitson Clark, *Churchmen and the Condition of England 1832–1885* (1973), 11.

page 79, line 17 E. Burke, *Reflections on the Revolution in France* (1790 edn), 359.

page 79, line 31 For a good discussion of 'the classless hierarchy' see H. Perkin, *The Origins of Modern English Society 1780–1880* (1972 edn), 17–38. J. S. Taylor, in his Stanford University Ph.D. dissertation (copy in Devon Record Office), 'Poverty in Rural Devon' (1966), 265, confirms this social picture of the West Country: 'Devon society during the Industrial Revolution was largely unaffected by the forces that were destroying the paternal structure in other areas of England.'

page 80, line 7   W. J. Rowe, *Cornwall in the Age of the Industrial Revolution* (Liverpool, 1953), 246.

page 80, line 11   Watson, 10 Nov. 1861.

page 80, line 15   M. Rutherford, *The Revolution in Tanner's Lane* (9th edn, 328. n.d.),

page 80, line 18   E. P. Thompson, *The Making of the English Working Class* (1963), 40.

page 80, line 27   Bodleian MS Eng. Lett. d. 223, f. 88.

page 81, line 14   Quoted by Thompson, *Making of the English Working Class* 232.

page 81, line 18   Byles, 73 and 118–19. For an excellent discussion of the deference principle see G. Best, *Mid-Victorian Britain 1851–1875* (1971), 233ff.

page 81, line 21   Quoted by L. Cazamian, *The Social Novel in England 1830–1850* (1973 edn), 265.

page 81, line 30   J. A. Froude, *Short Studies on Great Subjects* (1894 edn), IV, 240–41.

page 82, line 10   Watson, 5 May 1864.

page 82, line 11   Hawker, *Footprints*, 104. Though he did not write these words about himself there can be no doubt that Hawker considered they applied to him.

page 82, line 18   Watson, 24 July 1864.

page 82, line 26   Ibid., 26 June 1864.

page 82, line 33   R. Jefferies, *Hodge and his Masters* (1966 edn), I, 6 and 162.

page 83, line 11   Watson, 17 Mar. 1856.

page 83, line 17   Ibid., 27 Apr. 1862.

page 83, line 21   M. Collins, *Sweet and Twenty* (1875), II, 210. That Collins was referring to Hawker is revealed in F. Collins, *Mortimer Collins: His Letters and Friendships* (1877), II, 40.

Chapter 5

page 85, line 3   Watson, 27 July 1862.

page 85, line 18   Bodleian MS Eng. Lett. d. 226, f. 111.

page 86, line 8   Watson, 17 Apr. 1856.

page 86, line 22   Byles, 75.

page 87, line 7   Watson, 25 Mar. 1860.

page 87, line 9   Byles, 77.

page 87, line 13   (1827), 4.

page 87, line 14   Ibid., 3.
page 88, line 1   Bodleian MS Eng. Misc. b. 93, f. 126. For a slightly different version see Byles, 81.
page 88, line 12   Byles, 81.
page 88, line 14   Ibid., 82.
page 88, line 15   Ibid., 78.
page 89, line 6   *First Report* of Cross Commission (1886), 5.
page 89, line 9   St Mark's School Log.
page 89, line 16   Bodleian MS Eng. Lett. d. 225, f. 55.
page 89, line 19   Watson, 6 Apr. 1862.
page 89, line 21   St Mark's Log.
page 89, line 26   Watson, 6 Feb. 1859.
page 89, line 28   Ibid., 9 Feb. 1862.
page 90, line 4   R. J. E. Boggis, *A History of the Parish and Church of St. Mary Magdalene, Barnstaple* (Canterbury, 1915), 101.
page 90, line 6   St Mark's Log.
page 90, line 19   Bodleian MS Eng. Msic. d. 650/3, f. 67.
page 90, line 22   Ibid., Theol. d. 58, f. 32.
page 90, line 27   St Mark's Log.
page 90, line 32   Ibid.
page 91, line 2   Bodleian MS Eng. Lett. d. 223, f. 98.
page 91, line 11   Cornwall County Record Office, DD. EN. 2471. Hawker to J. Blight, 8 Dec. 1857.
page 91, line 24   D. McClatchey, *Oxfordshire Clergy 1777–1869* (Oxford 1960), 143.
page 91, line 32   L. C. Sanders (ed.), *Lord Melbourne's Papers* (1889), 384.
page 92, line 1   W. L. Mathieson, *English Church Reform 1815–1840* (1923), 34.
page 92, line 4   Dean Hole, *Memories* (n.d.), 146.
page 92, line 9   Mathieson, *English Church Reform*, 32.
page 92, line 20   Bodleian MS Eng. Misc. e. 593, f. 18. Cf. Byles, 344.
page 92, line 25   Bodleian MS Eng. Misc. e. 592, f. 91.
page 92, line 28   J.-J. Rousseau, *Émile* (Everyman edn, 1957), 220.
page 93, line 1   Bodleian MS Eng. Lett. d. 226, f. 96.
page 93, line 23   Kitson Clark, *Churchmen and the Condition of England*, 101–2.
page 93, line 26   Watson, 16 June 1861.
page 93, line 28   Quoted by Lawson and Silver, *Social History of Education*, 282.
page 94, line 14   Chadwick, *The Victorian Church*, 1, 521.
page 94, line 20   Baring-Gould, 155–6.
page 94, line 25   Byles, 156.
page 94, line 30   Ibid., 144.
page 95, line 6   Ibid., 150–51.

page 95, line 32   Bodleian MS Eng. Misc. d. 650/4, f. 9.
page 96, line 6   Watson, 8 June 1857.
page 96, line 8   Ibid., 23 Aug. 1857.
page 96, line 9   Bodleian MS Eng. Lett. d. 225, f. 4.
page 96, line 14   Byles, 144.
page 96, line 19   Watson, 14 Sept. 1862.
page 96, line 26   Baring-Gould, 203.
page 96, line 30   Bodleian MS Eng. Theol. d. 58, f. 3.
page 97, line 2   Watson, 31 July 1857.
page 97, line 4   J. F. White, *The Cambridge Movement* (Cambridge, 1962), 206
Hawker must have been the 'priest in the diocese of Exeter' referred to in
Hierurgia Anglicana. He was certainly having a chasuble made for him by
an Oxford tailor as early as 1846, and he apparently began to wear it that
year. *Notes & Queries* (Apr. 1904), 278 and (May 1904), 436. See also *Western
Morning News* (17 Nov. 1894).
page 97, line 17   Byles, 129.
page 97, line 18   Bodleian MS Eng. Misc. e. 590, f. 114.
page 97, line 18   Ibid., 595, f. 158.
page 97, line 20   Ibid., e. 590, f. 164.
page 97, line 21   Ibid., e. 594, f. 47.
page 97, line 23   Ibid., Theol. d. 57, f. 10.
page 97, line 27   Ibid., Misc. d. 650/3, f. 57.
page 97, line 28   Ibid., Theol. e. 161, f. 166. This Miltonic expression was a
favourite of Hawker's.
page 97, line 34   R. S. Hawker, *Stones Broken from the Rocks*, ed. E. R. Apple-
ton and C. E. Byles (Oxford, 1922), 111.
page 98, line 1   Bodleian MS Eng. Theol. d. 58, f. 68.
page 98, line 4   Ibid., f. 12.
page 98, line 7   Ibid., e. 161, f. 125.
page 98, line 13   *Stones*, 115.
page 98, line 14   Ibid., 114.
page 98, line 22   Byles, 206-7.
page 98, line 25   Ibid., 560.
page 98, line 35   Ibid., 604-5.
page 99, line 2   Watson, 10 Aug. 1862.
page 99, line 6   Ibid., 17 May 1868.
page 99, line 19   *Stones*, 118.
page 99, line 27   Watson, 15 June 1856.
page 100, line 10 Ibid., 16 Nov. 1862.
page 100, line 12 Byles, 399.
page 100, line 15 Ibid., 331.

page 100, line 24   Ibid., 150.
page 101, line 8   Bodleian MS Eng. Lett. d. 223, f. 137.
page 101, line 15   Ibid., Misc. d. 650/3, f. 13.
page 101, line 30   Breton, *Hawker of Morwenstow*, 36.
page 102, line 3   Watson, 3 July 1856.
page 102, line 4   Ibid.
page 102, line 16   A. Chandler, *A Dream of Order: The Medieval Ideal in Nineteenth-Century English Literature* (1971), passim.

Chapter 6

page 103, line 18   Bodleian MS Eng. Theol. e. 161, f. 20.
page 103, line 23   Quoted by Chadwick, *The Victorian Church*, 1, 353.
page 104, line 2   Bodleian MS Eng. Misc. e. 593, f. 181.
page 104, line 12   *The Times* (15 Nov. 1844), 4.
page 105, line 1   Cazamian, *The Social Novel in England*, 175.
page 105, line 6   Watson, 30 Nov. 1862.
page 105, line 8   Ibid., 7 Dec. 1862.
page 105, line 10   Ibid., 8 Nov. 1868.
page 105, line 29   *English Churchman* (24 Oct. 1844), 671.
page 107, line 7   *The Times* (15 Nov. 1844), 4.
page 107, line 20   Ibid. (25 Nov. 1844), 5.
page 108, line 3   Quoted by H. House, *The Dickens World* (1941), 73.
page 108, line 18   *The Times* (25 Nov. 1844), 5.
page 109, line 3   Byles, 175.
page 109, line 7   Ibid., 176.
page 110, line 1   M. Blaug, 'The Myth of the Old Poor Law and the Making of the New', *Journal of Economic History*, XXIII (June 1963), 177.
page 110, line 9   Byles, 224.
page 110, line 18   H. Spencer, *An Autobiography* (1904), 1, 30.
page 110, line 22   Bodleian MS Eng. Lett. d. 226, f. 106.
page 110, line 25   Ibid.
page 110, line 35   Ibid., 225, f. 185.
page 111, line 6   Ibid., f. 190.
page 111, line 16   Watson, 16 Mar. 1862 and n.d.
page 111, line 16   Ibid., 9 Dec. 1866. Actually the Tonacombe estate comprised more than 700 acres, to the Duchy of Cornwall's 400-plus. The Thynnes owned over 3,000 acres.
page 111, line 19   Ibid.9, 17 Mar. 1867.
page 111, line 30   Ibid., 29 Jan. 1865.

page 111, line 32   Ibid., 12 July 1863.
page 112, line 1   Baring-Gould, 68.
page 112, line 10   Watson, 1 Nov. 1863.
page 112, line 14   Bodleian MS Eng. Lett. d. 226, f. 45.
page 112, line 21   Byles, 227.
page 113, line 2   W. Tuckwell, *Reminiscences of a Radical Parson* (1905), 38.
page 113, line 5   L. Jenyns, *Memoir of the Rev. John Stevens Henslow* (1862), 91
page 113, line 7   Heath, *Peasant Life in the West of England*, 90.
page 113, line 14   R. S. Hawker, *Echoes of Old Cornwall* (1846), 47. Annotation
in Hawker's hand in the Truro Library copy.
page 113, line 26   Watson, 19 Oct. 1855.
page 113, line 30   Wallis, *Poetical Works of Hawker*, 61–5.
page 114, line 10   Watson, 19 Feb. 1865.
page 114, line 14   Bodleian MS Eng. Misc. e. 590, f. 75.
page 114, line 18   Ashby, *Joseph Ashby of Tysoe*, 206.
page 115, line 4   F. G. Heath, *The English Peasantry* (1874), 235.
page 115, line 11   M. A. Crowther, *Church Embattled* (Newton Abbot, 1970),
7 and 242.
page 115, line 12   A. Tindal Hart, *The Country Priest in English History* (1959),
67.
page 115, line 22   Watson, 29 Dec. 1867.
page 115, line 28   Bodleian MS. Eng. Misc. e. 592, f. 126.
page 115, line 30   Ibid., Lett. d. 225, f. 68.
page 116, line 3   Watson, 10 Nov. 1861.
page 116, line 8   Bodleian MS Eng. Lett. d. 223, f. 107.
page 116, line 9   Byles, 310.
page 116, line 17   Tonacombe Mnaor MSS, 2 Mar. 1871.
page 116, line 24   Bodleian MS Eng. Lett. e. 96, f. 6.
page 116, line 30   Byles, 120.
page 116, line 35   Baring-Gould, 74.
page 117, line 9   A. J. C. Hare, *Memorials of a Quiet Life* (1884 edn), II, 81.
page 117, line 12   A. J. C. Hare. *The Years with Mother*, ed. M. Barnes (1952),
35.
page 117, line 15   Watson, 18 Apr. 1856.
page 117, line 17   Ibid., 12 July 1863.
page 117, line 18   Ibid., 21 Dec. 1862.
page 117, line 20   Ibid., 29 Jan. 1865.
page 117, line 31   Pembroke College MSS, 2 Oct. 1855.
page 118, line 5   Watson, 29 Dec. 1869.
page 118, line 13   Bodleian MS Eng. Lett. d. 225, f. 203.
page 118, line 23   E. Huxley (compiler), *The Kingsleys* (1973), 37.

page 119, line 1   Watson, 30 Nov. 1862.
page 119, line 13   Bodleian MS Eng. Lett. d. 226, f. 120.

Chapter 7

page 120, line 12   Watson, 18 Apr. 1856.
page 121, line 1   Watson, 24 Apr. 1864.
page 121, line 9   B.M. Add. MSS 37826, ff. 42–50.
page 121, line 16   W. Page (ed.), *The Victoria County History of Cornwall* (1906). 1, 3.
page 121, line 20   Quoted by S. H. Burton, *The Coasts of Cornwall* (1955), 78.
page 121, line 22   A. G. Folliott-Stokes, *The Cornish Coast and Moors* (1912), 38.
page 121, line 25   Wallis, *Poetical Works of Hawker*, 47.
page 121, line 30   Hawker, *Footprints*, 213.
page 122, line 2   Byles, 167.
page 122, line 7   R. Duncan, *Devon and Cornwall* (1966), 178. Part of Duncan's account of Hawker is inaccurate, however. Tennyson did not stay at Hawker's vicarage 'on several occasions' (177). He visited Morwenstow once.
page 122, line 11   Watson, 2 Feb. 1868.
page 122, line 18   Hawker, *Footprints*, 202.
page 122, line 20   Byles, 319.
page 122, line 31   Watson, 16 Nov. 1862.
page 123, line 6   Hawker, *Footprints*, 190. For the interesting legend of Coppinger, as retailed by Hawker, see 125–44.
page 123, line 16   Byles, 63.
page 123, line 19   Halliday, *History of Cornwall*, 261.
page 123, line 19   Penn, *Cornish Notes and Queries*, 282.
page 124, line 1   Hawker, *Footprints*, 191–2.
page 124, line 16   Ibid., 204.
page 124, line 20   Wallis, *Poetical Works of Hawker*, 101.
page 125, line 2   Hawker, *Footprints*, 207.
page 125, line 7   Ibid., 210–11.
page 126, line 16   Ibid., 216.
page 126, line 30   Byles, 445.
page 127, line 3   Wallis, *Poetical Works of Hawker*, 125.
page 127, line 12   Ibid., 69.
page 127, line 12   J. H. Newman, *Sermons Chiefly on the Theory of Religious Beliefs* (1843), 350.
page 127, line 11   *Stones*, 44.

page 127, line 16   Ibid., 112.
page 127, line 23   Wallis, *Poetical Works of Hawker*, 134.
page 128, line 4   Byles, 395–6.
page 128, line 29   Watson, 31 Oct. 1862.
page 128, line 33   [Crofton], *Bencoolen to Capricorno*, 68.
page 129, line 4   Wallis, *Poetical Works of Hawker*, 169–70.
page 129, line 15   Bodleian MS Eng. Misc. d. 650/3, ff. 21–2.
page 131, line 3   Watson, 16 Nov. 1862.
page 131, line 11   Ibid., 15 Dec. 1861.
page 131, line 15   Bodleian MS Eng. Misc. e. 590, f. 55.
page 131, line 16   Ibid., e. 591, f. 68.
page 131, line 18   Watson, 19 May 1861.
page 131, line 19   Ibid., 20 Apr. 1857.
page 131, line 24   Ibid., 26 July 1863.
page 131, line 27   Ibid., 8 Nov. 1863.
page 132, line 10   Bodleian MS Eng. Misc. d. 650/3, f. 16.
page 133, line 2   Watson, 26 July 1863. Some details in this account differ
from those in Hawker's letter to Godwin. See Boyles, 459–62.
page 134, line 2   Byles, 463–4.
page 134, line 16   Ibid., 465.
page 134, line 20   Ibid., 483.
page 134, line 23   Watson, 1 Mar. 1868.
page 134, line 30   Byles, 582.
page 134, line 34   Ibid., 487.
page 135, line 1   Watson, 30 June 1867.
page 135, line 9   Byles, 532.
page 135, line 14   Pembroke College MSS, 11 Apr. 1860.
page 135, line 22   Watson, 25 Nov. 1860.
page 135, line 24   Ibid., 10 Sept. 1864.
page 135, line 25   Ibid., 24 Nov. 1861.

Chapter 8

page 136, line 12   Hawker, *Footprints*, 103–5.
page 137, line 9   R. J. E. Boggis, *I Remember* (Exeter, 1947), 185.
page 137, line 11   *The Book of Plymouth* (Plymouth, 1938), 173.
page 137, line 14   Halliday, *History of Cornwall*, 302.
page 137, line 17   D. Du Maurier, *Vanishing Cornwall* (1967). For this and
other examples of eccentric Cornish clergymen see 133–40.
page 137, line 18   Rowse, *A Cornish Childhood*, 134.

page 137, line 29   C. K. F. Brown, *A History of the English Clergy 1800–1900* (1953), 153.
page 137, line 31   Hart, *The Country Priest in English History*, 103.
page 138, line 9   Bodleian MS Eng. Lett. d. 226, f. 126.
page 138, line 18   R. M. Barton (ed.), *Life in Cornwall in the Mid Nineteenth Century* (1971), 182.
page 138, line 19   T. Carlyle, *Sartor Resartus* (1910 edn), 294.
page 138, line 22   Bodleian MS Eng. Misc. e. 592, f. 208.
page 138, line 30   Ibid., Lett. d. 223, f. 22.
page 139, line 3   Watson, 15 Oct. 1865.
page 139, line 9   Ibid., 2 Dec. 1860 and 22 May 1864.
page 139, line 10   Bodleian MS Eng. Misc. e. 592, f. 184.
page 139, line 14   Byles, 530.
page 139, line 20   Ibid., 83.
page 139, line 27   Bodleian MS Eng. Misc. d. 650/4, f. 6.
page 139, line 32   Watson, 23 Aug. 1857.
page 140, line 7   Byles, 84.
page 140, line 8   Ibid., 86.
page 140, line 10   *New York Times* (1 Apr. 1973).
page 140, line 17   Byles, 83–4.
page 140, line 25   Bodleian MS Eng. Misc. b. 93, f. 67.
page 140, line 27   Ibid., Lett. e. 96, f. 42.
page 140, line 30   Ibid., d. 224, f. 130.
page 141, line 6   Donovan, *After the Tractarians*, 33.
page 141, line 14   Kelly MSS, 8 May.
page 142, line 6   Watson, 6 Jan. 1861.
page 142, line 7   Bodleian MS Eng. Misc. e. 594, f. 22.
page 142, line 9   Ibid., d. 650/3, f. 58.
page 142, line 26   Watson, 6 Jan. 1861.
page 142, line 28   Ibid., n.d.
page 142, line 33   Bodleian MS Eng. Misc. d. 650/4, f. 9.
page 143, line 5   Watson, 24 Nov. 1861.
page 143, line 10   *The Times* (8 Apr. 1959), 11.
page 143, line 20   Watson, 24 Nov. 1861.
page 143, line 22   A. H. D. Acland (ed.), *Memoir and Letters of Sir Thomas Dyke Acland* (1902), 306.
page 143, line 24   Hart, *The Country Priest in English History*, 110.
page 143, line 28   Rowse, *Essays and Studies*, XII, 107.
page 143, line 32   Byles, 102–3.
page 144, line 3   Bodleian MS Eng. Misc. d. 650/4, f. 9.
page 144, line 13   Watson, 14 Mar. 1858.

page 144, line 15 Ibid., 1 Jan. 1857.
page 144, line 27 Byles, 99.
page 147, line 34 Bodleian MS Eng. Misc. d. 650/4, f. 9.
page 145, line 10 Ibid., Lett. d. 223, f. 113.
page 145, line 14 Ibid., Misc. d. 650/4, f. 6.
page 145, line 20 Watson, 26 June 1864.
page 145, line 21 Bodleian MS Eng. Misc. d. 650/4, f. 2. Cf. Byles, 101.
page 145, line 28 Watson, 26 June 1864.
page 145, line 29 Byles, 99.
page 146, line 5 Bodleian MS Eng. Misc. e. 592, f. 135.
page 146, line 10 Watson, 26 Feb. 1865.
page 146, line 12 Ibid., 20 Jan. 1867.
page 146, line 18 Bodleian MS Eng. Misc. b. 93, f. 106.
page 146, line 26 Ibid., Lett. d. 225, f. 136.
page 146, line 29 Ibid., Misc. e. 591, f. 136.
page 147, line 2 J. M. Campbell, *Dentistry Then and Now* (Glasgow, 1963), 238.
page 147, line 13 Watson, 10 Mar. 1861.
page 147, line 17 Ibid., 17 July 1864.
page 147, line 26 Ibid., 21 Aug.
page 147, line 33 H. Tennyson, *Alfred Lord Tennyson* (1897), I, 274.
page 148, line 4 Kelly MSS, 15 July 1862.
page 148, line 9 Lee, *Memorials of Hawker*, 50.
page 148, line 13 Bodleian MS Eng. Lett. d. 233, f. 113.
page 148, line 19 Byles, 92.
page 148, line 23 Watson, 31 Aug. 1862.
page 148, line 28 Pembroke College MSS, 26 Mar. 1861.
page 149, line 2 Bodleian MS Eng. Misc. d. 650/4, f. 9.
page 149, line 3 Ibid., Lett. d. 233, f. 114.
page 149, line 7 Tonacombe Manor MSS, 'Recollections' (1926).
page 149, line 14 *Western Morning Mercury* (25 Aug. 1875).
page 149, line 26 Collins, *Sweet and Twenty*, II, 215.
page 149, line 33 Bodleian MS Eng. Misc. d. 650/4, ff. 6–7.
page 150, line 33 *Western Morning Mercury* (25 Aug. 1875).
page 151, line 16 Watson, 19 Feb. 1865.
page 151, line 20 25 Feb. 1866.
page 151, line 21 8 Dec. 1867.
page 151, line 23 31 Dec. 1865.
page 151, line 24 20 Apr. 1857.
page 151, line 24 13 Nov. 1864.
page 151, line 27 Byles, 489.

page 151, line 32   Bodleian MS Eng. Misc. d. 650/3, f. 30.
page 152, line 14   Watson, 21 May 1865.
page 152, line 27   Bodleian MS Eng. Misc. d. 650/4, f. 9.
page 153, line 8   Quoted by Byles, 185.
page 153, line 33   Watson, 8 May 1867.
page 154, line 5   Collins, *Sweet and Twenty*, III, 227.
page 154, line 9   Watson, 18 Mar. 1858.
page 154, line 12   Byles, 100.
page 154, line 17   Bodleian MS Eng. Misc. d. 650/3, f. 19.
page 154, line 23   Lee, *Memorials of Hawker*, 62.
page 155, line 5   *Utilitarianism, Liberty and Representative Government* (Everyman edn, 1960), 124–5.
page 155, line 14   Bodleian MS Eng. Misc. e. 592, f. 167.
page 155, line 21   See the too schematic analysis of Hawker's character which mars M. F. Burrows's generally admirable book. She explains that 'all the anomalies in his character . . . and his eccentricities fall into place [when it is seen that] ... he was at once a mystic and an artist [who] ... failed to bring the two sides of his character into harmony with each other [and] ... was torn in two by the conflict.' (*Hawker*, 48–9).

Chapter 9

page 157, line 31   R. S. Hawker, *Rural Synods* (1844), 24.
page 157, line 33   Letter from Dr C. D. Peters to me, 22 Oct. 1973.
page 157, line 35   Pembroke College MSS, 3 Sept. 1854.
page 158, line 18   Byles, 327 and 574.
page 158, line 33   21 Feb. 1858.
page 159, line 6   Bodleian MS Eng. Misc. e. 590, f. 74.
page 159, line 10   1 Sept. and 3 Dec. 1840.
page 159, line 19   Watson, 22 Mar. 1863.
page 159, line 23   28 Jan.
page 159, line 29   Watson, 26 Jan. 1862.
page 160, line 6   3 July 1864.
page 160, line 11   Watson, 24 Aug. 1862.
page 160, line 12   Ibid., 29 Nov. 1863.
page 160, line 14   Ibid., 9 July 1865.
page 160, line 17   Ibid., 4 Nov. 1866.
page 160, line 18   Bodleian MS Eng. Lett. d. 225, f. 51.
page 160, line 27   Watson, 3 July 1864.
page 160, line 32   Ibid., 28 Jan. 1866.
page 161, line 3   16 June.

page 161, line 6   Bodleian MS Eng. Lett. d. 223, f. 88.
page 161, line 10   Watson, 10 Mar.
page 162, line 13   Ibid., 11 Nov. 1860.
page 162, line 18   Ibid., 14 June 1863.
page 162, line 22   Bodleian MS Eng. Lett. d. 225, f. 14.
page 162, line 26   Watson, 15 Aug. 1858.
page 163, line 5   Ibid., 11 Nov. 1860.
page 163, line 15   Pembroke College MSS, 20 Mar., 5 Apr. and 3 May 1852.
page 163, line 28   Bodleian MS Eng. Misc. d. 650/3, f. 22.
page 163, line 32   Ibid., f. 26.
page 163, line 33   Watson, 29 Mar.
page 164, line 4   Pembroke College MSS, 20 Mar. 1852.
page 164, line 10   F. C. C. Atkin, *The Parish Church of St. Michael and All Angels, Bude Haven* (1935), 47.
page 164, line 17   9 Feb.
page 164, line 20   Bodleian MS. Eng. Lett. d. 224, f. 162.
page 164, line 29   Watson, 27 Apr. 1862.
page 165, line 11   J. J. Hecht, *The Domestic Servant Class in Eighteenth-Century England* (1956), 74–5.
page 165, line 12   Watson, 3 May 1863.
page 165, line 14   Bodleian MS Eng. Lett. d. 223, f. 115.
page 165, line 32   Watson, 29 Mar. 1868.
page 165, line 33   Ibid., 7 May 1857.
page 166, line 1   Ibid., 31 May 1863.
page 166, line 5   Ibid., 5 Mar. 1862.
page 166, line 12   Ibid., 7 May 1859.
page 166, line 14   Pembroke College MSS, 28 May.
page 166, line 17   Ibid., 24 Feb.
page 166, line 28   Ibid., 28 July.
page 167, line 10   11 Nov. 1841.
page 167, line 13   K. Thomas, 'The Double Standard', *Journal of the History of Ideas*, xx (1959), 206.
page 167, line 22   M. Hewitt, *Wives and Mothers in Victorian Industry* (1958), 53.
page 168, line 4   Watson, 23 June 1861.
page 168, line 8   Bodleian MS Eng. Misc. d. 650/3, f. 47.
page 168, line 15   Watson, 31 May 1863.
page 168, line 24   Byles, 387.
page 168, line 31   Ibid., 153 and 528.
page 168, line 33   Lee, *Memorials of Hawker*, 48.

page 169, line 4   Bodleian MS Eng. Misc. e. 597, f. 26.
page 169, line 24   *Making of the English Working Class*, 368. It was not, however, an entirely original insight. See, e.g., D.L. Purves (ed.), *The Works of Jonathan Swift* (1889), 81, and D. P. Walker, *The Decline of Hell* (1964), 257.
page 169, line 26   W. James, *The Varieties of Religious Experience* (1919 edn), 11.
page 169, line 32   S. G. Dimond, *The Psychology of the Methodist Revival* (1926), 193–4.
page 169, line 34   S. Freud, *Moses and Monotheism* (1939), 183ff.
page 170, line 5   T. Shaw, *The Bible Christians 1815–1907* (1965), 85.
page 170, line 8   Baring-Gould, 146.
page 170, line 15   Shaw, *Bible Christians*, 85.
page 170, line 16   Ibid., 86.
page 170, line 17   Townsend, Workman and Eayrs, *History of Methodism*, I, 511.
page 170, line 23   Watson, 28 Oct. 1860.
page 170, line 25   G. H. Schofield, *The History of Methodism in Stratton and Bude* (Bude, 1922), 7.
page 170, line 34   Shaw, *Bible Christians*, 78.
page 171, line 6   Townsend, Workman and Eayrs, *History of Methodism*, I, 510.
page 171, line 18   E. J. Hobsbawm and G. Rudé, *Captain Swing* (1969), 187.
page 171, line 23   *Stones*, 101.
page 171, line 28   Townsend, Workman and Eayrs, *History of Methodism*, I 511.
page 171, line 34   Byles, 155.
page 172, line 4   M. Cook (ed.), 'The Diocese of Exeter in 1821', *Devon and Cornwall Record Society*, III (1958), 36.
page 172, line 12   Pembroke College MSS, 28 July 1856.
page 172, line 20   Ibid., 2 June 1854
page 172, line 25   Bodleian MS Eng. Lett. d. 226, f. 50.
page 173, line 5   Pembroke College MSS, n.d.
page 173, line 23   Byles, 604, 146–7 and 155.
page 173, line 27   M. Ward, *Robert Browning and His World: The Private Face* (1968), 26.
page 173, line 29   *Praeterita* (1949 edn), 245.
page 173, line 31   E. Gosse, *Father and Son* (1932 edn), 69.
page 174, line 18   Watson, 13 Aug. 1865.

Chapter 10

page 175, line 15   Quoted by R. Ellmann, *Golden Codgers* (1973), 1.
page 175, line 20   Fr. Rolfe, *Hadrian the Seventh* (1929 edn), 379.
page 176, line 2   Pembroke College MSS, 15 Feb. 1855.
page 176, line 13   F. C. Redlich and D. X. Freedman, *The Theory and Practice of Psychiatry* (New York, 1966), 482.
page 176, line 31   'The Fascination of the Paranoid Personality' in C. Woolf and B. Sewell (eds), *New Quests for Corvo* (Aylesford, 1961), 8.
page 177, line 6   See A. J. A. Symons, *The Quest for Corvo* (1955 edn) and D. Weeks, *Corvo* (1971), *passim.*
page 177, line 10   B. Fothergill, 'Rolfe and Benson' in Woolf and Sewell (eds), *Corvo*, 47.
page 177, line 22   Symons, *Quest for Corvo*, 190.
page 177, line 23   Watson, 15 Nov. 1857.
page 177, line 27   Pembroke College MSS, 15 Dec. 1854.
page 177, line 30   C. Woolf (ed.), *The Centenary Edition of the Letters of Frederick William Rolfe* (1962), III, 164.
page 178, line 8   Pembroke College MSS, 2 June 1854.
page 178, line 22   Ibid., undated fragment.
page 179, line 7   Ibid., 25 Oct. 1850.
page 179, line 19   Woolf, *Letters of Rolfe*, III, 164.
page 179, line 21   Watson, 18 March.
page 180, line 1   Pembroke College MSS, 10 April, and Byles, 108.
page 180, line 21   Pembroke College MSS, 28 July 1856 and undated fragment.
page 180, line 28   Exeter Public Library. Hawker to Editor of *Blackwood's Magazine*, 3 Jan. 1858.
page 180, line 31   Bodleian MS Eng. Lett. d. 224, f. 58.
page 181, line 3   Woolf, *Letters of Rolfe*, II, 35.
page 181, line 6   Byles, 589.
page 181, line 12   G. O. Trevelyan, *The Life and Letters of Lord Macaulay* (1895 edn), 518.
page 181, line 20   Bodleian MS Eng. Lett. d. 224, f. 139.
page 181, line 26   His emphasis. Woolf, *Letters of Rolfe*, II, 46.
page 181, line 27   Bodleian MS Eng. Lett. d. 224, f. 57.
page 181, line 32   Truro Library, 29 Jan. Cf. M. Williams who says, quite wrongly, that Hawker 'became one of the best-known, most talked-about clerics in the kingdom'. *Following the Famous in Cornwall* (Camborne, n.d.), 3. See also C. Woolf, 'Some Uncollected Authors XXXIX: Hawker of Morwenstow', *Book Collector*, XIV, no. 1. (Spring 1965), 63. Woolf explains

that Hawker's long neglect was chiefly caused by the fact that his work was never properly brought before the public. If so, it was certainly not for his want of trying.

page 182, line 13 Bodleian MS Eng. Lett. d. 223, ff. 15/16 and 32.
page 182, line 19 Watson, 10 May 1868.
page 182, line 24 Ibid., 6 June 1861.
page 182, line 26 Ibid., 4 May and 31 July 1858.
page 182, line 32 Pembroke College MSS, 19 May.
page 183, line 13 Watson, 8 May 1864.
page 183, line 20 Ibid., 31 Dec. 1865.
page 183, line 23 Letter to John Wickett, Stratton druggist, 1 Aug. 1838, in my possession.
page 184, line 1 Symons, *Quest for Corvo*, 214.
page 184, line 4 Pembroke College MSS, Postmark 1 April 1854.
page 184, line 13 Watson, 11 Dec. 1864.
page 184, line 18 Ibid., 6 July 1862.
page 184, line 20 Bodleian MS Eng. Lett. d. 224, f. 166.
page 184, line 21 7 Feb. 1869.
page 184, line 22 Bodleian MS Eng. Lett. d. 224, f. 108.
page 184, line 27 Ibid., d. 225, f. 79.
page 184, line 28 Byles, 267.
page 184, line 30 9 Feb. 1862.
page 184, line 34 Bodleian MS Eng. Lett. e. 96, f. 20.
page 185, line 4 Watson, 18 Aug. 1861 and 16 Oct. 1863.
page 185, line 17 Fr. Rolfe, *Don Renato*, ed. C. Woolf (1963), 15.
page 185, line 20 Bodleian MS Eng. Lett. d. 223, f. 77.
page 185, line 21 Ibid., f. 82.
page 185, line 22 Pembroke College MSS, undated fragment.
page 185, line 23 Bodleian MS Eng. Misc. e. 595, f. 116.
page 185, line 28 Ibid., Eng. Lett. d. 224, f. 103.
page 185, line 29 Ibid., d. 223, f. 6.
page 185, line 31 Ibid., f. 71.
page 185, line 32 Pembroke College MSS, undated fragment.
page 185, line 34 Bodleian MS Eng. Lett. d. 123, f. 36.
page 186, line 1 Ibid., d. 223, f. 6.
page 186, line 5 Ibid., f. 25.
page 186, line 11 Symons, *Quest for Corvo*, 60.
page 186, line 13 27 Apr. 1862 and 1 Mar. 1863.
page 186, line 24 Ibid., 14 Feb.
page 186, line 29 D. Weeks (ed.), *Baron Corvo: Letters to James Walsh* (1972), 21.

page 186, line 31   Ibid., 16.
page 187, line 1   Byles, 283.
page 187, line 4   Ibid., 328.
page 187, line 7   Watson, 30 May 1858.
page 187, line 14   L. E. Hinsie and R. J. Campbell, *Psychiatric Dictionary* (Oxford, 1970 edn), 623.
page 187, line 20   Bodleian MS Eng. Lett. d. 224, f. 131.
page 187, line 21   Ibid., 225, f. 90.
page 187, line 23   Pembroke College MSS, 30 Nov. 1854.
page 187, line 26   16 June 1863 and 15 Dec. 1861.
page 187, line 30   Bodleian MS Eng. Misc. d. 650/3, f. 41.
page 187, line 34   Byles, 188.
page 188, line 2   Watson, 2 Feb. 1862.
page 188, line 4   12 Jan.
page 188, line 12   Ibid., 20 July.
page 188, line 27   Byles, 188.
page 188, line 29   Watson, 24 Sept. 1864.
page 188, line 33   Ibid., 2 June 1867.
page 189, line 3   Pembroke College MSS, 15 Dec. 1854.
page 189, line 14   26 Feb. 1865.
page 189, line 14   Ibid., 19 Apr. 1868.
page 189, line 22   Weeks, *Corvo: Letters to Walsh*, 37.
page 189, line 24   Pembroke College MSS, 25 Feb. 1852.
page 190, line 21   Bodleian MS Eng. Lett. d. 226, f. 130.
page 191, line 32   B.M. Add. MSS 44382, f. 322.
page 192, line 2   Bodleian MS Eng. Misc. d. 650/3, f. 102.
page 192, line 6   Weeks, *Corvo: Letters to Walsh*, 25.
page 192, line 9   5 May.
page 192, line 18   Bodleian MS Eng. Lett. d. 226, f. 106.
page 192, line 18   Ibid., d. 225, f. 20.
page 192, line 24   Ibid., f. 132.
page 192, line 25   Ibid., f. 99.
page 192, line 31   Ibid., f. 76.
page 193, line 19   Watson, 25 Apr. 1857.
page 193, line 25   Symons, *Quest for Corvo*, 222.
page 193, line 31   E. H. Coleridge (ed.), *Letters of Samuel Taylor Coleridge* (1895 edn), I, 240. Quoted by M. Abrams, *The Milk of Paradise* (New York, 1970 edn), 3.

Chapter 11

page 194, line 11   Bodleian MS Eng. Misc. d. 649, f. 99.
page 194, line 14   Baring-Gould, 218.
page 195, line 5   Byles, 102.
page 195, line 14   A. Hayter, reviewing M. Lefebure, *Samuel Taylor Coleridge: A Bondage of Opium* (1974), *New Statesman* (26 July 1974), 123.
page 195, line 18   E. Schneider, *Coleridge, Opium and Kubla Khan* (Chicago, 1953), 37.
page 196, line 1   A. Hayter, *Opium and the Romantic Imagination* (1971 edn), 39.
page 196, line 4   Bodleian MS Eng. Misc. e. 592, f. 150.
page 196, line 6   G. Woodcock, *Dawn and the Darkest Hour* (1972), 275.
page 196, line 13   Hayter, *Opium and the Romantic Imagination*, 40.
page 196, line 18   Ibid., 41.
page 196, line 24   Godwin, *Poetical Works of Hawker*, 222.
page 196, line 32   T. De Quincey, *Confessions of an English Opium Eater*, ed. A. Hayter (1971), 71.
page 197, line 13   This letter is undated but from internal evidence it seems to have been sent in January 1857.
page 197, line 14   Watson, 5 Oct. 1856.
page 197, line 18   Ibid., 8 July 1860.
page 198, line 5   Tonacombe Manor MSS, n.d.
page 198, line 19   Bodleian MS Eng. Misc. e. 590, f. 74.
page 198, line 22   Watson, 1 Mar. 1863.
page 198, line 30   Ibid., 6 Mar. 1863.
page 198, line 31   Ibid., 22 Feb. 1863.
page 199, line 5   14 June 1863.
page 199, line 27   Ibid., 3 Dec. 1858.
page 199, line 30   Ibid., 12 July 1863.
page 199, line 33   Ibid., 4 Sept. 1864.
page 199, line 34   Ibid., 30 Aug. 1863.
page 200, line 14   E.g. compare Godwin, *Poetical Works of Hawker*, 241, with Bodleian MS Eng. Misc. e. 594, f. 118.
page 200, line 21   Cf. De Quincey in Hayter, *Opium and the Romantic Imagination*, 240ff.
page 200, line 22   Heath-Stubbs, *The Darkling Plain*, 82.
page 200, line 29   Bodleian MS Eng. Theol. f. 55, f. 92.
page 200, line 30   Byles, 327.
page 200, line 31   Bodleians MS Eng. Lett. d. 225, f. 147.
page 200, line 34   Ibid., Misc. e. 596, f. 136.

page 201, line 3   Ibid., d. 224, f. 120.
page 201, line 7   Burrows, *Hawker*, 125. The same verdict is reached by C. L. Wilkinson, *The Times Literary Supplement* (20 Dec. 1934). 902.
page 201, line 15   Bodleian MS Eng. Misc. e. 590, f. 147.
page 201, line 20   *Stones.*
page 201, line 26   Bodleian MS Eng. Misc. e. 590–96, *passim.*
page 204, line 5   Lee, *Memorials of Hawker*, 103–5.
page 204, line 8   Bodleian MS Eng. Theol. f. 56, ff. 61 and 29.
page 204, line 10   *Stones*, 26 and Byles, 366.
page 204, line 11   For a disparaging, but just, assessment of Hawker as mystic see Burrows, *Hawker*, especially 107 and 117ff.
page 204, line 11   Byles, 254–5.
page 204, line 22   Bodleian MS Eng. Lett. d. 226, f. 76.
page 204, line 24   Byles, 228. Cf. Lee, *Memorials of Hawker*, 107.
page 205, line 7   Bodleian MS Eng. Theol. e. 160, f. 100.
page 205, line 24   Byles, 351.
page 205, line 25   Bodleian MS Eng. Poet. d. 191, ff. 73ff.
page 205, line 28   Kelly MSS.
page 206, line 24   See e.g., J. A. Noble, *The Sonnet in England and Other Essays* (1893), 182–211.
page 207, line 5   Godwin, *Poetical Works of Hawker*, 20.
page 207, line 25   13 Dec. 1863.
page 207, line 31   T. De Quincey, *Suspiria de Profundis*, ed. G. Saintsbury (1927), 229.
page 208, line 3   Hayter, *Opium and the Romantic Imagination*, 160.
page 208, line 10   Ibid., 51.
page 208, line 17   Godwin, *Poetical Works of Hawker*, 242.
page 208, line 20   Ibid., 229–30.
page 208, line 22   De Quincey, *Confessions*, 103.
page 208, line 24   Watson, 14 Feb. 1864.
page 209, line 6   Godwin, *Poetical Works of Hawker*, 229–30.
page 209, line 15   Ibid., 237.
page 209, line 20   Ibid., 239.
page 210, line 2   Ibid., 243.
page 210, line 6   Ibid., 241.
page 210, line 29   19 May 1861.
page 210, line 31   18 Mar. 1860.
page 211, line 1   Byles, 220.
page 211, line 33   M. J. Gifford (ed.), *Pages from the Diary of an Oxford Lady 1843–1862* (Oxford, 1932), 8–9.
page 212, line 4   B.M. Add. MSS 37 825, f. 51.

page 212, line 14 Watson, 30 August 1863.
page 212, line 17 Byles, 471.
page 212, line 25 Watson, 17 Feb. 1867.
page 212, line 26 Bodleian MS Eng. Lett. d. 224, f. 97.
page 212, line 28 De Quincey, *Confessions*, 114.
page 212, line 29 W. J. Bate. *Coleridge* (1969), 128.
page 212, line 30 J. Cocteau, *Opium: The Diary of a Cure*, translated by M
   Crosland and S. Road (1957), 56.

Chapter 12

page 213, line 6   Bodleian MS Eng. Misc. d. 650/5, f. 1.
page 213, line 11 Ibid., Lett. e. 96, f. 38.
page 213, line 19 Baring-Gould, 172.
page 213, line 21 Bodleian MS Eng. Eng. Lett. d. 223, f. 121.
page 214, line 2   Watson, n.d.
page 214, line 6   Byles, 95.
page 214, line 26 Byles, 94–5.
page 214, line 31 Bodleian MS Eng. Lett. e. 96, f. 28.
page 215, line 6   Kelly MSS, 15 July.
page 215, line 16 Bodleian MS Eng. Lett. d. 650/3, f. 17.
page 215, line 18 Ibid., d. 223, f. 141.
page 215, line 24 Byles, 258.
page 216, line 5   Nov. 1869, 664.
page 216, line 7   Byles, 607.
page 216, line 14 Ibid., 444.
page 216, line 20 Watson, 11 Oct. 1863.
page 216, line 23 Byles, 448.
page 216, line 24 Watson, 20 Oct. 1863.
page 217, line 10 Bodleian MS Eng. Misc. d. 650/2, f. 65 and Byles, 413.
page 217, line 13 Byles, 490.
page 217, line 15 Ibid., 499.
page 217, line 19 Bodleian MS Eng. Theol. f. 57, ff. 19 and 23.
page 217, line 24 Ibid., Lett. d. 223, f. 143.
page 217, line 33 B.M. Add. MSS 37825, f. 43.
page 218, line 10 Bodleian MS Eng. Misc. d. 650/3, f. 96.
page 218, line 12 Watson, 25 Dec. 1864.
page 218, line 15 Ibid., 11 Dec. 1864.
page 218, line 21 Ibid., 4 Dec. 1864.
page 218, line 28 Ibid., 1 Jan. 1865.

page 219, line 18   Byles, 504–5.
page 219, line 22   Watson, 15 Dec. 1864.
page 219, line 26   Ibid., 30 Sept. 1860.
page 220, line 1   Byles, 500–501.
page 220, line 18   Watson, 25 Dec. 1864.
page 220, line 22   Ibid., 14 Feb. 1864.
page 220, line 25   Ibid., 29 Mar. 1863.
page 220, line 26   Ibid., 22 Mar. 1863.
page 220, line 33   Ibid., 24 Apr. 1864.
page 221, line 2   Ibid., 10 Nov. 1861.
page 221, line 9   Bodleian MS Eng. Lett. d. 224, f. 100.
page 221, line 11   Ibid., f. 73.
page 221, line 15   19 Nov. 1865.
page 221, line 22   Bodleian MS Eng. Lett. d. 224, f. 185.
page 221, line 23   Ibid., f. 188.
page 222, line 1   Ibid., Misc. b. 93, f. 64.
page 222, line 2   Byles, 558.
page 222, line 4   Watson, 8 Dec. 1867.
page 222, line 8   Bodleian MS Eng. Lett. d. 225, f. 37.
page 222, line 14   Watson, 2 Feb. 1868.
page 222, line 18   Bodleian MS Eng. Lett. d. 223, f. 147.
page 222, line 24   Ibid., f. 145.
page 222, line 33   Bodleian MS Eng. Lett. d. 225, f. 42.
page 223, line 6,   Ibid., d. 226, f. 107.
page 223, line 8   4 Feb. 1866.
page 223, line 16   Bodleian MS Eng. Lett. d. 225, ff. 28 and 49.
page 223, line 22   McClatchey, *Oxfordshire Clergy*, 23.
page 223, line 29   Bodleian MS Eng. Lett. d. 226, f. 109.
page 224, line 2   Ibid., d. 225, f. 187.
page 224, line 13   Ibid., f. 180.
page 224, line 17   Ibid., f. 138.
page 224, line 23   Watson, 13 Aug. 1865.
page 224, line 24   Ibid., 16 Mar. 1862.
page 224, line 27   Ibid., 9 Feb.
page 224, line 28   Ibid., 13 May 1866.
page 224, line 31   Ibid., 29 Nov. and 2 Feb. 1868.
page 224, line 34   Ibid., 17 May 1868.
page 225, line 11   17 June 1856
page 225, line 17   Ibid., 17 Mar.
page 225, line 32   Byles, 19.
page 226, line 4   *Essays and Reviews* (1860), 369.

page 226, line 9   *Stones*, 121.
page 226, line 11   Lee, *Memorials of Hawker*, 95.
page 226, line 16   Ibid., 104–5.
page 226, line 25   J. M. Keynes, *Essays in Biography*, ed. G. Keynes (1951), 134.
page 226, line 33   Watson, 21 Feb. 1864.
page 227, line 9   P. T. Marsh, *The Victorian Church in Decline* (1969), 41 and 50
page 227, line 15   G. M. Young, *Victorian England: Portrait of an Age* (1957 edn), 76.
page 227, line 21   Byles, 623.
page 227, line 27   Byles, 235–6.
page 227, line 31   Bodleian MS Eng. Misc. e. 595, f. 116.
page 227, line 34   Ibid., f. 29.
page 228, line 3   Ibid., e. 590, f. 8 and 591. f. 101. *Stones*, 123.
page 228, line 6   Ibid., e. 595, f. 155.
page 228, line 7   Byles, 388.
page 228, line 11   Bodleian MS Eng. Lett. d. 225, f. 32.
page 228, line 18   2 June.
page 228, line 26   Bodleian MS Eng. Lett. d. 225, f. 11.
page 229, line 2   Lee, *Memorials of Hawker*, 190.
page 229, line 13   B.M. Add. MSS 37825, f. 43.,
page 229, line 26   Ibid., f. 45.
page 229, line 30   Ibid., f. 46.
page 230, line 2   Ibid., f. 53.
page 230, line 7   Baring-Gould, 231.
page 230, line 8   B.M. Add. MSS 37825, f. 54.
page 230, line 13   Bodleian MS Eng. Misc. d. 650/3, f. 96.
page 230, line 31   Ibid., Eng. Lett. d. 225, f. 132.
page 231, line 2   Ibid., f. 135.
page 231, line 5   Ibid., f. 147.
page 231, line 13   B.M. Add. MSS 37825, f. 63.
page 231, line 15   Ibid., f. 1793.
page 231, line 16   Byles, 600–601.
page 231, line 29   Bodleian MS Eng. Lett. d. 226, f. 121.
page 231, line 32   Ibid., Theol. e. 161, f. 20.
page 232, line 1   Ibid., Misc. d. 649, f. 66. The lines are from Tennyson's *In Memoriam*, xxiii.
page 232, line 4   Ibid., Eng. Lett. d. 225, f. 198.
page 232, line 20   Watson, 31 Jan. 1869.
page 232, line 22   Byles, 449.

Index

Hawker, Caroline, *see* Dinham, Caroline

Hawker, Charlotte (née I'ans), 45–9, 76, 79, 86, 99, 101, 116, 120, 156, 178, 184, 197–8, 210, 217, 223

Hawker, Claud, 26, 91, 138, 157, 182, 186, 187, 194–5, 213, 230

Hawker, Jacob Stephen, 37–8

Hawker, Jane Elizabeth (née Drewitt), 37

Hawker, John, 36–7

Hawker, Juliot, 222

Hawker, Mary, 151, 198

Hawker, Morwenna Pauline, 217, 221

Hawker, Pauline (née Kuczynski), 140, 212, 216–22, 228, 229, 230–32

Hawker, Robert, D.D., 32–6, 37–9

Hawker, Robert Stephen, 16, 26, 29–30, 64; and his age, 15, 209, 224–5; his antiquarianism, 63, 150, 158; his attitude towards servants, 164–8; and Charlotte, 45–9, 197–8; and his children, 221–2; his daily round, 120, 199; his death and fear of it, 188, 231–2; his dress and appearance, 21, 97, 138–41, 211; his eccentricity, 18, 61, 94–5, 136–47, 155, 157; his enemies, 178–9, 185–6; his farming interests, 77, 162–4; his financial troubles, 188–93, 223; his friends, 177, 184–5; his humour, 40–42, 50, 58, 173, 213–14; his inspiration drawn from nature and the sea, 39, 44, 126–7; the legend, 23–5, 27, 28; his love of animals, 69, 142–4; his medievalism, 30, 102, 141, 153–4, 209, 215; his mendacity, 210–12; his mental health, 19, 112, 134–5, 174, 175–93, 196–7, 231; and Methodism associated with sexual feeling, 167–9; his millenarianism, 34, 72, 205, 210; his mysticism, 127, 196, 204–6, 226; and his neighbours, 156–74; and opium, 194–212, 224; the patriarch, 17, 81–2, 84, 111; and Pauline, 216–20; his physical health, 75, 112, 174, 231; his poetry, 20, 44, 55–7, 113, 200, 206–10, 214; his relations with Dissenters, 80, 100, 112, 116, 170–74, 178–9; his relations with his parishioners, 67–74, 80, 90;

and his relatives, 182–3; his religious views, 54–5, 96–9, 131–2, 159–60, 225, 227–30; as 'Reuben', 44; his secession, 228–30, 232; his seclusion, 58–9, 65, 66, 67, 78, 83, 160–61, 193, 232; and shipwrecks, 121–35; his socio-economic views, 104–10, 113–114; his superstitions, 62, 131, 150–53, 205; as a thinker, 53–4, 200–204; his vicarial and pastoral labours, 60, 77, 83, 85–119; and visitors to Morwenstow, 147–50; his youth and education, 32, 36–44, 52–5

Hawker, Rosalind, 222

Hawker, Stephen, 183

Hawker, Tom, 183

Hawker, Willy, 91

Hawkins, Sir Christopher, 64

Hayter, Alethea, 195, 196, 208

Heale, Nanny, 50–51

Heath, F. G., 115

Heath-Stubbs, John, 27

Heine, H., 186

Hellia, J., 149

Hennacliff, 63, 148

Henry (schoolboy), 90

Henslow, J. S., 113

Herbert, George, 102, 202

Herrick, Robert, 61

Hingeston-Randolph, F. C., 28, 212

Hitcham, 113

Hoare family, 185

Hodson, Mary (née Hawker), 38

Hodson, Thomas, 38

Holsworthy, 40, 72, 121, 141, 147

Holy Grail, 208

Holy Trinity Church, Paddington, 219

Home and Colonial Infant School Society, 93

Hortense, Queen, 206

Hoskins, W. G., 65

Howard, Thomas, 69

Howley, Archbishop W., 92

Hunt, T. F., 87

Huxley, Aldous, 196

I'ans, Charlotte, *see* Hawker, Charlotte

I'ans, Wrey, 46

Ignatius, Fr., *see* Lyne, Joseph

Immaculate Conception, Papal Bull on, 227